Complications of Diabetes

Dose schedules are being continually revised and new side-effects recognized. Oxford University Press makes no representation, express or implied, that the drug dosages in the book are correct. For these reasons the reader is strongly urged to consult the pharmaceutical company's printed instructions before administering any of the drugs recommended in this book.

Complications of Diabetes

Chapters from the Oxford Textbook of Endocrinology and Diabetes First Edition

Edited by

John A.H. Wass

Professor of Endocrinology, University of Oxford;
Consultant Physician, Radcliffe Infirmary;
Consultant Physician, Nuffield Orthopaedic Centre, Oxford

and

Stephen M. Shalet

Professor of Endocrinology, Christie Hospital, Manchester;
Professor of Medicine, University of Manchester

Diabetes section edited by

Edwin Gale and Stephanie A. Amiel

OXFORD
UNIVERSITY PRESS

OXFORD
UNIVERSITY PRESS

Great Clarendon Street, Oxford OX2 6DP

Oxford University Press is a department of the University of Oxford.
It furthers the University's objective of excellence in research,
scholarship, and education by publishing worldwide in

Oxford New York

Auckland Cape Town Dar es Salaam Hong Kong Karachi
Kuala Lumpur Madrid Melbourne Mexico City Nairobi
New Delhi Shanghai Taipei Toronto
With offices in
Argentina Austria Brazil Chile Czech Republic France Greece
Guatemala Hungary Italy Japan Poland Portugal Singapore
South Korea Switzerland Thailand Turkey Ukraine Vietnam
and an associated company in Berlin

Oxford is a registered trade mark of Oxford University Press
in the UK and in certain other countries

Published in the United States
by Oxford University Press Inc., New York

© Oxford University Press, 2002

British Library Cataloguing in Publication Data

Data available

Library of Congress Cataloging in Publication Data

Typeset in Minion by Newgen Imaging Systems (P) Ltd., Chennai, India
Printed in the UK
on acid-free paper by Ashford Colour Press, Ltd.

ISBN 978–0–19–954425–7

10 9 8 7 6 5 4 3 2 1

Contents

List of contributors

Amiel, Stephanie A Department of Diabetes, Endocrinology and Internal Medicine, Guy's, King's, and St Thomas's School of Medicine, King's College, London, UK

Carter, Angela M Academic Unit of Molecular Vascular Medicine, The General Infirmary, Leeds, UK

Edmonds, Michael Department of Diabetes, King's College Hospital, London, UK

Evans, Mark L Department of Diabetes, Endocrinology and Internal Medicine, Guy's, King's and St Thomas's School of Medicine, King's College, London, UK

Forrester, John V Department of Ophthalmology, University of Aberdeen Medical School, Aberdeen, UK

Foster, AVM Senior Podiatrist, King's College Hospital, London, UK

Grant, PJ Professor of Medicine, Head of Academic Unit of Molecular Vascular Medicine, Leeds General Infirmary, Leeds, UK

Hadden, David R Sir George E. Clarke Metabolic Unit, Regional Centre for Endocrinology and Diabetes, Royal Victoria Hospital, Belfast, UK

Kitabchi, Abbas E Professor of Medicine and Molecular Sciences; Director, Division of Endocrinology, Diabetes and Metabolism, The University of Tennessee, Memphis, Tennessee, USA

Lebovitz, Harold E Professor of Medicine, Division of Endocrinology, State University New York, Health Center at Brooklyn, New York, USA

MacKinnon, Jane R Department of Ophthalmology, University of Aberdeen Medical School, Aberdeen, UK

Murphy, Mary Beth Research Nurse Director, Division of Endocrinology, Diabetes and Metabolism, The University of Tennessee, Memphis, Tennessee, USA

Panahloo, Arshia Consultant, Diabetes and Endocrinology, St George's Hospital, London, UK

Silink, M Ray Williams Institute of Paediatric Endocrinology, Paramatta, New South Wales, Australia

Tesfaye, Solomon Consultant Physician, Diabetes and Endocrinology, Royal Hallamshire Hospital, Directorate of Medicine (Department of Diabetes), Sheffield, UK

Tooke, John Dean, Peninsula Medical School, Plymouth, UK

Trevisan, Roberto Divisione Malattie del Metabolismo, Universita di Padova, Clinica e Sperimentale, Padova, Italy

Viberti, Giancarlo Unit for Metabolic Medicine, Department of Diabetes, Endocrinology and Internal Medicine, Guy's, King's and St Thomas's School of Medicine, Division of Medicine, London, UK

Yudkin, John S Professor of Medicine, Diabetes and Cardiovascular Disease Academic Unit, University College London, London, UK

1 Hypoglycaemia

Mark L. Evans and Stephanie A. Amiel

Introduction

Hypoglycaemia is the most important acute complication of the pharmacological treatment of diabetes mellitus, principally because a low blood glucose impairs brain (and potentially cardiac) function. The brain has minimal endogenous stores of energy, with small amounts of glycogen in astroglial cells. The brain is therefore largely dependent on circulating glucose as the substrate to fuel cerebral metabolism and support cognitive performance. If blood glucose levels fall sufficiently, cognitive dysfunction is inevitable. Because of this effect on brain function, patients with diabetes rank fear of hypoglycaemia as highly as fear of chronic complications such as nephropathy or retinopathy.[1] Some will attempt to minimize risk of hypoglycaemia by relaxing blood glucose control. Thus, hypoglycaemia and its avoidance limit the degree to which glycaemic control can be intensified to reduce the risk of chronic complications of diabetes both for type 1 and type 2 diabetes.[2–4]

Definition of hypoglycaemia

Despite its importance, hypoglycaemia is surprisingly difficult to define. It may be defined *clinically* as an episode in which low blood glucose results in a characteristic symptom complex. Hypoglycaemia prevalence rates using symptoms to define an episode will obviously be dependent on subjective awareness of hypoglycaemia. In population studies, many symptomatic mild episodes will not be recalled, while normoglycaemic episodes that mimic symptoms of hypoglycaemia may be recorded. Such symptom-based definition systems may categorize episodes by degree: mild which is self-recognized and self-treated without disruption of normal activity; moderate, which is self-recognized but requires intervention that disrupts normal activity; and severe, where third party intervention is required.

Hypoglycaemia can be defined *biochemically* when the blood glucose falls below a certain level. Frequency will then be dependent upon frequency of monitoring. There is no universal threshold level for defining biochemical hypoglycaemia. The use of capillary, venous, venous arterialized (sampling from a distal venous cannula in a heated hand) or arterial samples will introduce variability between studies, as will the subsequent measurement of either whole blood or plasma values. Recent experimental work suggests that a plasma glucose of 3 mmol/l or less defines a glucose concentration at which important changes in brain function occur (evidence of cortical dysfunction and diminished responses to a subsequent episode of hypoglycaemia. Some authorities now cite a plasma glucose of 3 mmol/l or less as a definition of hypoglycaemia but other values are also used, usually in the range of 3–4 mmol/l. It is important to recognize that these levels are, and should be, higher than those used to define spontaneous hypoglycaemia in non-diabetic patients. A more robust definition for epidemiological study is that of *severe hypoglycaemia*, usually taken as an episode of low blood glucose requiring third party rescue.[3] An alternative definition of severe hypoglycaemia is an episode of low blood glucose resulting in coma or requiring intravenous glucose or glucagon rescue.[5] This definition will result in apparently lower rates of severe hypoglycaemia but is likely to have the most accurate recall in retrospective analyses.

Incidence of hypoglycaemia

Even allowing for the differences in definition, the incidence of severe hypoglycaemia varies considerably from centre to centre (Table 1). For example, in the large prospective Diabetes Control and

Table 1 Rates of severe hypoglycaemia and effect of intensifying diabetes therapy

	Study	n	Incidence of severe hypoglycaemia (events per 100 patient years)
Type 1 diabetes	DCCT study[6] 1997	1441	
		730 conventional	18.7
		711 intensified	61.2
	Dusseldorf group[5] 1997	Conventional (historical)	28
		538 intensified	17
	Stockholm study[38] 1994	96	
		52 conventional	37
		44 intensified	110
Type 2 diabetes	UKPDS[4] 1998	3876 randomized	
		Rates by therapy	
		Diet	0.1
		Chlorpropamide	0.4
		Glibenclamide	0.6
		Insulin	2.3

Complications Trial (DCCT) study of type 1 diabetes, there was an overall rate of 18.7 episodes per 100 patient years on conventional therapy and 61.2 episodes per 100 patient years during intensified treatment.[6] However, the risk between treatment centres within the study varied from 0 to 150 episodes per 100 patient years. The incidence of severe hypoglycaemia in type 2 diabetes is lower than in type 1. In both type 1 and type 2 diabetes, risk of hypoglycaemia is markedly increased by intensified glucose control, but severe hypoglycaemia can complicate diabetes treatment at any level of glycaemic control.

Biochemical hypoglycaemia at night is probably common in all insulin treated diabetes. It is often asymptomatic. In a study of type 1 patients, Gale and Tattersall found that 22 of 39 had at least one glucose result below 2 mmol/l during the night[7] and more recent studies suggest that the problem remains.[8] Physiological responses to hypoglycaemia are reduced during sleep.[9] The significance and consequences of nocturnal biochemical hypoglycaemia are unknown.

Physiological responses to hypoglycaemia

Responses to hypoglycaemia in health

In health, hypoglycaemia sufficient to cause significant impairment of cognitive function does not occur. A series of defensive neuro-humoral changes limit the extent to which blood glucose can fall. These counterregulatory responses stimulate endogenous glucose production and tend to reduce peripheral utilization of glucose. Normally, counterregulation and symptoms of hypoglycaemia occur before brain performance becomes impaired so that a protective hierarchy of responses to a falling glucose exists.[10] Figure 1 shows the hierarchy of responses to a falling glucose from a number of studies.

Although the liver is the major source of endogenous glucose production, there is increasing evidence that the kidneys are able to produce significant amounts of glucose by gluconeogenesis and in

hypoglycaemia up to 40 per cent of the body's glucose production may be renal in origin.[11] Like hepatic glucose production, renal glucose output may be stimulated directly by neural activation and indirectly by changes in circulating amounts of gluconeogenic precursors. It is also insulin sensitive.

As glucose levels start to fall, the first change in the non-diabetic is the cessation of pancreatic insulin release and stimulation of glucagon release. Hepatic glucose output rises as a result. The role of hepatic autoregulation, in which hepatic glucose production rises in response to a falling blood glucose level independently of hormonal stimulation, is unclear. It is likely that insulin and glucagon alone can protect against continuing hypoglycaemia. Adrenaline also rises rapidly in acute hypoglycaemia, stimulating hepatic glucose output both directly and indirectly by peripheral effects to increase hepatic delivery of gluconeogenic precursors such as alanine, glycerol and lactate. The sympathetic and parasympathetic autonomic nervous systems are stimulated. Their activation can be measured indirectly by rises in blood noradrenaline and pancreatic polypeptide respectively. Sympathetic nerves directly stimulate endogenous hepatic glucose production. The adrenal and autonomic responses to hypoglycaemia can compensate for defective glucagon responses in experimental studies. Growth hormone and cortisol are probably of secondary importance in acute counterregulation, acting predominantly to reduce peripheral glucose utilization. Other endocrine changes during hypoglycaemia include increased plasma renin activity and rises in prolactin, vasopressin, oxytocin and β-endorphin. The role of these hormones in glucose regulation is uncertain.

In the non-diabetic, early counterregulatory changes will normally restore blood glucose levels rapidly to normal before further changes develop. These responses can be examined experimentally by infusing insulin to overcome counterregulatory changes and prolong the glucose fall. A simultaneous glucose infusion is often used to control the rate and extent of the hypoglycaemia. As glucose levels are lowered, warning symptoms of hypoglycaemia develop (Table 2). These are often divided into autonomic symptoms (resulting from counterregulatory neurohumoral responses) and neuroglycopenic symptoms (resulting directly from the effects of glucose deprivation on the brain). Classification into autonomic and neuroglycopenic groups may be either on the basis of the known aetiology of the symptom (for example, sweating due to cholinergic sympathetic outflow) or by using statistical techniques such as principal component analysis. Groups of symptoms that tend to cluster together can be identified by principal component analysis, either during experimental hypoglycaemia, or from population-based studies in people with diabetes.[12] Hunger is a particularly useful symptom, since it both

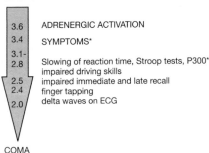

NORMAL

3.6	ADRENERGIC ACTIVATION
3.4	SYMPTOMS*
3.1–2.8	Slowing of reaction time, Stroop tests, P300*
	impaired driving skills
2.5	impaired immediate and late recall
2.4	finger tapping
2.0	delta waves on ECG

COMA

Fig. 1 Hypoglycaemia awareness: the normal protective hierarchy of responses against progressive hypoglycaemia in which neurohumoral and symptomatic responses (capitals) occur before the onset of cognitive dysfunction (lower case). Of these, the Stroop test measures speed of reading lists of colour names written in appropriately and, later, incongruously coloured ink and P300 is an evoked potential recorded in response to a stimulus by scalp electrodes. *=in some studies of poorly controlled diabetes these parameters have been found to change at even higher glucose levels. Plasma glucose levels are given in mmol/l.

Table 2 Symptoms of acute hypoglycaemia in diabetic adults

Autonomic	Neuroglycopenic	Other	Miscellaneous
Sweating	Dizziness	Hunger	Palpitations
Tremor	Confusion	Blurred vision	Shivering
Warmth	Tiredness	Drowsiness	
Anxiety	Difficulty in speaking	Tiredness	
Nausea	Headache		

Adapted from Reference (12).

warns of hypoglycaemia and promotes eating and restoration of glucose levels.

If glucose levels are lowered below the levels for activation of the described protective responses, cognitive performance will become impaired. Reductions in glucose such as this do not occur in health except in extreme circumstances such as prolonged vigorous exercise. Starvation, for example, does not cause loss of consciousness. In experimental hypoglycaemia, a wide range of cognitive tests has been used to measure brain function and show deterioration at quite modest degrees of hypoglycaemia.[13] Deteriorated performance of complex tasks requiring cognitive input such as complex reaction times and operation of driving simulators, may be detectable at an arterialized plasma glucose of around 3 mmol/l. Memory tasks which are a little more resilient, and simpler tasks, such as finger tapping, deteriorate at around 2.4 mmol/l.

In theory, if glucose levels are lowered far enough, brain function becomes further impaired, so that drowsiness and even seizures or coma may eventually develop. This occurred in insulin-shock therapy used in psychiatry during the first half of the nineteenth century.

Responses to hypoglycaemia in diabetes

In diabetes, endogenous protection against hypoglycaemia is impaired. With injection of insulin or ingestion of sulphonylureas, the ability of the pancreas to modify insulin release is lost. Most type 1 diabetic patients will also develop deficient glucagon responses to hypoglycaemia (although not to other secretagogues) within the first five years of diabetes.[14] This is probably because intact β-cell function is needed for α-cell responses. The primary humoral defence against hypoglycaemia is then adrenaline.[15] A number of studies have shown deficiencies in adrenaline secretion in otherwise healthy diabetic subjects, particularly associated with disease duration.[14] In some patients, significant abnormalities in counterregulatory neurohumoral responses to hypoglycaemia are associated with reduced awareness of hypoglycaemia. This greatly increases the risk of recurrent severe hypoglycaemia.[16] Patients with type 2 diabetes are less prone to hypoglycaemia,[4] at least until later in their disease. This is probably related to residual insulin secretion and preservation of glucagon responses. As one might anticipate, these responses become defective towards the end of the evolution of the type 2 disease.

Although defective in some degree, patients with diabetes do make significant neuroendocrine responses to acute hypoglycaemia. As in health, these are hyperglycaemic in nature. The blood glucose-elevating effects of the neuroendocrine responses to hypoglycaemia may cause hyperglycaemia continuing into the next day. This is in spite of the significant risk of a second severe hypoglycaemic episode within 24 h of an index episode.

Symptoms of hypoglycaemia alter with age. In diabetic children, symptoms of hypoglycaemia may be different from those reported by adults and behavioural problems are more prominent.[17] With young children, signs of hypoglycaemia observed by parents assume more importance. Healthy elderly subjects are less symptomatic during induced hypoglycaemia,[18] and elderly diabetic patients treated with insulin report more light-headedness and unsteadiness during hypoglycaemia than younger subjects.[19] In particular, statistical analysis identifies a group of incoordination/dysarticulation symptoms that may become as prominent as the classical autonomic and neuroglycopenic groups described above.[19]

Failure of counterregulatory mechanisms, especially failure to experience the symptoms of hypoglycaemia (failed generation, failed perception or too rapid a progression of the hypoglycaemia), exposes the patient to risk of significant cognitive dysfunction. This can present as confusion, slurred speech, irrational behaviour, emotional lability, or even loss of consciousness or seizure. This is dangerous, exposing the patient to embarrassment, potential danger (if occurring during driving or operating machinery or in a hazardous environment) and possibly permanent physical or cerebral injury. The cognitive effects of hypoglycaemia may persist for up to 60 minutes after correction of the circulating glucose level.[20] Patients should therefore be warned against driving soon.

Sensing of hypoglycaemia

For counterregulatory and symptomatic responses to be initiated, the body must first detect hypoglycaemia. There is evidence for some peripheral sensing of low glucose levels in the liver/hepatic vein[21] but selective catheterization studies in animals have shown that the predominant glucose-sensor for hypoglycaemia is located within the cerebral circulation.[22] Further work using microdialysis has identified the ventromedial hypothalamus as an important area, at least in rats,[23] and recent work suggests a similar location in man.[24] As blood glucose levels fall, the cerebral metabolic rate for glucose falls. It may be a fall in the metabolic rate in sensitive areas of the brain – possibly the ventromedial hypothalamus – that triggers counterregulatory responses.

Causes of hypoglycaemia

The major underlying cause of hypoglycaemia in patients with diabetes is the inadequacy of medical treatments for diabetes, compared with the normal exquisite control of insulin secretion from the healthy pancreas. Treatment of type 2 diabetes with sulphonylureas or other agents which stimulate insulin release results in a loss of feedback control compared with the healthy non-diabetic pancreas. This will often result in episodes of relative hyperinsulinaemia, particularly if long-acting agents (for example, chlorpropamide or glibenclamide) are used in elderly patients.

The use of exogenous insulin creates a further hazard, especially in patients with little or no residual insulin secretory capacity (type 1 and late type 2 diabetes). Subcutaneous insulin therapy delivers insulin systemically rather than into the portal circulation. Absorption of subcutaneous insulin is unpredictable, depending on factors such as skin blood flow (and therefore site of injection), but also has considerable unexplained variability. This will affect insulin kinetics, affecting time to peak action and duration of the effects of an injection. Subcutaneous injection of a bolus of conventional soluble (rapid-acting) insulin results in a delay before the peak onset of action compared with the healthy pancreas response to food. Injection should therefore be taken 30–60 min before meals, creating a risk of preprandial hypoglycaemia if the meal is delayed. Soluble insulin also has a relatively prolonged postprandial action, with relative hyperinsulinaemia after the meal, so that many insulin-treated patients will need to snack between meals. Conversely, the relatively short action of intermediate acting insulin used to control glucose overnight means that these insulins have a marked peak in their action 4–8 h after they are administered. Nocturnal hypoglycaemia may result either from the continued action of soluble insulin from the daytime, and/or the dose of intermediate acting insulin used to control morning fasting glucose levels. Attempts to reduce these problems by synthesizing artificial insulins with more physiological kinetics have been partially successful.[25]

A cause may or may not be identifiable for individual episodes of hypoglycaemia. Exercise, missed meals/snacks, treatment errors and alcohol are the most commonly reported causes of severe hypoglycaemia (Box 1).[26] Exercise, especially if unaccustomed, vigorous or

---

Box 1 Risk factors and associations for individual and recurrent episodes of hypoglycaemia

- ◆ Common causes of single episodes of hypoglycaemia
  - Missed or inadequate meals/snacks
  - Exercise
  - Drug or insulin error
  - Alcohol
  - Change in absorption from injection for example, hot bath, sauna, change in injection site
- ◆ Risk factors for recurrent hypoglycaemia
  - History of severe hypoglycaemia
  - Hypoglycaemia unawareness/deficient counterregulation
  - Long duration of diabetes
  - C peptide deficiency
  - Under age 5
  - Nocturnal hypoglycaemia
  - Intensified glycaemic control (insulin or drug treatment)
  - Inappropriate insulin/drug regimen for example, long-acting sulphonylurea in elderly
- ◆ Other risk factors for problematic hypoglycaemia
  - Manipulation of diabetes/'brittle diabetes' (includes suicide/parasuicide and obsessive fear of hyperglycaemia)
  - Endocrine causes
    - Addison's disease
    - Hypopituitarism
    - Hypothyroidism or hypothyroid medications
  - Renal failure (decreased clearance of insulin, glibenclamide, chlorpropamide)
  - Liver failure
  - Other drugs
    - ? Angiotensin-converting enzyme inhibitors
    - Anti-hypertensive medication
    - Cessation of steroid therapy
  - Postpartum/breast feeding
  - Dieting and anorexia
  - Insulin antibodies

---

prolonged not only causes immediate hypoglycaemia but continues to lower blood glucose over the next 12–24 h as expended muscle and liver glycogen stores are replaced. The possibility that exercise may cause hypoglycaemia many hours later is often not appreciated. Alcohol may contribute to hypoglycaemia, both at the time of drinking and also by causing later hypoglycaemia. Alcohol increases the risk of hypoglycaemia by inhibiting gluconeogenesis needed to maintain blood glucose levels after fasting. Alcohol also causes neglect of self-care of diabetes (affecting compliance with medical treatment and dietary regimens), decreases perception of symptoms of early hypoglycaemia and may impair the ability to take appropriate action to recover from a low glucose.

Intensified glycaemic control in both type 1 and type 2 diabetes significantly increases the risk of severe hypoglycaemia in most centres.[2–4] This is especially true if an unrealistic attempt is made to impose intensified glycaemic control on a patient who is unable or unwilling to achieve improved glucose targets. Other inappropriate treatment regimens, such as the use of long-acting sulphonylureas in elderly subjects, may also contribute to hypoglycaemia risk. Renal failure and hypothyroidism (decreased insulin clearance) and hypoadrenalism from Addison's or hypopituitarism (reduced insulin antagonism) are rare causes of recurrent hypoglycaemia. Insulin treated patients on adrenal replacement therapy may be most safely managed on longer acting agents, for example, prednisolone rather than hydrocortisone, to avoid periods of very low corticosteroid levels at night. Drugs which have been reported to increase hypoglycaemia risk in treated diabetic patients include angiotensin-converting enzyme-inhibitors in type 1 patients, any hypertensive therapy in type 2 diabetes (possibly reflecting more active medical management rather than a direct effect of a particular drug), anti-thyroid treatment and cessation of steroid treatment. Recurrent hypoglycaemia, or mixed hypoglycaemia/ketoacidosis occur in some subjects labelled as suffering from 'brittle diabetes'. Psychosocial factors may contribute to this presentation and some patients may chose to run their blood glucose obsessively at near-hypoglycaemic levels.

Hypoglycaemia unawareness/impaired counterregulation

In addition to the inability to alter insulin secretion and diminished glucagon responses to hypoglycaemia described above, some patients with diabetes develop further deficiencies in neurohumoral responses. The adrenaline responses to hypoglycaemia may also be delayed and diminished. Associated with this impaired counterregulation is a diminution and delay in the symptoms that warn of a low glucose. The normal protective hierarchy of responses to hypoglycaemia is disturbed so that protective responses start with or even after cognitive impairment (Fig. 2). These patients have a significantly increased risk of severe hypoglycaemia.[16]

In addition to the evidence for defective initiation of counterregulatory responses to hypoglycaemia in patients with impaired ability to recognize hypoglycaemia, there is also some evidence of impaired peripheral sensitivity to any responses that do occur, compounding the problem.[27]

Risk factors for hypoglycaemia unawareness/impaired counterregulation include increased duration of diabetes and intensified glycaemic control. Amiel et al. demonstrated defective counterregulation in intensively treated patients[28] and showed that 2–6 months of

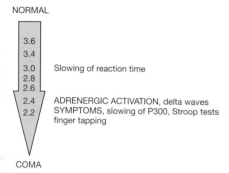

NORMAL

3.6
3.4
3.0   Slowing of reaction time
2.8
2.6
2.4   ADRENERGIC ACTIVATION, delta waves
2.2   SYMPTOMS, slowing of P300, Stroop tests
         finger tapping

COMA

Fig. 2 Hypoglycaemia unawareness: the abnormal hierarchy of responses against progressive hypoglycaemia in deficient counterregulation/hypoglycaemia unawareness in which protective neurohumoral and symptomatic responses (capitals) are delayed and occur with or after cognitive impairment (lower case). Plasma glucose levels are given in mmol/l. Stroop and P300 defined as in Fig. 1.

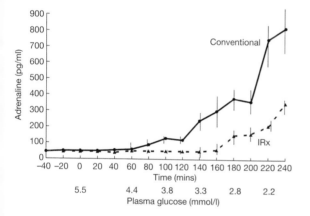

Fig. 3 Intensified control and impaired counterregulation (reproduced with permission from Amiel SA, Sherwin RS, Simonson DC, Tamborlane WV. Effect of intensive insulin therapy on glycemic thresholds for counter-regulatory hormone release. *Diabetes*, 1988; **37**: 901–7). Adrenaline responses to a controlled stepped reduction in plasma glucose from 5–2.4 mmol/l in young people with type 1 diabetes before (solid line) and after (dashed line) intensification of therapy.

intensified insulin therapy sufficient to lower HbA_{1c} levels from 9.6–7.1 per cent resulted in delayed and diminished counterregulatory responses to a controlled hypoglycaemic challenge (Fig. 3).[29] However, not all intensified insulin therapy regimens appear to carry the same risks.[30]

Mechanism of hypoglycaemia unawareness/impaired counterregulation

It was long believed that hypoglycaemia unawareness/impaired counterregulation was a consequence of a specific diabetic autonomic neuropathy. However, the phenomenon is distinct from the classical diabetic autonomic neuropathy and patients with hypoglycaemia

unawareness and impaired counterregulation to hypoglycaemia may be otherwise intact on autonomic function testing.

Whereas hyperglycaemia is a major risk factor for classical diabetic autonomic neuropathy, hypoglycaemia itself seems to be a major factor in the loss of neurohumoral activation and symptomatic responses. Brief exposure to experimental mild hypoglycaemia in non-diabetic and diabetic subjects reduces subsequent responses to hypoglycaemia.[31] This may explain the increased risk of a second severe hypoglycaemic episode occurring within 24 h of an index event. Although the hypoglycaemia-induced defect in counterregulation is transient, exposure to recurrent episodes may underlie the clinical syndrome of hypoglycaemia unawareness in many cases.

Insulin species

Whether human insulin, manufactured by genetic recombinant technology, is associated with more or different hypoglycaemia in diabetes remains controversial. There have been a number of anecdotal reports of loss of hypoglycaemia awareness and episodes of severe hypoglycaemia from patients after switching to human insulin. Subtle pharmacokinetic differences do exist between human and pork insulin after subcutaneous injection and these differences are greater when the comparison is made between human insulins and the older 'dirty' animal insulins. However, research studies have failed to find consistent differences in hypoglycaemic frequency and/or counterregulatory differences to hypoglycaemia when human rather than highly purified animal insulins are used.[32] Such studies cannot however conclusively exclude idiosyncratic or very small differences that might be clinically relevant to susceptible patients.

The debate about human insulin is emotive and has been fuelled on occasions by media interest and diverse pressure groups. Currently, most clinicians will tread a middle path, tending to use human insulin in most patients, but recognizing the right of the patient to opt for animal insulins if he or she feels more comfortable with them. Apart from the source of the material, there are no major disadvantages known to be exclusive to the highly purified animal insulins not shared by the human forms. An important caveat to this is that merely switching to pork insulin will not resolve problems with hypoglycaemia unawareness. As described below, strategies for reversing hypoglycaemia unawareness/impaired glucose counterregulation should be considered regardless of the insulin species used and can be successful without need to change.

Pregnancy

Hypoglycaemia may become a particular problem in pregnancy, where diabetic women strive for very tight control and are generally restricted to the use of conventional insulins. Recurrent asymptomatic severe hypoglycaemic episodes are significant for the mother, but apparently have no negative impact on the fetus. Careful attention to achieving (not exceeding) the lower limits of the glucose targets (fasting plasma glucose 3.5 mmol/l for pregnancy) and, if necessary, acceptance of a slightly higher pre-bed glucose (7 to 9 mmol/l) may help. Inspection of eating, especially snacking, patterns may indicate times where problems exist. The insulin resistance of late pregnancy resolves with delivery of the placenta and labour ward protocols for blood glucose control should reflect this, allowing reduction in insulin administration immediately postpartum, to avoid maternal hypoglycaemia. Because of the imperfections of our ability to control blood glucose in the diabetic mother, their babies are at risk for hypoglycaemia, probably secondary to fetal hyperinsulinaemia before and during labour. Breast feeding is an energy-consuming activity and maternal insulin doses may need further reduction during lactation.

Consequences of hypoglycaemia

Acute episodes

Acute episodes of hypoglycaemia resulting in cognitive impairment may result in accidents. If glucose levels fall low enough, drowsiness, coma and/or epileptic seizures may result in hospital admission. Altered behaviour may manifest as aggression, or may mimic alcohol intoxication. In the UK, hypoglycaemia is not accepted by courts as a valid medicolegal explanation for driving offences, and the onus is on the individual to ensure that hypoglycaemia does not occur behind the steering wheel. Although diabetic patients have accident rates similar to those of the non-diabetic driver, up to 16 per cent of those accidents they may experience are related to hypoglycaemia at the wheel.[33] Most of the documentation of accident risk in diabetes predates the drive for tight glycaemic control. Patients with a current history of severe hypoglycaemia or asymptomatic hypoglycaemia with high risk of severe hypoglycaemia must be told not to drive at all, and steps should be taken immediately to attempt to restore hypoglycaemia awareness and protection.

Acute hypoglycaemia may result in transient neurological sequelae, such as hemiplegia, which may mimic a cerebrovascular event (hemiplegic hypoglycaemia). Rarely hypoglycaemia may be followed by cerebral oedema, which may require management in an intensive care unit. Persistent neurological damage may follow very severe and prolonged hypoglycaemia, usually after a major insulin overdose.

Mortality resulting from acute hypoglycaemia is difficult to quantify accurately. Each year, 25–30 deaths are recorded in the UK as being directly related to hypoglycaemia. Population studies suggest that this may be higher, with perhaps 1–2 per cent of deaths in type 1 patients caused by hypoglycaemia.[34] Some of these may present as the distressing 'dead in bed' syndrome, in which, often young, type 1 patients are discovered in the morning to have died during sleep. One estimate suggests that 6 per cent of deaths in diabetic people under the age of 40 may be of this nature.[35] The death is often attributed to hypoglycaemia and/or a cardiac arrhythmia related to an autonomic neuropathy, but the difficulties in diagnosing these problems at post-mortem are obvious.

ECG changes have been identified during acute experimental hypoglycaemia which may predispose to arrhythmias. These may relate to changes in catecholamines and/or potassium associated with the hypoglycaemia. It is possible that some patients are at higher risk of such events.[36] It is too early to know if such changes observed in experimental settings are relevant clinically.

Recurrent episodes

Recurrent hypoglycaemia, especially if asymptomatic, may have social, financial and employment implications. Employers may be unsympathetic, and those with recurrent hypoglycaemia without warning will be barred from driving. Some may avoid social contact for fear of embarrassment if hypoglycaemia occurs.

The chronic effects of recurrent hypoglycaemia from which apparently full recovery is made at the time, are unknown. Other repeated brain insults, for example, trauma in boxers, may lead on to irreversible brain damage. Neonatal hypoglycaemia (not usually diabetic) is known to be associated with impaired brain function later and in young children below the age of seven, recurrent hypoglycaemia with seizures in early life is associated with slowed mental development, and may reduce subsequent adult IQ levels (as will other causes of seizure).[37] In adults, prospective studies of intensified therapy, with its associated increased risk of severe hypoglycaemia, have failed to show any deficit in those with recurrent hypoglycaemia. However, these studies were relatively short, with an average of 6.5 years follow-up in the DCCT and 7.5 years in the smaller Stockholm Diabetes Intervention Study.[38,39] Early cross-sectional studies were small and no adjustments were made for the chronic effects of illness. Later studies in adult populations have attempted to estimate the decrement in IQ performance by subtracting performance IQ (representing 'fluid intelligence', which deteriorates with ageing) from a reading assessment (the National Adult Reading Test, representing 'stored intelligence' thought to be stable once attained). The methodology is open to criticism, but studies suggested that recurrent severe hypoglycaemia (5 or more episodes) was associated with a modest decrement in IQ of about five points.[40] Reaction time has been found to be slower in very tightly controlled type 1 diabetic patients but equally so in poorly controlled people.[41] Other studies have failed to show an association or found it only in patients with chronic complications such as neuropathy,[42] suggesting that hyperglycaemia rather than hypoglycaemia may be important in causing a diabetic 'encephalopathy'. A significant criticism of cross-sectional studies is that they cannot directly address causality. Neuroimaging has not yet resolved the problem as although white matter changes have been identified in diabetic patients with recurrent severe hypoglycaemia, they are not specific for hypoglycaemia.

Management of hypoglycaemia

Acute episodes

Most episodes of hypoglycaemia are self-managed with oral carbohydrate. Glucose tablets such as dextrosol (3.1 g/tablet) or liquid preparations such as Lucozade (19 g/100 ml) and fresh fruit juice are widely recommended but any palatable sources of concentrated glucose can be used. About 20 g of rapidly absorbed carbohydrate is usually needed and this can be repeated after 10 min if necessary. Complex carbohydrate is not always necessary – for example, preprandial hypoglycaemia may be managed by bringing the meal forward. The American Diabetic Association currently recommends 15 g of fast acting carbohydrate, repeated after 15–20 min if glucose levels are still below 3.8 mmol/l. A glycaemic response should occur rapidly to oral carbohydrate, within 10–15 min. If refined glucose is used, most authorities recommend a starchy snack should also be ingested to avoid glucose levels dropping again after rapid absorption of available glucose from the stomach. This may be achieved by expediting the next meal. In children who may be reluctant to eat or drink, concentrated glucose preparations such as Hypostop (Diabetic BioDiagnositics 32 g/100 ml) or honey can be squeezed inside the

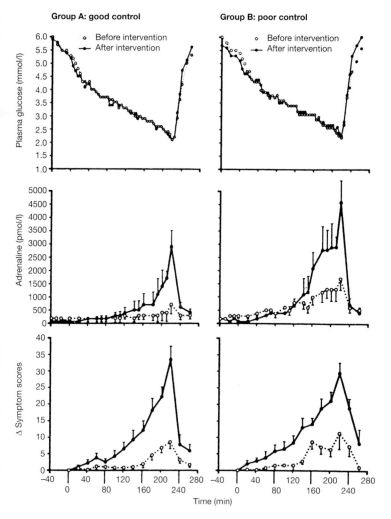

Fig. 4 Restoration of hormone responses and symptomatic awareness of hypoglycaemia in long standing type 1 diabetes with hypoglycaemia unawareness: plasma glucose profiles, adrenaline responses and symptoms before and after a period of avoidance of hypoglycaemia. (Reproduced with permission from Cranston I, Lomas J, Maran A, Macdonald IA, Amiel SA. Restoration of hypoglycaemia awareness in patients with long-standing insulin dependant diabetes. *Lancet*, 1994; **344**: 283–7.)

cheek. The absorption of this is probably by the concentrated glucose trickling back down the oropharynx and inducing reflex swallowing. Such therapies should not be attempted in the unconscious, where parenteral glucose or glucagon should be used.

Glucagon can be given intravenously, subcutaneously or intra-muscularly. It mobilises hepatic glycogen. It is ineffective in conditions such as liver disease where there may be inadequate hepatic glycogen stores. It is available as a 1 mg injection pack for emergency intra-muscular injection by a third party at home. The effect will be short-lived, so that the recovered patient should take oral carbohydrate to prevent glucose levels from falling again. Intravenous glucose injection will rapidly elevate blood glucose levels and is the standard emergency department treatment for hypoglycaemia that cannot be managed by oral intake. 25 ml of 50 per cent glucose contains 14.5 g of glucose but is hyperviscous, difficult to administer, may result in a thrombophlebitis and has caused limb loss when injected into a peripheral vein. Larger volumes (65 ml) of 20 per cent glucose or even 125 ml of 10 per cent are to be recommended instead.

Having treated the acute episode, an attempt should be made to identify the underlying cause (missed meals, exercise) and to give advice/education as appropriate. If there is a history of repeated hypoglycaemia and/or unawareness of hypoglycaemia, the patient should be formally reviewed by a specialist diabetes team. Finally it should be remembered that recovery of cognitive functioning may lag behind restoration of blood glucose levels and even symptomatic recovery.[20] People who self-treat a hypoglycaemic attack while driving should not resume driving for about 20 min. Patients who become hypoglycaemic on sulphonylurea therapy will require monitoring and probably additional glucose support for up to 48 h as the hypoglycaemia is recurrent and prolonged.

Avoidance of hypoglycaemia

In addition to advice about managing acute episodes, patients need advice about avoiding future hypoglycaemia. Appropriate education should be given about the common precipitants of hypoglycaemia such as exercise or alcohol. Patients may increase their carbohydrate intake and/or adjust insulin doses before and after exercise to avoid low blood glucose. Unaccustomed, vigorous or prolonged exercise necessitates a further reduction in the overnight insulin dose between 15 and 50 per cent in a well-controlled patient. Alcohol, with its ability to cause delayed hypoglycaemia, taken with exercise (for example dancing and drinking at parties) may be particularly dangerous. In insulin-treated patients, consideration of the insulin kinetics will identify times of high risk of hypoglycaemia, for example, 2–3 h post-meals and in the night. Between meal snacking and/or the use of the new ultra short-acting insulin analogues may be the only way to achieve good postprandial glucose levels without hypoglycaemia before the next meal. Hypoglycaemia at night is a particular danger and many insulin-treated patients experience asymptomatic nocturnal hypoglycaemia.[7,8] A bedtime snack (including perhaps uncooked cornstarch) has been advocated[43] and use of very short-acting insulins for the evening meal may help overcome hypoglycaemia during the first few hours of sleep. Although the evidence base is lacking, injecting the evening intermediate acting insulin at bedtime may help achieve fasting normoglycaemia with diminished risk of nocturnal hypoglycaemia. Insulin injection sites and the timing of sulphonylurea doses should be checked, as lipohypertrophy and inappropriate timing of drug therapy (sulphonylurea taken at bedtime) may be easily corrected.

The correct targets for glucose control in both type 1 and type 2 diabetes are to intensify glycaemic control *without inducing hypoglycaemia*. To achieve this, treatment regimens should be tailored for individuals. For example, striving for perfect glycaemia in an elderly patient who lives alone may expose that patient to an unacceptable risk of hypoglycaemia. The use of multiple insulin injection regimens and/or subcutaneous insulin pump therapy in type 1 diabetes, and choice of appropriate treatment in type 2 diabetes may aid this. Many type 1 patients will be empowered to adjust their own insulin doses in combination with home blood glucose monitoring. A suitable target for home glycaemia is to avoid glucose results of below 4 mmol/l as avidly as avoiding hyperglycaemia, in order to defend against glucose levels associated with cognitive impairment and hypoglycaemia unawareness (see below).

Reversibility of hypoglycaemia unawareness

If deficient counterregulatory and symptomatic responses are caused by a hypoglycaemia-induced adaptation, then the abnormality should be reversible by avoiding hypoglycaemia. The ability to restore counterregulatory responses and symptomatic awareness, at least partially, to patients with counterregulatory failure, and hypoglycaemia unawareness by strict avoidance of hypoglycaemia was first demonstrated in short duration patients.[44] Cranston *et al.* showed that strict avoidance of all plasma glucose results of below 3 mmol/l was able to restore counterregulatory responses and symptomatic awareness to induced hypoglycaemia in small groups of long duration type 1 diabetes. This included both those in good control with near normal HbA_{1c} and those in chronically poor control with recurrent severe hypoglycaemia.[45] This was the first suggestion of a common aetiology for such counterregulatory failure (Fig. 4). Importantly the protective hierarchy of responses to hypoglycaemia was restored, with hormonal and symptomatic responses occurring

again before cognitive impairment. These results were achieved without a deterioration in overall glycaemic control, confirming the primacy of avoiding hypoglycaemia rather than a need for simply 'relaxing control'. Such patient management is very labour intensive and not all patients succeed in eliminating hypoglycaemia from their daily lives. However, careful investigation, seeking asymptomatic episodes of plasma glucose below 3 mmol/l in daily life, may help identify strategies to reduce their frequency and work towards restoring hypoglycaemia awareness.

References

1. **Pramming S, Thorsteinsson B, Bendtson I, Binder C.** Symptomatic hypoglycaemia in 411 type 1 patients with insulin dependent diabetic patients. *Diabetic Medicine*, 1991; **8**: 217–22.

2. **Wan PH, Lau J, Chalmore TC.** Meta-analysis of effects of intensive blood glucose control on the development of the microvascular complications of the type 1 diabetes. *Lancet*, 1993; **341**: 1306–9.

3. **The Diabetes Control and Complications Trial (DCCT) Research Group.** The effect of intensive treatment of diabetes on the development and progression of long-term complications in insulin-dependent diabetes mellitus. *New England Journal of Medicine*, 1993; **329**: 977–86.

4. **UK Prospective Diabetes Study (UKPDS) Group.** Intensive blood glucose control with sulphonylureas or insulin compared with conventional treatment and risk of complications in patients with type 2 diabetes (UKPDS 33). *Lancet*, 1998; **352**: 837–53.

5. **Bott S, Bott U, Berger M, Muhlhauser I.** Intensified insulin therapy and the risk of severe hypoglycaemia. *Diabetologia*, 1997; **40**: 926–32.

6. **The Diabetes Control and Complications Research Group.** Hypoglycemia in the Diabetes Control and Complications Trial. *Diabetes*, 1997; **46**: 271–86.

7. **Gale EAM, Tattersall RB.** Unrecognised nocturnal hypoglycaemia in insulin-treated diabetics. *Lancet*, 1979; **i**: 1049–52.

8. **Vervoort G, Goldschmidt HM, van Doorn LG.** Nocturnal blood glucose profiles in patients with type 1 diabetes mellitus on multiple (> or = 4) daily insulin injection regimens. *Diabetic Medicine*, 1996; **13**: 794–9.

9. **Jones TW** *et al.* Decreased epinephrine responses to hypoglycemia during sleep. *New England Journal of Medicine*, 1998; **338**: 1657–62.

10. **Mitrakou A** *et al.* Hierarchy of glycemic thresholds for counter-regulatory hormone secretion, symptoms and cerebral dysfunction. *American Journal of Physiology*, 1991; **23**: E67–74.

11. **Cersosimo E, Garlick P, Ferretti J.** Renal glucose production during hypoglycemia in humans. *Diabetes*, 1999; **48**: 261–6.

12. **Deary IJ, Hepburn DA, MacLeod KM, Frier BM.** Partitioning the symptoms of hypoglycaemia using multi-sample confirmatory factor analysis. *Diabetologia*, 1993; **36**: 771–7.

13. **Heller S, Macdonald I.** The measurement of cognitive function during acute hypoglycaemia: experimental limitations and their effect on the study of hypoglycaemia unawareness. *Diabetic Medicine*, 1996; **13**: 607–15.

14. **Bolli G** *et al.* Abnormal glucose counterregulation in insulin-dependent diabetes mellitus. Interaction of anti-insulin antibodies and impaired glucagon secretion. *Diabetes*, 1983; **32**: 134–41.

15. **Rizza RA, Cryer PE, Gerich JE.** Role of glucagon, catecholamines, and growth hormone in human glucose counterregulation: effects of somatostatin and combined alpha- and beta-blockade on plasma glucose recovery and glucose flux rates following insulin induced hypoglycaemia. *Journal of Clinical Investigation*, 1979; **64**: 62–71.

16. **Gold AE, MacLeod KM, Frier BM.** Frequency of severe hypoglycemia in patients with type I diabetes with impaired awareness of hypoglycemia. *Diabetes Care*, 1994; **17**: 697–703.

17. Ross LA, McCrimmon RJ, Frier BM, Kelnar CJ, Deary IJ. Hypoglycaemic symptoms reported by children with type 1 diabetes mellitus and by their parents. *Diabetic Medicine*, 1998; **15**: 836–43.

18. Matyka K, Evans M, Lomas J, Cranston I, Macdonald I, Amiel SA. Altered hierarchy of protective responses against severe hypoglycemia in normal aging in healthy men. *Diabetes Care*, 1997; **20**: 135–41.

19. Jaap AJ, Jones GC, McCrimmon RJ, Deary IJ, Frier BM. Perceived symptoms of hypoglycaemia in elderly type 2 diabetic patients treated with insulin. *Diabetic Medicine*, 1998; **15**: 398–401.

20. Tallroth G, Lindgren M, Stenberg G, Rosen I, Agarch CD. Neurophysiological changes during insulin induced hypoglycaemia and in the recovery period following glucose infusion in type 1 (insulin-dependent) diabetes mellitus and in normal men. *Diabetologia*, 1990; **33**: 319–23.

21. Hevener AL, Bergman RN, Donovan CM. Novel glucosensor for hypoglycemic detection localized to the portal vein. *Diabetes*, 1997; **46**: 1521–5.

22. Biggers DW *et al.* Role of brain in counterregulation of insulin induced hypoglycaemia in dogs. *Diabetes*, 1989; **38**: 7–16.

23. Borg M, Sherwin R, Borg W, Tamborlane W, Shulman G. Local ventromedial glucose perfusion blocks counterregulation during hypoglycaemia in awake rats. *Journal of Clinical Investigation*, 1997; **99**: 361–5.

24. Reed L, Cranston IA, Marsden PM, Amiel SA.

25. Ahmed AB, Home PD. The effect of the insulin analog lispro on nighttime blood glucose control in type 1 diabetic patients. *Diabetes Care*, 1998; **21**: 32–7.

26. Feher MD, Grout P, Kennedy A, Elkeles RS, Touquet R. Hypoglycaemia in an inner-city accident and emergency department: a 12-month survey. *Archives of Emergency Medicine*, 1989; **6**: 183–8.

27. Hilsted J *et al.* Metabolic and cardiovascular responses to epinephrine in diabetic autonomic neuropathy. *New England Journal of Medicine*, 1987; **317**: 421–6.

28. Amiel SA, Tamborlane WV, Simonson DC, Sherwin RS. Defective glucose counterregulation after strict control of insulin-dependent diabetes mellitus. *New England Journal of Medicine*, 1987; **316**: 1376–83.

29. Amiel SA, Sherwin RS, Simonson DC, Tamborlane WV. Effect of intensive insulin therapy on glycaemic thresholds for counter regulatory hormone release. *Diabetes*, 1988; **37**: 901–7.

30. Berger M, Muhlhauser I. Implementation of intensified insulin therapy: a European perspective. *Diabetic Medicine*, 1995; **12**: 201–8.

31. Amiel SA. Ernst-Friedrich-Pfeiffer-Memorial lecture. Hypoglycaemia associated syndrome. *Acta Diabetologica*, 1998; **35**: 226–31.

32. Amiel SA. Human insulin in hypoglycemia. A new arena? *Diabetes*, 1995; **44**: 257–60.

33. MacLeod KM. Diabetes and driving: towards equitable, evidence-based decision-making. *Diabetic Medicine*, 1999; **16**: 282–90.

34. Sovik O, Thordarson H. Dead-in-bed syndrome in young diabetic patients. *Diabetes Care*, 1999; **22**(suppl. 2): B40–2.

35. Laing SP *et al.* The British Diabetic Association Cohort Study, II: cause-specific mortality in patients with insulin-treated diabetes mellitus *Diabetic Medicine*, 1999; **16**: 466–71.

36. Marques JL *et al.* Altered ventricular repolarization during hypoglycaemia in patients with diabetes. *Diabetic Medicine*, 1997; **14**: 648–54.

37. Rovet JE, Ehrlich RM, Hoppe M. Intellectual deficits associated with early onset of insulin dependent diabetes mellitus in children. *Diabetes Care*, 1987; **10**: 510–5.

38. Reichard P, Pihl M. Mortality and treatment side effects during long term intensified conventional insulin treatment in the Stockholm Diabetes Intervention Study. *Diabetes*, 1994; **43**: 313–7.

39. The Diabetes Control and Complications Trial (DCCT) Research Group. Effects of intensive diabetes therapy on neuropsychological function in adults in the diabetes control and complications study. *Annals of Internal Medicine*, 1996; **124**: 379–88.

40. Langan SJ, Deary IJ, Hepburn DA, Frier BM. Cumulative cognitive impairment following recurrent severe hypoglycaemia in adult patients with insulin-treated diabetes mellitus. *Diabetologia*, 1991; **34**: 337–44.

41. Maran A, Lomas J, Macdonald IA, Amiel SA. Lack of preservation of higher brain function during hypoglycaemia in patients with intensively-treated IDDM. *Diabetologia*, 1995; **38**: 1412–8.

42. Ryan CM, Williams Finegold DN, Orchard TJ. Cognitive dysfunction in adults with Type 1 diabetes mellitus of long duration: effects of recurrent hypoglycaemia and other chronic complications. *Diabetologia*, 1993; **36**: 329–34.

43. Kaufman FR, Devgan S. Use of uncooked cornstarch to avert nocturnal hypoglycaemia in children and adolescents with type 1 diabetes. *Journal of Diabetes Complications*, 1996; **10**: 84–7.

44. Fanelli CG *et al.* Meticulous prevention of hypoglycemia normalizes glycemic thresholds and magnitude of most of the neuroendocrine responses to, and symptoms of, and cognitive function during hypoglycaemia in intensively-treated patients with short-term IDDM. *Diabetes*, 1993; **42**: 1683–9.

45. Cranston I, Lomas J, Maran A, Macdonald IA, Amiel SA. Restoration of hypoglycaemia awareness in patients with long-standing insulin dependent diabetes. *Lancet*, 1994; **344**: 283–7.

Further reading

Maran A, Amiel SA. Research methodologies in hypoglycaemia: counter-regulatory phenomena and nerve-brain dysfunction. In: Mogensen CE, Standl E. Walter de Gruyter, eds. New York: 1994: 171–90.

Frier BM, Fisher M. *Hypoglycaemia and Diabetes: Clinical and Physiological Aspects*. London: Edward Arnold, 1993.

2.1 Diabetic ketoacidosis in childhood and adolescence

M. Silink

Diabetic ketoacidosis (DKA) may occur at the time of diagnosis of diabetes or at any time subsequently. It is the cause of very significant morbidity and remains the most common cause of death in childhood and adolescent diabetes.[1–3]

Type 1 diabetes occurs in childhood with an incidence which varies from over 40 per 100 000 children under the age of 15 years in Finland to less than 1 per 100 000 in Asia. The mean age at diagnosis is usually 10–12 years, though in a number of countries this seems to be declining. The younger the child is at diagnosis the more aggressive the autoimmune mediated destruction of the pancreatic beta-cell and the more rapid the progression to complete insulin dependence. Children are thus more liable to DKA than adults. Furthermore, children experience more viral infections than do adults and the metabolic stresses associated with these infections increase their risk of developing diabetic ketoacidosis.

Diabetic ketoacidosis has traditionally been considered to occur only in type 1 diabetes. Although the vast majority of diabetes in childhood and adolescence is type 1 diabetes there has been a worldwide trend to the earlier development of type 2 diabetes, especially in certain at-risk ethnic groups (for example, Asian, African-Americans, Hispanic-Americans). Diabetic ketoacidosis is also being encountered in these obese adolescents with type 2 diabetes, especially when there are associated stress factors such as infection. The treatment of DKA in these patients is the same as for those with type 1 diabetes; however the subsequent course of the treatment usually differs and most patients are able to stop insulin and be treated with oral hypoglycaemic agents, weight reduction, exercise, and an appropriate food plan.

Diabetic ketoacidosis

Diabetic ketoacidosis develops only in those in whom there is a profound deficiency of insulin action. The two factors which contribute to this are a true deficiency of insulin and the presence of insulin resistance (Box 1).[4] The hallmarks of DKA are hyperglycaemia, hyperketonaemia, and acidosis. A useful definition of DKA is a serum bicarbonate less than 15 mmol/l and hyperglycaemia above 15 mmol/l. The pH under these circumstances is usually below 7.3 and this is frequently included in the definition.

Insulin deficiency

With increased awareness of diabetes, DKA at diagnosis is becoming less frequent (less than 20 per cent in countries like Australia). The incidence is usually higher in the very young in whom the diagnosis of diabetes is usually not considered because of its rarity in that age group and because the child may be too young for symptoms such as polydipsia and polyuria to be appreciated as abnormal.

In patients with known diabetes, insulin deficiency may be due to insulin omission, with this occurring most frequently in the turbulent years of adolescence when psychosocial factors play an important role. Poor compliance with insulin injections may also be precipitated if the demands of an intensive insulin regimen exceed the child's or adolescent's ability to cope. A four per day injection regimen, which involves a pre-lunch dose at school, may prove to be

Box 1 Pathogenesis of diabetic ketoacidosis

- ◆ Insulin deficiency
  - ▪ Beta-cell damage
  - ▪ Insulin omission
  - ▪ Insulin under-dosage
- ◆ Insulin resistance
  - ▪ Acidosis
  - ▪ Electrolyte imbalance
  - ▪ Hypertonicity
  - ▪ Glucotoxicity
  - ▪ Infections
  - ▪ Stress hormones
  - ▪ Cytokines
  - ▪ Intrinsic insulin resistance

too demanding for the child or adolescent and a three injection per day regimen, not involving an injection at school, may prove more acceptable. Insulin deficiency can also occur when the need for an increased dosage is not appreciated because of infrequent monitoring of blood glucose levels. This occurs especially during puberty when insulin dosages need to be increased substantially at the time of rapid body growth and pubertal development or intermittantly in association with intercurrent infection. Occasionally, meter malfunction or improper testing techniques may result in false low blood glucose levels being obtained and consequent insulin under-dosage.

Insulin resistance

Insulin resistance is the hallmark of type 2 diabetes, but it also contributes to the development of DKA in type 1 diabetes by reducing the effectiveness of any insulin which may be present. Factors leading to the development of insulin resistance include increased levels of stress hormones (adrenaline, glucagon, hydrocortisone and growth hormone) and certain cytokines (such as IL-1β), all of which are raised in infections.[4] As the metabolic derangement of DKA progresses (acidosis, electrolytes disturbances, hyperosmolality[5] and elevated glucose levels), insulin resistance occurs because of secondary effects on signal transduction in insulin responsive target tissues.[4,5]

Recurrent diabetic ketoacidosis

Recurrent DKA is unusual in the very young or the school age child because the management of their diabetes is the responsibility of the parents. The situation changes in adolescence when the quest for independence clashes with risk-taking behaviour, peer pressure, experimentation with alcohol, drugs and other factors. Insulin omission is not infrequent in this age group and is the predominant cause of recurrent ketoacidosis. Insulin omission may be a cry for attention, a desire to be admitted to the relative safety of a hospital, or even a mark of severe underlying depression with suicidal ideation. The adolescent with recurrent admissions for diabetic ketoacidosis runs a serious risk of causing harm to himself or herself. Removing the right of the adolescent to be responsible for his or her insulin injections usually, dramatically, reduces the frequency of recurrent DKA.[6] Although this is a practical solution to the problem of insulin omission, it does not address the underlying psychological problem and expert psychiatric help is essential.

Development of diabetic ketoacidosis

The crisis in an evolving episode of DKA is usually precipitated when vomiting supervenes. Children, in general, vomit more readily with any illness than do adults. Because of vomiting, oral fluids can no longer replace the large volumes of water lost by the polyuria and dehydration rapidly supervenes. The signs of dehydration are shown in Table 1. Despite the rapid development of life-threatening dehydration, urinary output remains high because of the osmotic diuresis caused by the glucosuria.

Table 1 Signs of dehydration

Mild up to 5% loss of weight	Moderate 6–9% loss of weight	Severe 10+% loss of weight
Thirst	Decreased skin turgor	Hypotension
Tachycardia	Sunken fontanelle in babies	Shock
Dry mouth	Sunken eyes Decreased capillary return Cool periphery	Cyanosis
	Altered sensorium disoriented, agitated or apathetic	

Evolution of diabetic ketoacidosis

The evolution of DKA is characterized by increasing hyperglycaemia and hyperketonaemia.[4] The biochemical mechanisms are discussed in Chapter 2.2. Occasionally, in children, a craving for sweet drinks is a feature of the early stages of diabetes and the consumption of large volumes of sweet fluids may greatly elevate blood glucose levels. Particularly in very young, especially obese, babies, in whom there has been vomiting and poor intake for several days, diabetic ketoacidosis can occur in the absence of markedly raised blood glucose levels (that is, levels of 12–15 mmol/l).

The hyperketonaemia is the product of increased peripheral lipolysis, the increased conversion of these free fatty acids to ketoacids (acetoacetic and beta-hydroxybutyric acids) by the liver, and the decreased peripheral utilization of ketoacids as energy substrates.[4] The diagnosis of DKA is readily suspected by a simple urine test demonstrating glycosuria and ketonuria. However, diabetic ketoacidosis needs to be confirmed by a blood test demonstrating an elevated blood glucose level together with a reduced bicarbonate level or lowered pH.

Defences against acidosis

The increased production of the ketoacids initially causes ketosis without acidosis. However, eventually the body's defences against metabolic acidosis are overwhelmed. These homeostatic defences depend on three mechanisms, namely, buffering, respiratory compensation and renal correction.[4] Buffering systems are very quick, with 85 per cent of the buffering occurring intracellularly. The clinical hallmark of respiratory compensation is hyperventilation (Kussmaul respiration) which is the result of acidosis stimulating the respiratory centre. Respiratory compensation is effective in the short term in maintaining pH because of the unique nature of the bicarbonate buffering system and because the extracellular pH is largely determined by this system (pH = a constant $(pK_a = 6.1) + \log(HCO_3^-/H_2CO_3))$. This form of compensation is limited by the fact that for every H^+ ion eliminated from the body as CO_2 there is the concomitant loss of a HCO_3^- ion ($H^+ + HCO_3^- \leftrightarrow H_2CO_3 \leftrightarrow CO_2 + H_2O$). As diabetic ketoacidosis progresses, the metabolic load of H^+ ions rises to several hundred mmol per day, thereby exceeding the kidney's abilities to generate sufficient HCO_3^- ions and acidosis rapidly develops. Respiratory compensation is fragile and rapid falls in pH can occur with small decrements in HCO_3^- or with small increases in pCO_2 if hyperventilation decreases through exhaustion (for example, a rise in the pCO_2 from 10 to 20 mmHg in a patient with a serum bicarbonate of 4 mmol/l will cause the pH to fall from 7.22 to 7.0).

Diabetic ketoacidosis is a life-threatening disorder which is typically associated with the major deficits in water and electrolytes (Table 2). The extent of these deficits varies greatly and will depend on various factors, the most important being the length of time taken to become acidotic and whether vomiting has supervened. The initial biochemical results of the 91 consecutive episodes of diabetic ketoacidosis severe enough to warrant admission to the intensive care unit of the Royal Alexandra Hospital for Children, Sydney, Australia, in the 10-year-period 1987–96 is shown in Table 3 (unpublished data).

Warning signs in diabetic ketoacidosis

The frequency of DKA in childhood and adolescent diabetes is decreasing because of earlier diagnosis of patients with newly presenting type 1 diabetes and better management of those with established diabetes; however, it remains a problem with significant morbidity and mortality. Warning signs of possible problems should be noted on presentation[6] and include:

- diabetic ketoacidosis in very young patients
- severe dehydration
- shock

Table 2 Deficits in diabetic ketoacidosis

Constituent	Deficit
Water	50–100 ml/kg
Sodium	7–10 mmol/kg
Potassium	5–7 mmol/kg
Chloride	4–7 mmol/kg
Phosphate	2–4 mmol/kg

- pH less than 7.0
- low potassium
- hypernatraemia
- hyperosmolality
- extremely high blood glucose levels
- hyperlipidaemia
- deterioration in consciousness

Successful treatment is dependent on having access to paediatric units of expertise where there are intensive care units and personnel capable of providing the required nursing, laboratory, and medical services (Box 2).[6,7]

Treatment of diabetic ketoacidosis

The aims of therapy in the treatment of diabetic ketoacidosis[6–9] are contained in Box 3.

Treatment of shock

The treatment of shock is accomplished by increasing the intravascular volume so that perfusion of body tissues is improved. Signs of shock include low blood pressure, tachycardia, oliguria, peripheral cyanosis, cold and mottled extremities and the central manifestations of shock

Box 2 Clinical observations in care of diabetic ketoacidosis

- ◆ Hourly pulse rate
- ◆ Hourly respiratory rate
- ◆ Hourly BP initially
- ◆ Hourly neurological observations initially
- ◆ Hourly blood glucose levels whilst on insulin infusion
- ◆ Accurate fluid balance charting (may need urinary catheter)
- ◆ 2–4 hourly temperature
- ◆ Urine testing until negative for ketones

Table 3 Details of 91 consecutive admissions with DKA to intensive care (RAHC, Sydney) 1987–96

	Age (years)	BGl (mmols/l)	Na (mmols/l)	Cor Na (mmols/l)	K (mmols/l)	Osm (mOsm/l)	HCO₃ (mmols/l)	pH
Mean	8.82	36	134	143	4.6	312	6	7.09
25th cent	2.80	26	130	138	4.0	295	4	7.01
75th cent	12.83	40	138	148	5.1	324	8	7.17
Median	10.30	32	134	142	4.6	306	6	7.09
Range	0.33–18.06	17–126	118–153	127–166	2.3–7.6	281–405	1–14	6.80–7.37

BGl: blood glucose; Na: sodium; Cor Na: corrected sodium; K: potassium; Osm: osmolality; HCO₃: bicarbonate.

Box 3 Treatment of diabetic ketoacidosis

- Treatment of shock
- Correction of dehydration
- Replacement of continuing losses
- Maintenance fluids
- Correction of deficits of electrolytes
- Correction of hyperglycaemia
- Correction of acidosis
- Treatment of sepsis if present

Box 4 Calculated sodium and osmolality

- Calculated serum sodium = measured sodium + 1.6/5.5 × (serum glucose − 5.5)
- (an alternate formula widely used for calculated sodium is measured sodium + 0.5(blood glucose − 5.6)) however this gives more elevated values when used in diabetes)
- Calculated plasma osmolality = plasma sodium × 2 + plasma urea (mmol/l) + plasma glucose (mmol/l).

which include disorientation and being semi-comatose. Usually, repeated intravenous bolus doses of 10 ml/kg body weight of normal saline (0.9 per cent saline) are given until blood pressure and signs of tissue perfusion are normalized. As the main cause of the shock is volume depletion due to loss of water, treatment with crystalloids (normal saline) suffices in most instances and colloids (such as albumin or polygeline) should be avoided. In instances of life-threatening shock when plasma volume expanders are required urgently, one can use 10–20 ml/kg of 5 per cent albumin in normal saline or the equivalent of polygeline or infusion of 0.5–1.0 gm/kg of albumin followed by 10–20 ml/kg of normal saline (5 per cent albumin is approximately equivalent to 3.5 per cent polygeline). In addition to fluid replacement, shocked patients should receive oxygen by facial mask.[6]

The correction of poor tissue perfusion is a very important part of the treatment of DKA. Without adequate tissue perfusion insulin would not be able to reach its target tissues. Furthermore, under-perfused tissues are hypoxic and this results in secondary lactic acidosis which adds to the acidosis caused by the accumulation of ketoacids.[10] Dehydration, *per se*, is a physiological stress and leads to elevation of the stress hormones which contribute to the development and maintenance of insulin resistance.[10]

Correction of dehydration

The correction of dehydration commences after the treatment of shock has been accomplished and is a direct function of body mass. The basic rule of rehydration in DKA, as in adults, is to correct the deficit over 24–48 h.[6–9] The degree of dehydration is assessed clinically and the deficit which needs to be made up is calculated by percentage dehydration × body weight, for example, a 40 kg child who is 10 per cent dehydrated requires 4 l of fluid for repair of dehydration. Some protocols suggest that half the calculated deficit should be corrected over the first 8 h with the rest over the following 16 h, however, the safer alternative is for the deficit to be corrected evenly. The more sick the child, the more slow should be the rate of rehydration. A useful guide to the rate of rehydration is to use the calculated total osmolality from the biochemical parameters on admission (Box 4). If the calculated osmolality is 320–360, rehydration should take 36 h. For calculated total osmolalities in excess of 360, rehydration should take 48 h, unless cerebral oedema occurs as a complication when rehydration should be slowed even further.

Maintenance fluid requirements

Maintenance fluid requirements are not directly proportional to body weight but to energy expenditure per unit mass. Caloric or energy expenditure is thus influenced by factors such as age, mass, body temperature, level of activity, environmental activity, humidity, etc. As it is not convenient in practice to measure an individual's caloric expenditure to determine water requirement, an algorithm is used to calculate maintenance fluid requirements. Table 4 expresses water requirements per kg according to age whilst another alogarithm independent of age but giving very similar results is 1500 ml/m²/day. Modifying factors increasing these requirements include fever, hyperventilation and high environmental temperature. Obvious ongoing excessive losses (for example, osmotic diuresis associated with hyperglycaemia, diarrhoea if present) need to be replaced also over and above the calculated maintenance requirements.

It should be recognized that while the correction of the fluid deficits involves three separate considerations (the emergency management of shock, correction of dehydration, and the provision of maintenance fluid requirements) there are various protocols which serve to accomplish these aims. The volume required for the treatment of shock is always dependent on clinical judgement and is based on correcting the vital signs indicating under-perfusion. However, experience has shown that a simplified approach can be applied to the calculation of the volume of fluid required to correct dehydration and provide maintenance requirements. This is to replace the dehydration and maintenance fluid volumes at a rate of 3 l/m² body surface area/day, which approximates 2–2.5 times the normal maintenance requirements and replaces half of the usual 10 per cent fluid deficit over 24 h. The surface of a child or adolescent can be calculated by the use of a nomogram or by the following formula:

$$Body\ surface\ area = square\ root\ of\ the\ sum\ of\ height\ (in\ cm) \times weight\ (in\ kg)\ divided\ by\ 3600.$$

Regardless of which protocol is used to prescribe fluid management, it is essential to review the fluid balance, the electrolyte profile as well as the clinical condition of the patient every 2–4 h.

Fluids used for rehydration and maintenance

Normal saline or 0.9 per cent sodium chloride (sodium 154 mmol/l and chloride 154 mmol/l) is the most widely used fluid for rehydration

Table 4 Maintenance water requirements

	ml/kg/day	ml/kg/h
3rd day of life to 9 months	120–140	5–6
12 months	90–100	3.75–4.0
2 years	80–90	3.33–3.75
4 years	70–80	3.0–3.33
8 years	60–70	2.5–3.0
12 years	50–60	2.0–2.5

in diabetic ketoacidosis.[6,7] If hypernatraemia is a complicating feature then half-normal saline (0.45 per cent saline) needs to be used. Hypernatraemia is present if the calculated serum sodium is above 150 mmol/l (Box 3). The use of normal saline as the basic rehydrating solution will correct the body deficit of sodium, but inevitably will lead to an over-correction of chloride deficits. This contributes to a subsequent hyperchloraemic state, in which a compensated hyperchloraemic metabolic acidosis exists. There is no evidence that there are any adverse outcomes of the hyperchloraemic state which can persist for several days until renal correction restores homeostasis.

Once the blood glucose levels decrease to below 12 mmol/l, glucose needs to be added to the rehydrating fluid. This usually coincides with the major part of the fluid and electrolyte deficits having been repaired and hence there is a lower requirement for ongoing salt replacement. The infusion fluid is therefore changed to half-normal saline containing glucose made up to 5 per cent (0.45 per cent saline +5 per cent dextrose). The addition of glucose to the intravenous fluids allows the continuation of adequate insulin amounts to be given to correct the acidosis. Failure to give glucose containing fluids at this stage will result in inadequate amounts of insulin being infused with the resulting danger of worsening ketoacidosis. Children and adolescents seem to have a greater need for continued insulin at this stage of diabetes ketacidosis management than do adults.

Insulin replacement

Insulin controls the acidosis by inhibiting the production of the metabolic acid load (ketoacids) in diabetic ketoacidosis as well as stimulating the peripheral metabolism of ketoacids. For every molecule of ketoacid anion metabolized one H^+ ion is consumed (for example, $H^+ + Acetoacetate^- \rightarrow$ Acetoacetic acid $\rightarrow H^+ + HCO_3^- \rightarrow H_2O + CO_2$). Insulin reverses the hyperglycaemia by inhibiting the release of hepatic glucose and promoting the uptake of glucose into stores. Thus, the key to reversing diabetic ketoacidosis is insulin. Despite this statement, insulin replacement does not take precedence over correction of shock and the commencement of rehydration. Insulin replacement is best delivered by 'low-dose' insulin infusion and given as a side infusion of short-acting insulin at an initial rate of 0.1 unit/kg/h.[6,7] (It is be possible to administer repeated intramuscular bolus doses of 10–20 per cent of the total daily dose of insulin every 2–4 h but responses are not as predictable as with continuous low-dose intravenous infusions).[11] The desired rate of fall in the blood glucose is 5 mmol/l/h, although a greater fall than this is acceptable in the first 2 hours of treatment as rehydration starts. In children a

loading dose of insulin has not been shown to be of proven benefit, probably because even the so-called low dose insulin infusion results in supraphysiological plasma insulin levels of 100–200 mU/l. These levels are sufficient to inhibit hepatic glucose release, stimulate peripheral glucose utilization, inhibit the release of non-esterified fatty acids (which are the substrates for ketoacid synthesis) as well as to stimulate peripheral ketoacid utilization. The insulin infusion rate can be adjusted hourly (by 10 per cent increments) according to bedside blood glucose readings so as to maintain the fall in the blood glucose levels of 5 mmol/l/h. As mentioned previously, when the blood glucose levels fall below 12 mmol/l, the intravenous fluids are changed to 5 per cent dextrose in 0.45 per cent normal saline and the insulin infusion continued at 0.05 unit/kg/h to keep the blood glucose levels 5–10 mmol/l until ketones are cleared from the urine and the patient is able to tolerate oral food. When oral food is tolerated, the intravenous fluid can be phased out and the insulin can be given subcutaneously. The optimal time to change from intravenous to subcutaneous insulin is before a meal. The first dose of subcutaneous short acting insulin (typically 2/7 of the total daily dose if the patient is known to have diabetes or 2/7 of a total daily dose of 1 unit/kg/day in newly diagnosed patients) is given half an hour before the meal. The infusion is stopped one hour after the meal by which time the subcutaneous short-acting insulin will have taken over.

Potassium

Potassium replacement can safely be started after shock has been corrected and as soon as rehydration commences (unless the patient is known to have renal failure). Potassium replacement at a dose of 5 mmol/kg/day is usually given as potassium chloride or a mixture of potassium chloride/potassium phosphate or potassium chloride/potassium acetate, which is added to the normal saline using concentrations of 40 mmol potassium/l. Repeated electrolyte measurements at 2–4 h intervals are required to monitor potassium replacement. Occasionally, hypokalaemia is a feature of DKA (see clinical case) and higher concentrations of potassium need to be given (with ECG monitoring) as this indicates more profound potassium deficiency. Under these circumstances frequent electrolyte measurements (for example, hourly) are needed.

Bicarbonate

As in adults (see Chapter 2.2), bicarbonate is not generally needed to correct the acidosis of DKA and the main indication for its use is in the dire emergency situation when acidosis is so profound that it may adversely be affecting cardiac output (pH less than 7.0 and/or HCO_3 less than 5 mmol/l). Bicarbonate usage has the potential to cause overshoot alkalosis; hypernatraemia; hypokalaemia; paradoxical cerebral acidosis; decreased tissue oxygenation and stimulation of ketoacid production and hence should be used rarely.[4,6,7,12] If needed, the amount can be calculated from the base deficit derived in the arterial blood gas results by the following formula: dose of bicarbonate = $0.3 \times$ base deficit $\times$ body weight (kg) however it is recommended that only one-third of this be used and given over 30 min (in severe acidosis associated with poor peripheral perfusion arterial blood gases are preferred over venous blood gases). Further doses should only be given after full re-evaluation including a repeat of the arterial blood gases.

Phosphorus replacement

Phosphorus levels (present as phosphate), usually low or low-normal at presentation, fall to very low levels with the start of treatment, because of underlying phosphorus depletion, movement of phosphorus intracellularly and the formation of various intracellular phosphory-lated compounds. As in adults (see Chapter 2. 2) in practice additional phosphorus supplementation is rarely needed and intravenous phos-phate supplementation has been associated with adverse outcomes.[13] The use of potassium phosphate for one-third of the potassium replacement is therefore a logical and a safe way of replacing some of the phosphorus deficits.

Cerebral oedema

Mild cerebral oedema is probably a very frequent,[14] but not univer-sal,[15] phenomenon in the recovery from DKA as demonstrated by serial CT scans, however, life-threatening cerebral oedema remains an albeit rare but much feared complication. While there are known contributing factors to the development of cerebral oedema (over-rapid rehydration, fluid over-load, severity of acidosis, degree of hyperosmolality due to hyperglycaemia and hypernatraemia), many instances have no obvious cause and are idiosyncratic.[16-20] Cerebral oedema tends to present after treatment has started (12–48 h later) but it has been reported prior to the start of intravenous therapy. Patients should be monitored neurologically hourly and, because cerebral oedema may be rapid in onset, mannitol should be readily available. Cerebral oedema demands immediate emergency measures to combat it (intravenous mannitol 1 gm/kg over 15 min followed by a further dose over the next 2 h, fluid restriction, dexamethasone, possibly endotracheal intubation and paralysis, and, rarely neurosur-gical relief of pressure). Relevant monitoring includes CT scanning and inserting of intracranial pressure monitoring.[6,7] The details of the one case of cerebral oedema seen at the Royal Alexandra Hospital for Children in Sydney in 1987–96 are presented in the clinical case (unpublished data).

Other adverse outcomes

Most DKA episodes in childhood and adolescence are successfully treated without complications; however diabetic ketoacidosis remains a potential cause of morbidity or mortality.[1,2] There may be long-term morbidity due to cerebral, hypothalamic, pituitary or spinal cord infarctions.[21-24] The underlying cause of death may be over-whelming acidosis, dehydration, cerebral oedema or interstitial pulmonary oedema.[25] Transient myocardial arrhythmias, usually supra-ventricular tachycardias, may complicate the recovery period of diabetic ketoacidosis. The adverse outcomes of the 1987–96 series from the Royal Alexandra Hospital for Children, Sydney included one instance of a frontal lobe infarct and two instances of persistent upper motor neurone signs in the legs (unpublished data).

Hyperosmolar hyperglycaemic nonketotic coma

This condition, in which the blood glucose is grossly elevated (above 33 mmol/l) in the absence or only trace amounts of ketosis, is rare in childhood. IVS management is considered in Chapter 2.2. Treatment is similar to that of DKA, however, greater emphasis on a more gradual reduction in glucose levels is needed (for example, 2 mmol/h instead of 5 mmol/h).[4,26]

Conclusion

In summary, the successful treatment of DKA in childhood and adolescence is dependent on access to expert nursing and medical care. The condition should be treated within a facility able to provide paediatric intensive care facilities by physicians expert in the care of childhood diabetes and whilst outcomes are generally very favour-able, diabetic ketoacidosis is still a potential cause of death and significant morbidity.

Clinical history

A boy of 12 years, known to have diabetes for three years was found by his mother to be most unwell. Compliance with insulin injections (twice daily isophane/soluble) was always problematic. He was taken to the local hospital several hours later. On physical examination he was semicomatose, afebrile, more than 10 per cent dehydrated, hyperventilating (respiratory rate 85/min), tachycardic (186 beats/min) with a BP 90/70 and a cold mottled periphery marked by poor capillary return. The bladder was palpable almost to the umbilicus. The liver span was enlarged (12.5 cm) and felt to be due to a fatty liver. Urinalysis revealed $+ + + +$ glycosuria (above 110 mmol/l) with $+ + + +$ ketonuria (over 16 mmol/l). The specimen of plasma was inspected and no lipaemia was detected. Biochemical analysis revealed: glucose 126 mmol/l, sodium 126 mmol/l, potassium 3.2 mmol/l, bicarbonate 2 mmol/l, urea 14 mmol/l, creatinine 220 mmol/l, phosphate 1.4 mmol/l. Arterial blood gases revealed a pH of 6.92, pO_2 of 100 mm Hg, pCO_2 10 mm Hg, base deficit greater than -28. Despite the measured low sodium, the corrected plasma sodium was markedly elevated at 161 mmol/l and the calculated plasma osmolality was 392 mmol/l (see formulae). A septic work-up was instituted (blood cultures, urine culture and chest X-ray) and he was started on broad spectrum antibiotics.

He was given three bolus doses of 10 ml/kg body weight of normal saline over the first hour before perfusion improved. In the first hour the BGL fell to 106 mmol/l. Because of the need to have a strict fluid balance he was catheterized. He was then started on a rehydrating and maintenance replacement schedule of normal saline over 48 h (main-tenance plus 10 per cent dehydration = 160 ml/kg/h (2 ml/kg/h for maintenance plus 2 ml/kg/h to replace 4000 ml in 48 h – see Box 4)). As hypokalaemia in the presence of acidosis indicated severe total body potassium deficiency, potassium chloride, 60 mmol/l, was added to the normal saline. A side-drip provided an insulin infusion (made by adding 50 units of short acting insulin to 500 ml of normal saline) at the rate of 0.1 unit/kg/h. This was adjusted hourly to maintain a fall of blood glucose of 5–7 mmol/l/h. After 4 h he seemed much improved. The blood tests at this stage showed the following parameters: glucose 92 mmol/l, sodium 146 mmol/l, potassium 2.8 mmol/l, urea 12 mmol/l, bicarbonate 3 mmol/l, phosphorus 0.5 mmol/l, arterial pH 7.1, pCO_2 10, base deficit greater than -28. Potassium replacement in the normal saline solution was increased to 80 mmol/l and cardiac monitoring intensified. At about 8 h his consciousness deteriorated and, following endotracheal intubation, he was transferred to a major paediatric centre, where on arrival (at 9 h) he was comatose with virtually the same biochemical parameters as at 8 h apart from the potassium rising to 3.4 mmol/l. Emergency therapy for cerebral oedema in the form of reduced intravenous fluid replacement, IV mannitol (1 gm/kg given over 15 min followed by an equal dose over the next 2 h) and IV dexamethasone in neurosurgical doses (4 mg every 4 h) was instituted immediately. Cerebral oedema was confirmed by CT scanning and a subdural pressure monitor (Comino bolt) was installed by the neuro-surgeons and intracranial pressure monitoring started. With this therapy intracranial pressure stabilized at an acceptable level. The rehydration schedule was slowed to over 96 h and the maintenance volumes halved. Because of calculated hypernatraemia (calculated sodium 171 mmol/l – see formula) the rehydrating solution was changed to 0.5 N saline (0.45 per cent saline) and the rate of insulin infusion controlled to maintain a fall in the blood glucose of 5 mmol/l/h. When the blood glucose level reached 12 mmol/l, glucose was added to the rehydrating and maintenance fluids to create 5 per cent glucose solutions and the insulin infusion adjusted to maintain levels of 5–10 mmol/l. He remained comatose for 48 h before slowly regaining consciousness. Initially, he exhibited the organic brain syndrome together with upper motor neurone signs in his legs. Over the next seven days there was a gradual resolution with the dexa-methasone being gradually weaned before being ceased. The insulin infusion was continued for a total of four days at an approximate infusion rate of 0.05 units/kg/h with glucose levels being maintained at 5–10 mmol/l with a 5 per cent glucose infusion in 0.225 per cent saline (the 0.45 per cent saline being changed to 0.225 per cent saline after 48 h). Antibiotics were ceased when the septic work-up revealed no bacterial growth in any cultures. When oral food was tolerated, he was changed over to a six hourly subcutaneous dosage of regular insulin for 24 h and then to his twice daily mixture of isophane and regular insulin. On day four his blood glucose was 8.0 mmol/l, sodium 139 mmol/l, chloride 120 mmol/l, potassium 4 mmol/l, bicarbonate 14 mmol/l indicative of a compensated hyperchloraemic metabolic acidosis. By day eight these parameters were normal.

References

1. Scibilia J, Finegold D, Dorman J, Becker D, Drash A. Why do children with diabetes die? *Acta Endocrinologica* (suppl.) 1986; **279**: 326–33.

2. Modan M, Karp M, Bauman B, Gordon O, Danon YL, Laron Z. Mortality in Israeli Jewish patients with type 1 (insulin-dependent) diabetes mellitus diagnosed prior to 18 years of age: a population based study. *Diabetologia*, 1991; **34**(7): 515–20.

3. Rosenbloom AL. Intracerebral crises during treatment of diabetic ketoacidosis. *Diabetes Care*, 1990; **13**(1): 22–33.

4. DeFronzo RA, Matsuda M, Barrett EJ. Diabetic ketoacidosis. A combined metabolic-nephrologic approach to therapy. *Diabetes Reviews*, 1994; **2**: 209–38.

5. Bratusch-Marrain PR, DeFronzo RA. Impairment of insulin-mediated glucose metabolism by hyperosmolality in man. *Diabetes*, 1983; **32**: 1028–34.

6. Silink M, ed. The management of diabetic ketoacidosis. In: APEG Handbook on childhood and adolescent diabetes. Published NSW Govt Printer. Distributed Child Health Promotion Unit, RAHC, Parramatta Sydney, 1996 (Ch. 7, pp. 36–42).

7. Rosenbloom A, Hanas R. Diabetic ketoacidosis (Diabetic Ketoacidosis). Treatment Guidelines. *Clinical Pediatrics*, 1996; **35**: 261–6.

8. Sperling MA, ed. Diabetes Mellitus. In: *Paediatric Endocrinology*. Philadelphia: WB Saunders and Co., 1996 (Ch. 7, pp. 229–64).

9. Edge JA. Management of ketoacidosis in childhood. *British Journal of Hospital Medicine*, 1996; **55**(8): 508–12.

10. Waldheusl W, Kleinberger G, Korn A, Dudcza R, Bratusch-Marrain P, Nowatny P. Severe hyperglycaemia: effects of rehydration on endocrine derangements and blood glucose concentration. *Diabetes*, 1979; **28**: 577–84.

11. Butkiewicz EK, Leibson CL, O'Brien PC, Palumbo PJ, Rizza RA. Insulin therapy for diabetic ketoacidosis. Bolus insulin injection versus continuous insulin infusion. *Diabetes Care*, 1995; **18**(8): 1187–90.

12. Hale PJ, Crase J, Nattrass M. Metabolic effect of bicarbonate in the treatment of diabetic ketoacidosis. *British Medical Journal*, 1984; **289**: 1035–8.

13. Winter RI, Harris CJ, Phillips LS, Green OC. Diabetic ketoacidosis. Induction of hypocalcaemia and hypomagnesemia by phosphate therapy. *American Medical Journal*, 1979; **67**: 897–900.

14. Krane J, Rockoff MA, Wallman JK, Wolfsdorf JI. Subclinical brain swelling in children during treatment of diabetic ketoacidosis. *New England Journal of Medicine*, 1985; **312**: 1147–51.

15. Smedman L, Escobar R, Hesser U, Persson B. Sub-clinical cerebral oedema does not occur regulary during treatment for diabetic ketoacidosis. *Acta Paediatrica*, 1997; **86**(11): 1172–6.

16. Edge JA, Dunger DB. Variations in the management of diabetic ketoacidosis in children. *Diabetic Medicine*, 1994; **11**(10): 984–6.

17. Hale PM, Rezvani I, Braunstein AW, Lipman TH, Martinez N, Garibaldi L. Factors predicting cerebral edema in young children with diabetic ketoacidosis and new onset type 1 diabetes. *Acta Paediatrica*, 1997; **86**(6): 626–31.

18. Mel JM, Werther GA. Incidence and outcome of cerebral oedema in childhood: are there predictors? *Journal of Paediatric Child Health*, 1995; **31**: 17–20.

19. Harris GD, Fiordalisi I, Harris WL, Mosovich LL, Finberg L. Minimizing the risk of brain herniation during treatment of diabetic ketoacidemia: a retrospective and prospective study. *Journal of Pediatrics*, 1990; **117**: 22–31.

20. Hammond P, Wallis S. Cerebral oedema in diabetic ketoacidosis. *British Medical Journal*, 1992; **305**: 203–4.

21. Roger B, Sills I, Cohen M, Seidel FG. Diabetic ketoacidosis. Neurologic collapse during treatment followed by severe developmental morbidity. *Clinical Pediatrics*, 1990; **29**(8): 451–6.

22. Roe TF, Crawford TO, Huff KR, Costin G, Kaufman FR, Nelson MD. Brain infarction in children with diabetic ketoacidosis. *Journal of Diabetes and its Complications*, 1996; **12**(2): 100–8.

23. Atkin SL, Coady AM, Horton D, Sutaria N, Sellars L, Walton C. Multiple cerebral haematomata and peripheral nerve palsies associated with a case of juvenile diabetic ketoacidosis. *Diabetic Medicine*, 1995; **12**(3): 267–70.

24. Tubiana-Rufi N, Thizon-de Gaulle I, Czernichow P. Hypothalamopituitary deficiency and precocious puberty following hyperhydration in diabetic ketoacidosis. *Hormone Research*, 1992; **37**(1–2): 60–3.

25. **Hoffmann WL** *et al.* Interstitial pulmonary oedema in children and adolescents with diabetic ketoacidosis. *Journal of Diabetes and its Complications*, 1988; **12**(6): 314–20.

26. **Ellis EN**. Concepts of fluid therapy in diabetic ketoacidosis and hyperosmolar hyperglycemic nonketotic coma. *Pediatric Clinics of North America*, 1990; **37**(2): 313–21.

2.2 Hyperglycaemic crises in adult patients with diabetes mellitus

Abbas E. Kitabchi and Mary Beth Murphy

Introduction

Diabetic Ketoacidosis (DKA) and the hyperosmolar non-ketotic state (HONK, also referred to in the USA as hyperosmolar hyperglycaemic state or HHS) are the two most serious acute hyperglycaemic metabolic complications of diabetes mellitus, even if managed properly. These disorders can occur in type 1 and type 2 diabetes. In the USA, the annual incidence rate for DKA from population-based studies ranges from 4.6–8 episodes per 1000 patients with diabetes.[1] There is evidence that hospitalizations for DKA have been increasing during the past two decades,[2] with DKA currently accounting for 4–9 per cent of all hospital discharge summaries among patients with diabetes.[3] The incidence of HONK is difficult to determine because of the lack of population-based studies and the multiple combined illnesses often found in these patients. In general, it is estimated that the rate of hospital admissions due to HONK is lower than DKA and accounts for less than one per cent of all primary diabetic admissions.[3–4]

The mortality rate in patients with DKA has significantly decreased to less than five per cent in experienced centres since the advent of low-dose insulin treatment regimens and appropriate fluid/electrolyte replacement protocols; however, the mortality rate of patients with HONK still remains high at approximately 15 per cent. The prognosis of both conditions is substantially worsened with increased age, presence of coma and hypotension.[5–7]

Definition of terms

DKA is a metabolic derangement seen in type 1 or type 2 diabetes which is caused by an absolute or relative deficiency of insulin resulting in hyperglycaemia, dehydration, ketonaemia, and metabolic acidosis. The laboratory diagnosis of DKA includes a plasma glucose above 13.9 mmol/l; a serum bicarbonate below 15 mmol/l, an arterial pH less than 7.3 and moderate to large ketones on serum or urine dipstick. From an historical perspective, HONK has been identified by several acronyms including: hyperglycaemic hyperosmolar non-ketotic coma (HHNC), hyperglycaemic hyperosmolar non-ketotic state (HHNK), and hyperosmolar non-ketotic coma (HNOK) and, most recently, in the USA, as HHS. All of these terms attempt to

define a state in which there is severe hyperglycaemia resulting in dehydration and hyperosmolarity with minimal ketosis and with or without coma. Because of the variability of the ketosis and mental status, the term HHS is probably the most appropriate term since ketosis is usually minimal but may not be absent and mental status can vary from moderate mental status changes to coma. However, we have retained the more familiar HONK for this article. The laboratory diagnosis of HONK includes a plasma glucose above 33 mmol/l (600 mg/dl), serum bicarbonate above 15 mmol/l, venous pH greater than 7.3 and small ketones on serum or urine dipstick. HONK characteristically complicates type 2 diabetes and may be present at the time of presentation. Table 1 compares the laboratory characteristics and fluid/anion/cation deficiencies in these two conditions.

Precipitating factors

Insulin hyposecretion, with or without peripheral insulin resistance and anti-insulin stress responses are the *sine qua non* of acute, severe hyperglycaemic states. Infection is the most common precipitating factor in the development of DKA and HONK. Other precipitating factors include omission or inadequate use of insulin and other stressful conditions such as cerebrovascular accident, alcohol abuse, pancreatitis, myocardial infarction, trauma, and drugs. New onset type 1 diabetes, not recognized early enough, can lead to the development of DKA. New onset diabetes occurring in the elderly (particularly residents of nursing homes) or people who become hyperglycaemic and are unaware or unable to treat the ensuing dehydration (or worse, treat their symptoms with proprietary drinks with high sugar content) are at risk for the development of HONK.[6]

Drugs that affect carbohydrate metabolism such as corticosteroids, thiazides, and sympathomimetic agents such as dobutamine and terbutaline may precipitate the development of HONK and DKA in susceptible individuals. In young patients with type 1 diabetes, psychological problems complicated by eating disorders may be a contributing factor in 20 per cent of recurrent ketoacidosis. Other factors that may lead to insulin omission and DKA in younger patients include fear of gaining weight with good metabolic control, fear of hypoglycaemia, rebellion from authority, and the stress of chronic disease.[8]

Pathogenesis

DKA and HONK are extreme manifestations of the impaired metabolic regulation that occurs in diabetes, resulting in abnormal metabolism of carbohydrate, protein and fat and disturbances of fluid and electrolyte balance. Although the pathogenesis of DKA is better understood than that of HONK, the basic underlying mechanism for both is a reduction in the net effective action of circulating insulin, coupled with a concomitant elevation of counter-regulatory stress hormones such as glucagon, catecholamines, cortisol, and growth hormone. In HONK, there is a residual insulin secretion which minimizes ketosis but does not control hyperglycaemia. This leads to severe dehydration, which is exacerbated by inadequate fluid intake and ensuing impaired renal function which leads to decreased excretion of glucose. These factors, coupled with a stressful condition, result in a more severe hyperglycaemic/hyperosmolar state than seen in DKA. Figure 1 depicts the pathogenic pathway of both DKA

Table 1 Diagnostic criteria and typical total body deficits of water and electrolytes in diabetic ketoacidosis (DKA) and hyperosmolar non-ketotic state (HONK)

	DKA			HONK
	Mild	**Moderate**	**Severe**	
Plasma glucose (mmol/l)	>13.9	>13.9	>13.9	>33.3
Arterial pH	7.25–7.30	7.00–<7.24	<7.00	>7.30
Serum bicarbonate (mmol/l)	15–18	10–<15	<10	>15
Urine ketone*	Small	Moderate	Large	Small
Serum ketone*	Small	Moderate	Large	Small
Effective serum osmolality**	Variable	Variable	Variable	>320 mOsml/kg
Anion Gap***	Wide (>10)	Wide (>12)	Wide (>12)	Normal to slightly wide (<12)
Alteration in sensorium or mental obtundation	Alert	Alert/drowsy	Stupor/coma	Stupor/coma
Typical Deficit‡				
Total water (l)	6			9
Water (ml/kg)†	100			100–200
Na^+ (mmol/kg)	7–10			5–13
Cl^- (mmol/kg)	3–5			5–15
K^+ (mmol/kg)	3–5			4–6
PO_4 (mmol/kg)	5–7			3–7
Mg^{++} (mmol/kg)	2–4			2–4
Ca^{++} (mmol/kg)	2–4			2–4

* Nitroprusside reaction method.

** Calculation: Effective serum osmolality: 2 (measured Na mEq/l) + glucose (mmol/l).

*** Calculation: Anion Gap: $(Na^+) - (Cl^- + HCO_3^-)$ mmol/l.

† Per kg of body weight.

‡ Data from References (27) and (12).

and HONK. Inadequate or ineffective insulin and increased levels of stress (counter-regulatory) hormones result in alterations of metabolism in carbohydrate, fat, and protein which are described below.[9]

Carbohydrate metabolism

When insulin is deficient (absolutely or relatively), hyperglycaemia results from: increased gluconeogenesis, accelerated glycogenolysis, and impaired glucose utilization by peripheral tissues.[10–12] Increased hepatic glucose production results from increased activity of rate-limiting gluconeogenic enzymes including fructose 1,6 biphosphatase, phosphoenolpyruvate carboxykinase (PEPCK), glucose 6 phosphatase, and pyruvate carboxylase which are stimulated by an increased glucagon/insulin ratio and hypercortisolism.[13] Furthermore, levels of gluconeogenic precursors rise, including:

(1) amino acids (alanine and glutamine) as a result of accelerated proteolysis and decreased protein synthesis;

(2) lactate as a result of increased muscle glycogenolysis and

(3) glycerol as a result of increased lipolysis.[11]

Although increased hepatic gluconeogenesis is the main mechanism of hyperglycaemia in severe ketoacidosis, recent studies have shown a significant portion of gluconeogenesis may be renal.[14] The decreased insulin availability and partial insulin resistance of DKA and HONK also contribute to decreased peripheral glucose utilization which adds to the overall hyperglycaemic state. Plasma glucose levels are always very high in HONK but can be mildly elevated in DKA, when renal function is good and causes major glycosuria.

Lipid and ketone metabolism

The increased production of non-esterified (free) fatty acids (NEFA) in DKA is the result of a combination of insulin deficiency and increased concentrations of counter-regulatory hormones, particularly adrenaline, which leads to the activation of hormone-sensitive lipase in the adipose tissue.[15,16] This breaks triglyceride into glycerol and NEFA. Although glycerol is used as a substrate for gluconeogenesis in the liver and the kidney, the massive release of NEFA assumes pathophysiological predominance in the liver. NEFA are oxidized to ketone bodies in the liver, a process predominantly stimulated by glucagon. They are also converted to diacylglycerol which may result in hyperlipidaemia and increased very-low-density lipoproteins (VLDL).[17] Glucagon increases hepatic carnitine levels and decreases hepatic malonyl CoA, stimulating carnitine acyltransferase (CAT1), the rate-limiting enzyme in ketogenesis. In addition to increased production of ketone bodies, clearance of ketones is decreased in DKA,[18–19] secondary to low insulin concentrations, increased glucocorticoids, and decreased peripheral glucose utilization.[20]

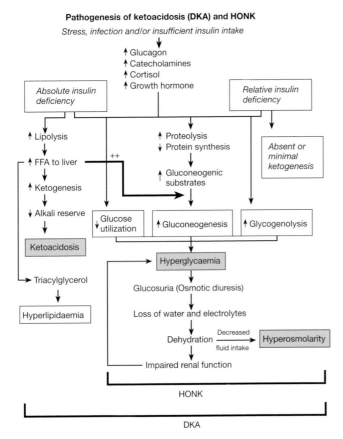

Fig. 1 Pathogenic pathway of DKA and HHS.

Growth hormone (GH) may also play a prominent role in ketogenesis. Even modest physiological doses of growth hormone can markedly increase circulating levels of NEFA and ketone bodies.[21] Spontaneous DKA is characterized by simultaneous elevations of multiple insulin-antagonizing (counter-regulatory) hormones[22,23] in the face of reduced insulin which converts the body from a carbohydrate metabolizing system to a lipid metabolizing system, the hallmark of DKA.

HONK on the other hand may be due to plasma insulin concentrations inadequate to facilitate glucose utilization by insulin sensitive tissues, but adequate (as determined by residual C-peptide) to prevent cellular lipolysis and subsequent ketogenesis.[24] There are few data in HONK to conclude whether or not differences in the level of stress hormones contribute to the less prominent ketosis seen in this state. Available data are consistent with multiple contributing factors with the most consistent differences being lower growth hormone and higher insulin in HONK than DKA (Table 2).[25] The higher insulin levels in HONK than DKA suggest that enough insulin may be available to inhibit cellular lipolysis but not enough for optimal carbohydrate metabolism.[17,26]

Water and electrolyte disturbances

Estimated electrolyte deficiencies in DKA and HONK are summarized in Table 1. As can be seen, the two states differ in the magnitude of dehydration and degree of ketosis and acidosis. Hyperglycaemia leads to an osmotic diuresis in both, with loss of water, sodium, potassium, and other electrolytes. Ketoanion excretion, which obligates urinary cation excretion, as sodium, potassium, and ammonium salts, also contributes to a solute diuresis. The extent of dehydration however is typically greater in HONK. At first this seems paradoxical, as patients with DKA experience the dual osmotic load of ketones and glucose. However, urinary ketoanion excretion on a molar basis is generally less than half that of glucose.[27–32] Factors which contribute to excessive volume losses in HONK include a protracted length of metabolic decompensation, impaired fluid intake, diuretic use, concomitant fever and gastrointestinal upset.[6,27,33,34] The more severe dehydration, together with the older average age of patients with HONK and the presence of other co-morbidities almost certainly accounts for the higher mortality of HONK.[34]

The osmotic diuresis in DKA and HONK promotes the net loss of multiple minerals and electrolytes (Na, K, Ca, Mg, Cl, and PO_4). While some of these can be replaced rapidly during treatment (Na, K, and Cl), others require days or weeks to restore losses and achieve balance.[35]

Abnormalities in intravascular potassium (K) in hyperglycaemic crises occur as a result of: increased plasma tonicity resulting in intracellular water and potassium shifts into the extracellular space; protein catabolism with resultant potassium shift into the extracellular space;[36] decreased potassium re-entry into the cell secondary to insulinopenia and significant renal potassium losses as a result of osmotic diuresis and ketonuria. Progressive volume depletion leads to decreased glomerular

Table 2 Biochemical data on admission in patients with diabetes admitted for hyperosmolar non-ketotic state (HONK) or diabetic ketoacidosis (DKA)

Value	Mean ± SEM	
	HONK (n=12)	DKA (n=22)
Glucose (mmol/l)	51.6 ± 4.6	34.2 ± 2.0
Na⁺ (mmol/l)	149.0 ± 3.2	134.4 ± 1.0
K⁺ (mmol/l)	3.9 ± 0.2	4.5 ± 0.13
BUN (mmol/l)	23.4 ± 3.8	11.7 ± 1.0
Creatinine (μmol/l)	123.9 ± 6.6	97.3 ± 3.7
PH	7.33 ± 0.03	7.12 ± 0.04
Bicarbonate (mmol/l)	18.0 ± 1.1	9.4 ± 1.4
Lactate (mmol/l)	3.9 ± 0.4	2.4 ± 0.2
3-β-hydroxybutyrate (mmol/l)	1.0 ± 0.2	9.10 ± 0.85
Osmolality*	380.0 ± 5.7	323.3 ± 2.5
IRI (nmol/l)	0.08 ± 0.01	0.07 ± 0.01
C-peptide (nmol/l)	1.14 ± 0.10	0.21 ± 0.03
FFA (nmol/l)	1.5 ± 0.19	1.6 ± 0.16
Glucagon (ng/ml)	1.9 ± 0.2	6.1 ± 1.2
Cortisol (ng/ml)	570.0 ± 49	500.0 ± 61
IRI (nmol/l)†	0.27 ± 0.05	0.09 ± 0.01
C-peptide (nmol/l)†	1.75 ± 0.23	0.25 ± 0.05

Reprinted with permission from Chupin M, Charbonnel B, Chupin F. C-peptide blood levels in ketoacidosis and in hyperosmolar non-ketotic diabetic coma. *Acta Diabetologica*, 1981; **18**: 123–8.

IRI = Immunoreactive insulin, BUN = Blood urea nitrogen, FAA = Free fatty acids.

* According to the formula 2(Na + K) + urea + glucose (mM).

† Values following intravenous administration of tolbutamide.

filtration rate and a greater retention of glucose and ketoanions in plasma which exacerbates plasma tonicity. Thus, in DKA a considerable percentage of patients exhibit concomitant hyperosmolarity. In one study, approximately 36 per cent of the DKA patients demonstrated elevated plasma osmolality.[37] Patients with a better history of food, salt and fluid intake prior to and during DKA have better preservation of kidney function, greater ketonuria and lower ketonaemia, a lower anion gap and are less hyperosmolar.

During treatment of DKA with insulin, hydrogen ions are consumed as ketoanion metabolism is facilitated. This regenerates bicarbonate which improves metabolic acidosis and decreases the plasma anion gap. The urinary loss of ketoanions, as sodium and potassium salts, therefore, represents the loss of potential bicarbonate, which is gradually recovered within a few days or weeks.[35]

Diagnosis

History and physical examination

The evolution of the acute DKA episode in type 1 or type 2 diabetes is typically very short while the process of HONK may evolve symptomatically over several days to weeks. For both, the classical clinical picture includes a history of polyuria, polydipsia, polyphagia, weight loss, vomiting, abdominal pain (only in DKA), dehydration, weakness, clouding of sensorium and finally coma. Findings on physical examination include poor skin turgor, Kussmaul respirations in DKA, tachycardia and, if unrecognized and left untreated, hypotension, alteration in mental status, shock and ultimately coma. Mental status can vary from full alertness to profound lethargy or coma, with the latter being more frequent in HONK. Although infection is a common precipitating factor for both conditions, patients can be normothermic or even hypothermic primarily due to peripheral vasodilatation and low fuel substrate availability. Hypothermia is a poor prognostic sign.[6] Patients may complain of abdominal pain on presentation which could be the result or cause (particularly in younger patients) of DKA. Further evaluation is necessary if this complaint does not resolve with resolution of dehydration and metabolic acidosis. Guaiac-positive coffee-ground emesis is found in up to 25 per cent of DKA patients, due to haemorrhagic gastritis.[33]

Laboratory evaluation

The initial laboratory evaluation of patients with suspected DKA or HONK should include:

(1) Plasma glucose

(2) Electrolytes, urea, creatinine with calculated anion gap $(Na^+ + K^+) - (Cl^- + HCO_3^-)$

(3) Serum and/or urine 'ketone' by dipstick

(4) Effective plasma osmolality $2 \times (Na^+) +$ glucose in mmol/l

(5) Urinalysis for glucose, ketones, and leukocytes

(6) Initial arterial blood gases

(7) Electrocardiogram (ECG) – to rule out an acute cardiac event as the precipitating cause as well as to monitor the effects of electrolyte replacement therapy

(8) Complete blood count with differential count

(9) Bacterial cultures of urine, blood, throat etc., if infection is suspected and chest X-ray if indicated.[38]

Additionally, a HbA₁c may be useful in determining whether this acute event is the result of chronic hyperglycaemia in a poorly-controlled or unrecognized diabetic or an isolated acute episode in an otherwise well-controlled patient. Table 1 depicts typical laboratory findings of patients with DKA and HONK.

The majority of patients with hyperglycaemic emergencies present with leukocytosis which is proportional to blood ketone body concentration and does not necessarily indicate infection. The serum sodium concentration is usually decreased because of the osmotic flux of water from the intracellular to the extracellular space in the presence of hyperglycaemia. This value can be corrected by adding 1.6 mmol/l of sodium for every 5.6 mmol/l of glucose above 5.6 mmol/l. Measured serum sodium and glucose concentrations may be falsely lowered by severe hypertriglyceridaemia in laboratories using volumetric testing or dilution of samples with ion-specific electrodes.[39,40] The serum potassium concentration may be elevated because of an extracellular shift of potassium due to insulin deficiency, hypertonicity and acidaemia. Patients with low-normal or low serum potassium concentration upon admission require very careful cardiac monitoring and more vigorous potassium replacement, as treatment lowers potassium further and can provoke cardiac dysrhythmia. Therefore, insulin should not be given until the serum potassium is greater than or equal to 3.3 mmol/l.

The accumulation of ketoacids results in metabolic acidosis which increases the plasma anion gap. In the past, normal anion gap was reported as 12 mmol/l;[12] however, serum sodium and chloride measured by ion-specific electrodes measures 2–6 mmol/l higher than earlier techniques, so currently the normal anion gap methodology is 7–9 mmol/l.[41,42] Therefore, an anion gap over 10–12 mmol/l indicates an increased anion gap acidosis.[41,42] Measured serum creatinine may be falsely elevated by interference with the assay by elevated acetoacetate.[43,44] This elevation should be monitored during hydration and following correction of acidosis. Total osmolality is calculated by the following formula: 2 (measured Na^+ mmol/l) + glucose (mmol/l) + urea (mmol/l). However, urea is an ineffective osmole, therefore, effective osmolality is a more accurate indicator of plasma tonicity and may be calculated as above. Total and effective osmolality correlate with mental status. As shown in Fig. 2, typically, patients who are stuporous or comatose have total and effective osmolalities of 340 and 320 mOsml/kg H_2O, respectively.[33,37] The occurrence of stupor or coma in diabetic patients in the absence of definitive elevation of effective osmolality (more than 320 mOsml/kg) demands immediate consideration of other causes of mental status change. Amylase levels are elevated in the majority of patients with DKA, but this may be due to non-pancreatic sources, such as the parotid gland. A serum lipase may be beneficial in the differential diagnosis of pancreatitis but may also be elevated in DKA. Abdominal pain and elevation of serum amylase and liver enzymes are more commonly noted in DKA than HONK.

Differential diagnosis

Ketoacidosis not only occurs in DKA but also in starvation ketosis and alcoholic ketoacidosis (AKA). These are distinguished by clinical history and by plasma glucose concentrations that range from mildly elevated (rarely above 13.9 mmol/l) to hypoglycaemia. In addition,

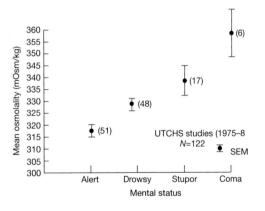

Fig. 2 Relationship of calculated serum osmolality on admission in 122 ketoacidotic patients to mental status. With permission from Kitabchi AE, Fischer IN. Insulin therapy of diabetic ketoacidosis: physiologic versus pharmacologic doses of insulin and their routes of administration. In: Brownlee M, ed. *Handbook of Diabetes Mellitus.* New York: Garland ATPM Press, 1981: 95–149.

while AKA can result in profound acidosis, with starvation ketosis the serum bicarbonate concentration is usually not lower than 18 mmol/l. DKA must also be distinguished from other causes of high anion gap metabolic acidosis including lactic acidosis, ingestion of drugs such as salicylate, methanol, ethylene glycol and paraldehyde and chronic renal failure (which is more typically hyperchloraemic rather than high anion gap). Clinical history of previous drug intoxications, or metformin use should be sought. Measurement of blood lactate, serum salicylate and blood methanol levels can be helpful in these situations. Ethylene glycol (antifreeze) is suggested by the presence of calcium oxalate and hippurate crystals in the urine. Paraldehyde ingestion is suspected by its characteristic strong odour in the breath. As each of these intoxicants result from the ingestion of low-molecular weight organic compounds, they can produce an osmolar gap in addition to the anion-gap acidosis.[24,27,28] Table 3 outlines the laboratory values and metabolic causes of various conditions associated with acidosis and coma.

Treatment

Therapeutic goals for the successful treatment of DKA and HONK include:

(a) improving circulatory volume and tissue perfusion

(b) decreasing serum glucose and plasma osmolality at a steady rate

(c) clearing the serum and urine of ketones

(d) correcting electrolyte imbalances

(e) identifying and treating precipitating factors

As has been clearly demonstrated in the past, hydration alone can affect clinical outcome by replacing fluid deficits, decreasing the level of counter-regulatory hormones and improving the hyperosmolar state which decreases insulin resistance.[23,45] Therefore, a low dose insulin regimen is more effective when preceded by hydration.

Fluid therapy

Initial fluid therapy is directed toward expansion of the intravascular and extravascular volume and restoration of renal perfusion. In the absence of cardiac compromise, isotonic saline (0.9 per cent NaCl), is infused at a rate of 15–20 ml/kg body weight/h or greater during the first hour (up to 1.5 l in the average adult). Subsequent choice for fluid replacement depends on the state of hydration, serum electrolyte levels and urinary output, but in general 4–14 ml/kg/h of 0.9 per cent NaCl if the corrected serum sodium is normal or low, 0.45 per cent NaCl at a similar rate can be used if corrected serum sodium is high. Once plasma glucose has fallen to about 14 mmol/l, glucose solutions should be used to continue fluid and insulin replacement. After the first litre of saline, potassium should be added at the rate of 20–40 mmol/l (two-thirds potassium chloride and one-third potassium phosphate) until the patient is stable and can tolerate oral supplementation. Potassium phosphate is best used in conjunction with potassium chloride (2 : 1), to decrease the chloride load as well as to replace intracellular losses of phosphate.

Adequate progress with fluid replacement is judged by haemodynamic improvement (BP), measurement of fluid input/output and clinical examination. Fluid replacement should correct estimated deficits slowly within the first 24 h. The induced change in serum osmolality should not exceed 3 mOsml/kg H_2O per h.[24,27,32,46] In patients with

Table 3 Laboratory evaluation of metabolic causes of acidosis and coma

	Starvation of high fat intake	DKA	Lactic acidosis	Uremic acidosis	Alcoholic ketosis (starvation)	Salicylate intoxication	Methanol or ethylene glycol intoxication	Hyperosmolar coma	Hypoglycaemic coma	Rhabdomyolysis
pH	Normal	↓	↑	Mild ↓	↓↑	↓↑*	↓	Normal	Normal	Mild ↓ may be ↓↓
Plasma glucose	Normal	↑	Normal	Normal	↓ or normal	Normal or ↓	Normal	↑↑ >27.8 mmol/l	↓↓ <1.7 mmol/l	Normal
Glycosuria	Negative	++	Negative	Negative	Negative	Negative†	Negative	++	Negative	Negative
Total plasma ketones‡	Slight ↑	↑↑	Normal	Normal	Slight to moderate ↑	Normal	Normal	Normal or slight ↑	Normal	Normal
Anion gap	Slight ↑	↑	↑	Slight ↑	↑	↑	↑	Normal or slight ↑	Normal	↑↑
Osmolality	Normal	↑	Normal	↑	Normal	Normal	↑↑	↑↑ >330 mOsml/kg	Normal	Normal or slight ↑
Uric acid	Mild ↑ (starvation)	↑	Normal	Normal ↑	↑	Normal	Normal	Normal	Normal	↑
Miscellaneous		May give false positive for ethylene glycol	Serum lactate >7 mmol/l	Urea >11.1 mmol/l		Serum salicylate +	Serum levels positive			Myoglobinuria, Haemoglobinuria

Data printed with permission from Fishbein HA, Palumbo PJ. Acute metabolic complications in diabetes. *Diabetes in America (National Diabetes Data Group)*. National Institute of Health, 1995. (NIH Publication No. 95–1468), 283–91.

DKA = diabetic ketoacidosis; + = positive; − = negative.

* Acetest and Ketostix measure acetoacetic acid only. Thus, misleading low values may be obtained because the majority of 'ketone bodies' are β-hydroxybutyrate.

† Respiratory alkalosis/metabolic acidosis.

‡ May get false-positive or false-negative urinary glucose caused by the presence of salicylate or its metabolites.

renal or cardiac compromise, monitoring of serum osmolarity and frequent assessment of cardiac, renal and mental status must be performed during fluid resuscitation to avoid iatrogenic fluid overload.[24,27,32,46] Measurement of central venous pressure may be needed.

Insulin therapy

Low dose insulin therapy proposed in the early 1970s[47,48] is now accepted as the optimal method of treatment of DKA after randomized prospective studies demonstrated similar outcomes in conventional high dose insulin treatment protocols versus low dose treatment protocols[24] (Fig. 3A). Hypoglycaemia and hypokalaemia are less frequent in low dose treatment regimens.

The optimal route of insulin therapy was also evaluated during this period and it was found that regardless of the route (intravenous (i.v.), subcutaneous (s.c.), intramuscular (i.m.)), recovery parameters were found to be similar in the three treatment groups (Fig. 3B). However, i.v. therapy demonstrated a greater decline in plasma glucose and

ketone bodies in the first two hours of treatment and the number of patients in the i.m. and s.c. groups who required additional priming doses of insulin were greater than in the i.v. therapy group. The rate of decline in blood glucose and ketone bodies after the first two hours remained comparable in all the three groups (Fig. 3B). In a subsequent study, the efficacy of an intravenous loading dose was evaluated in a low dose i.v. and i.m. treatment protocol. The results demonstrated that the initial delay in response to insulin therapy may be overcome by utilizing an intravenous loading dose of insulin (Fig. 3C), suggesting an intravenous loading dose of insulin is desirable regardless of the route of subsequent insulin administration.[24]

In moderate to severe DKA or DKA with mental obtundation (as defined in Table 1), regular intravenous insulin by continuous infusion is the treatment of choice. Once hypokalaemia (K^+ below 3.3 mmol/l) is excluded, an intravenous bolus of soluble insulin of 0.15 U/kg of body weight, followed by a continuous infusion at a dose of 0.1 U/kg/h (5–7 U/h in adults) should be administered. This low dose insulin usually decreases plasma glucose concentration at

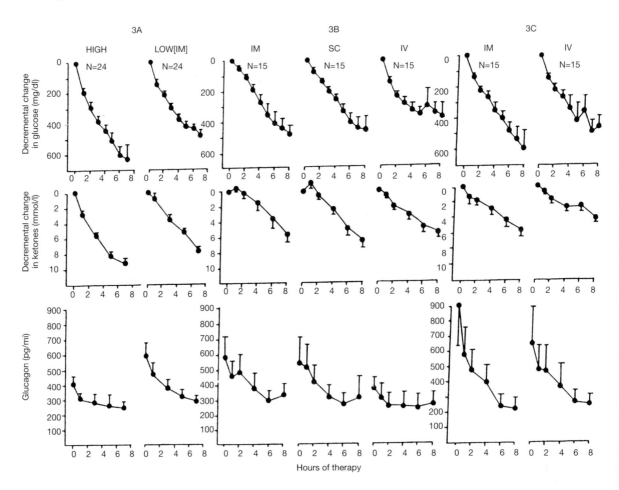

Fig. 3 Decremental changes in plasma glucose (mmol/l) and ketone bodies (mmol/l) and fall in plasma glucagon (pcg/ml). Conventional method of insulin therapy is compared with six methods of low dose regimens in seven groups of patients (total of 123 patients). With permission from Kitabchi AE, Fisher IN. Insulin therapy of diabetic ketoacidosis: physiologic versus pharmacologic doses of insulin and their routes of administration. In: Brownlee M, ed. *Handbook of Diabetes Mellitus*. New York: Garland ATPM Press, 1981: 95–149. To convert glucagon values from pcg/ml to ng/l, multiply by 1.0.

a rate of 2.8–3.5 mmol/l/h.[49] If plasma glucose does not fall by 2.8 mmol/l from the initial value in the first hour, check hydration status and, if acceptable, the insulin infusion may be doubled every hour until a steady glucose decline between 2.8–3.9 mmol/l is achieved. When the plasma glucose reaches 13.9 mmol/l (in DKA) or 17 mmol/l (in HONK), the insulin infusion rate can be decreased to 0.05–0.1 U/kg/ h (3–6 U/h), and glucose (5–10 per cent) added to the intravenous fluids. Thereafter, the rate of glucose administration may need to be adjusted to maintain blood glucose values of 8.3–11.1 mmol/l until metabolic control is achieved. In HONK, the insulin infusion may be a better means of maintaining stable plasma glucose levels until resolution of mental obtundation and hyperosmolality.

In cases of mild DKA, soluble insulin given i.m. or s.c. every hour is as effective as intravenous administration in lowering blood glucose and ketone bodies.[24] Such patients should first receive a 'priming' dose of soluble insulin of 0.4–0.6 U/kg weight, half as an i.v. bolus and half as i.m. or s.c. insulin.[46] Thereafter 0.1 U/kg/h of regular insulin i.m. or s.c. should be given.

Resolution of ketonaemia typically takes longer to clear than hyperglycaemia. β-hydroxybutyrare (βOHB) is the strongest and most prevalent acid in DKA. The nitroprusside method only measures acetoacetic acid and acetone. During therapy, βOHB (which is not measured with the nitroprusside test as 'ketones') is converted to acetoacetic acid (which is measured as 'ketones' with the nitroprusside test). This may lead the clinician to believe that ketosis has worsened. Therefore, qualitative ketone levels by the nitroprusside method should not be used as an indicator of response to therapy.

During therapy for DKA and HONK, blood should be drawn every hour for glucose estimation: every 2–4 hours for determination of serum electrolytes, glucose, blood urea nitrogen, creatinine, osmolality and venous pH (for DKA). During follow up, if repeat arterial blood gases are unnecessary, venous pH, which is usually 0.03 U lower than arterial pH, or venous bicarbonate (if excess chloride infusion is avoided) can be followed to avoid repeated arterial punctures. A flowsheet similar to the one depicted in Fig. 4 is essential in recording results and patient responses to treatment. Criteria for resolution of ketoacidosis include a blood glucose lower than 11 mmol/l, a serum bicarbonate level equal to or greater than 18 mmol/l, and a venous pH greater than 7.3. In DKA, subcutaneous insulin regimens can be started after resolution, a useful clinical

SUGGESTED DKA/HONK FLOWSHEET

Height: _____
Weight: _____
0° _____
24° _____

	DATE: HOUR:	ER											
	MENTAL STATUS*												
	TEMPERATURE												
	PULSE												
	RESPIRATION/DEPTH**												
	BLOOD PRESSURE												
	SERUM GLUCOSE (mM)												
	SERUM "KETONES"												
	URINE "KETONES"												
ELECTROLYTES	SERUM Na+ (mmol/l)												
	SERUM K+ (mmol/l)												
	SERUM CL− (mmol/l)												
	SERUM HCO3− (mmol/l)												
	UREA (mmol/l)												
	EFFECTIVE OSMOLALITY 2[measured Na (mmol/l)+ Glucose (mmol/l)												
	ANION GAP												
A.B.G.	pH VENOUS (V) ARTERIAL (A)												
	pO2												
	pCO2												
	O2 SAT												
INSULIN	UNITS PAST HOUR												
	ROUTE												
INTAKE FLUID/METABOLITES	0.45% NaCl (ml) PAST HOUR												
	0.9% NaCl (ml) PAST HOUR												
	5% DEXTROSE (ml) PAST HOUR												
	KCL (mmol) PAST HOUR												
	PO4 (mmol) PAST HOUR												
	OTHER												
OUTPUT	URINE (ml)												
	OTHER												

* A-ALERT   D-DROWSY   S-STUPOROUS   C-COMATOSE or GLASGOW COMA SCALE
** D-DEEP   S-SHALLOW   N-NORMAL

Adapted by permission from Kitabchi, *et al.*, In: Joslin's *Diabetes mellitus*. 1994 (23).

Fig. 4 DKA/HONK flowsheet for the documentation of clinical parameters, fluid and electrolytes, laboratory values, insulin therapy, and urinary output.

guideline is 24 hours after resolution of the ketosis. Subcutaneous regimens are best started once the patient is eating, with the regimen tailored to the meal pattern.

Low-dose insulin therapy provides a circulating insulin concentration of approximately 60–100 μU/ml. However, due to the short half-life of intravenous soluble insulin, sudden interruption of insulin infusion can lead to rapid lowering of insulin concentration resulting in relapse. Therefore, overlap should occur in intravenous insulin therapy and the initiation of the subcutaneous insulin regimen. Furthermore, frequent monitoring of the patient should be continued during this transition period.

Patients with known diabetes may be given insulin at the dosage they were receiving before the onset of DKA and further adjusted using a multiple daily injection (MDI) regimen. In patients with newly-diagnosed diabetes the initial total insulin dose should be approximately 0.6 U/kg/day divided into at least three doses of a mixed regimen including short and long-acting insulin until an optimal dose is established. Some type 2 patients may be discharged on oral agents and dietary therapy.

Potassium

Potassium deficit is the most serious of the electrolyte disturbances and is usually about 3–5 mmol/l body weight, although a deficit of as much as 10 mmol/l per kg has been reported.[12,50–52] Despite total body potassium depletion, mild to moderate hyperkalaemia is not uncommon in patients with hyperglycaemic crises. Insulin therapy, correction of acidosis, and volume expansion decrease serum potassium concentration. To prevent hypokalaemia, potassium replacement is initiated after serum levels fall below 5.5 mmol/l, assuming the presence of adequate urine output. Generally, 20–40 mEq of potassium (two-thirds potassium chloride and one-third potassium phosphate) in each litre of infusion fluid is sufficient to maintain a serum potassium concentration within the normal range of 4–5 mmol/l. Rarely, DKA patients may present with significant hypokalaemia. In such cases, potassium replacement should begin with initial fluid therapy and insulin treatment delayed until potassium concentration is restored above 3.3 mmol/l to avoid arrhythmias/cardiac arrest and respiratory muscle weakness.

Bicarbonate

Bicarbonate use in DKA remains controversial.[53] Its use was based on the assumption that severe metabolic acidosis is associated with intracellular acidosis which could contribute to organ dysfunction, such as in the heart, liver or brain, increasing morbidity and mortality. Potential adverse effects of alkali therapy include worsened hypokalaemia, worsened intracellular acidosis due to increased carbon dioxide production, delay of ketoanion metabolism, and development of paradoxical central nervous system acidosis.[53] At a pH above 7.0, re-establishing insulin activity blocks lipolysis and resolves ketoacidosis without any added bicarbonate. Prospective randomized studies have failed to show either beneficial or deleterious changes in morbidity or mortality with bicarbonate therapy in DKA patients with pH between 6.9 and 7.1[54] (Table 4). No prospective, randomized studies concerning the use of bicarbonate in DKA with pH values less than 6.9 have been reported. Given that severe acidosis may lead to a myriad of adverse vascular effects, it seems prudent that for patients with a pH below 6.9, 100 mmol of sodium bicarbonate be added to 400 ml of sterile water and given at a rate of 200 ml/h. In patients with a pH of 6.9–7.0, 50 mmol of sodium bicarbonate is diluted in 200 ml of sterile water and infused at a rate of 200 ml/h. No bicarbonate is necessary if pH is greater or equal to 7.0. Bicarbonate therapy lowers serum potassium; therefore, potassium supplementation should be maintained in intravenous fluid as described above and carefully monitored. (See Fig. 5 for guidelines.) Thereafter, venous pH should be assessed every two hours until the pH rises to 7.0, and treatment repeated every two hours, if necessary.

Phosphate

Phosphate shifts with potassium from the intracellular to the extracellular compartment in response to hyperglycaemia and hyperosmolarity. Osmotic diuresis subsequently enhances urinary phosphate loss (Table 1). Because of the extracellular shift, serum levels of phosphate at presentation with DKA and HONK are typically normal or increased despite whole body phosphate deficits in DKA that average about 1.0 mmol/kg of body weight.[55–58] During insulin therapy, phosphate re-enters the intracellular compartment leading to mild–moderate reductions in serum phosphate

Table 4 Response to therapy with phosphate and bicarbonate in diabetic ketoacidosis

Response to therapy	Phosphate treatment			Bicarbonate treatment		
	No	Yes	p value	No	Yes	p value
Time (h) to recovery (mean ± SEM)						
Glucose ≤ 13.9 mmol/l	3.6 ± 0.8	5.4 ± 1.4	NS	4.2 ± 1.0	4.9 ± 1.3	NS
HCO₃ ≥ 15 mmol/l	10.5 ± 0.8	12.7 ± 1.8	NS	21.0 ± 4.0	21.0 ± 4.3	NS
pH ≥ 7.3	11.3 ± 1.4	8.3 ± 1.2	NS	15.6 ± 2.5	13.1 ± 2.5	NS
Rate of decline						
Glucose (mmol/h)	5.2	5.0	NS			
Ketone bodies (mmol/h)	0.64	0.8	NS			

Reprinted with permission Kitabchi AE, Fisher JN, Murphy MB, Rumbak MJ. Diabetic ketoacidosis and the hyperglycaemic hyperosmolar nonketotic state. In: Kahn CR, Weir GC, eds. *Joslin's Diabetes Mellitus*, 13th edn. Philadelphia: Lea and Febiger, 1994: 738–70.
NS = Not significant.

PROTOCOL FOR MANAGEMENT OF ADULT PATIENTS WITH DKA

Initial Evaluation: After history and physical examination, obtain arterial blood gases, complete blood count with differential, urinalysis, blood glucose, BUN, electrolytes, chemistry profile and creatinine levels STAT as well as an EKG. Chest X-ray and cultures as needed. Start IV fluid, 1.0 L of 0.9% NaCl per hour initially (15-20 ml/kg/hour).
Diagnostic criteria: DKA: blood glucose >13.9 mmol/l arterial pH <7.3, bicarbonate <15 mmol/l, moderate ketonuria or ketonemia.

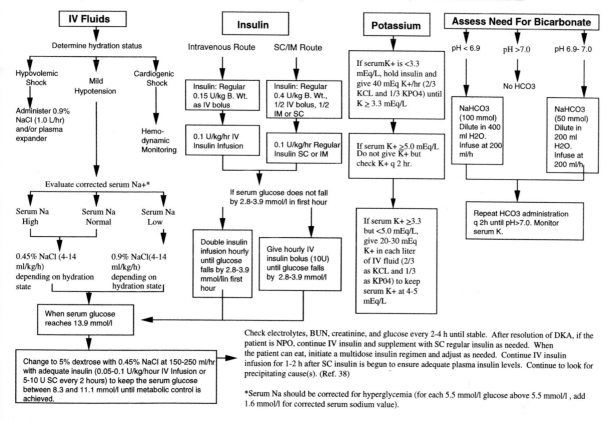

Fig. 5 Protocol for the management of patients with diabetic ketoacidosis (DKA).

concentrations. Adverse complications of hypophosphataemia are uncommon, occurring primarily in the setting of severe hypophosphataemia. Potential complications then include respiratory and skeletal muscle weakness, haemolytic anaemia, and worsened cardiac systolic per-formance.[58] Phosphate depletion may also contribute to decreased concentrations of 2,3-diphosphoglycerate (2,3-DPG), shifting the oxygen dissociation curve to the left and limiting tissue oxygen delivery.[58]

Prospective randomized studies have failed to show any beneficial effect of phosphate replacement on the clinical outcome in DKA[55,58] and overzealous phosphate therapy can cause hypocalcaemia with no evidence of tetany.[29,55] Table 4 summarizes the results of two prospective studies from our centre on the use of bicarbonate[54] and phosphate.[55] (The differences seen in baseline glucose and bicarbonate in the bicarbonate group compared to the phosphate group is due to the inclusion of more severe DKA patients in the bicarbonate study).[24] To avoid cardiac and skeletal muscle weakness and respiratory depression due to hypophosphataemia, careful phosphate replacement may sometimes be indicated in patients with cardiac dysfunction, anaemia, respiratory depression, and in those with serum phosphate concentration lower than 1.0 mg/dl. To replace

phosphate stores and to avoid chloride load, intravenous potassium supplementation can be given in a ratio of two-thirds potassium chloride and one-third potassium phosphate. No studies are available on the use of phosphate in the treatment of HONK.

Figures 5 and 6 summarize the step by step general guidelines for management of patients with DKA and HONK.

Complications

Common complications of DKA and HONK include:

(1) Hypoglycaemia due to overzealous treatment with insulin

(2) Hypokalaemia due to the use of large doses of insulin and treatment of acidosis with bicarbonate

(3) Hyperglycaemia secondary to interruption/discontinuance of intravenous insulin therapy following recovery without subsequent coverage with subcutaneous insulin

(4) Hyperchloraemia due to the use of excessive saline for fluid and electrolyte replacement which results in a transient non-anion gap metabolic acidosis as chloride from intravenous fluids replaces ketoanions lost as sodium and potassium salts during

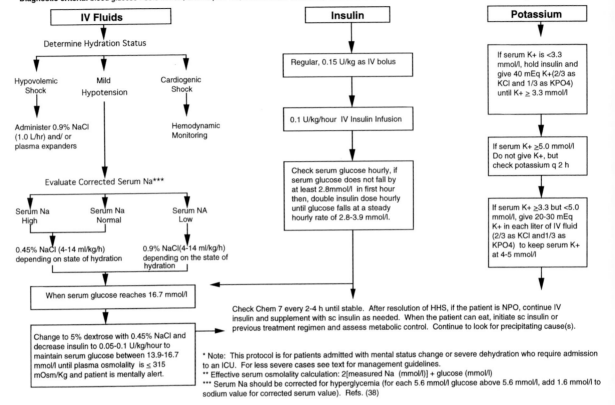

Fig. 6 Protocol for the management of patients with hyperosmolar non-ketotic (HONK) state.

osmotic diuresis. These biochemical abnormalities are transient and not clinically significant except for cases of acute renal failure or extreme oliguria

(5) Persistant ketosis, secondary to premature reduction in insulin administration. Some of the rare complications of DKA are outlined below.

Cerebral oedema

Cerebral oedema is a rare and sometimes fatal complication of DKA that is most commonly seen in paediatric patients with newly diagnosed diabetes. Clinically it is characterized by headache and lethargy followed by seizures and the development of papilloedema and other signs of increased intracranial pressure. Although the mechanism is not known, it probably results from osmotically driven movement of water into the CNS when plasma osmolality declines too rapidly with treatment of DKA. Fatal cases have also been reported with HONK. There is a lack of data regarding cerebral oedema morbidity in adult patients, therefore, recommendations are based on clinical judgement rather than scientific evidence.

Preventive measures that may decrease the risk of cerebral oedema in high-risk patients include:

(a) a gradual replacement of sodium and water deficits in patients who are hyperosmolar (maximal reduction in osmolality 3 mOsml/kg H2O/h)

(b) the use of hyposmolar solution (0 .45 per cent saline) or glucose infusions if corrected serum sodium concentration is high

(c) the addition of glucose to the hydrating solution once blood glucose reaches 14 mmol/l.

(d) maintenance of a glucose level of 14 mmol/l (DKA) or 17 mmol/l (HONK) until hyperosmolality and mental status improves and the patient becomes clinically stable.[59]

Adult respiratory distress syndrome (ARDS)

Hypoxaemia and rarely non-cardiogenic pulmonary oedema may complicate the treatment of DKA. Hypoxaemia is attributed to a reduction in colloid osmotic pressure that results in increased lung water content and decreased lung compliance. Patients with DKA who have a widened alveolo-arteriolar (A-a) oxygen gradient noted on initial blood gases, or with pulmonary crackles on physical examination appear to be at higher risk for the development of pulmonary oedema.

Prevention

The two major precipitating factors in the development of DKA are infection and inadequate insulin treatment (including noncompliance). Discontinuation of insulin for economic reasons is a common precipitant of DKA in urban African Americans[4] and in other less prosperous parts of the world. Such events should be avoidable by better utilization of medical care including affordable insulin, easier access to a health care provider, intensive patient education and timely and effective communication with a health care provider during an intercurrent illness.

Furthermore, sick-day management should be reviewed periodically with all patients and should include: specific information on how and when to contact a health care provider; clearly defined blood glucose goals and methods of use of supplemental short-acting insulin during illness; information on how to suppress a fever and treat an infection; initiation of an easily-digestible liquid diet containing carbohydrates and salt; instructions to never discontinue insulin and to seek professional advice early in the course of an illness.

Successful sick-day management requires effective communication with a health care professional and involvement by the patient and/or a family member. Variables that must be accurately recorded and communicated include: blood glucose, urine 'ketone' determination (when blood glucose is above or equal to 300 mg/dl), insulin administered, intake, temperature, respiratory and pulse rate and body weight.

As mentioned previously, many of the admissions for HONK are nursing home residents or the elderly or those who do not readily access health care, who become dehydrated and are unaware or unable to treat the increasingly dehydrated state. Better education of care givers as well as patients regarding signs and symptoms of new onset diabetes, the importance of adequate hydration, conditions/procedures/medications which worsen diabetes control; and the use of glucose monitoring could potentially decrease the incidence and severity of HONK.

References

1. Faich GA, Fishbein HA, Ellis SE. The epidemiology of diabetic acidosis: a population-based study. *American Journal of Epidemiology*, 1983; **117**: 551. Annual incidence rates for DKA.

2. **Centers for Disease Control, Division of Diabetes Translations**. *Diabetes Surveillance, 1991*. Washington DC, U.S. Goverment Printing Office, 1992; 635–1150. Epidemiological studies on hospitalization rates for DKA.

3. Fishbein HA, Palumbo PJ. Acute metabolic complications in diabetes. *Diabetes in America* (*National Diabetes Data Group*). National Institute of Health, 1995. (NIH Publication No. 95–1468), 283–91. Hospitalization rates for HONK and DKA.

4. **Umpierrez GE, Kelly JP, Navarrete JE, Casals MMC, Kitabchi AE.** Hyperglycaemic crises in Urban Blacks. *Archives of Internal Medicine*, 1997; **157**: 669–75. Hospitalization rates in urban blacks for hyperglycaemic crises.

5. DeFronzo RA, Matsuda M, Barret E. Diabetic ketoacidosis. A combined metabolic-nephrologic approach to therapy. *Diabetes Review*, 1994; **2**: 209–38. Review article on DKA.

6. Matz R. Hyperosmolar nonacidotic diabetes (HNAD). In: Porte D Jr, Sherwin RS, eds. *Diabetes Mellitus: Theory and Practice*, 5th edn. Amsterdam: Elsevier, 1997: 845–60. Review article HONK.

7. Morris LE, Kitabchi AE. Coma in the diabetic. In: Schnatz JD, ed. *Diabetes Mellitus: Problems in Management*. Menlo Park: Addison-Wesley, 1982: 234–51. Review article on coma in the diabetic; causes and management.

8. Polonsky WH, Anderson BJ, Lohrer PA, Aponte JE, Jacobson AM, Cole CF. Insulin omission in women with IDDM. *Diabetes Care*, 1994; **17**: 1178–85. Precipitating factors for hyperglycaemia in women.

9. Kitabchi AE, Umpierrez GE, Murphy MB, Barrett EJ, Kreisburg RA, Malone JI, Wall BM. Management of hyperglycemic crises in patients with diabetes. *Diabetes Care*, 2001; **24**: 131–53.

10. Felig P *et al.* Hormonal interactions in the regulation of blood glucose. *Recent Progress in Hormone Research*, 1979; **35**: 501–32. Hormonal interaction in the control of blood glucose.

11. Miles JM, Rizza RA, Haymond MW, Gerich JE. Effects of acute insulin deficiency on glucose and ketone body turnover in man: evidence for the primacy overproduction of glucose and ketone bodies in the genesis of diabetic ketoacidosis. *Diabetes*, 1980; **29**: 926–30. Role of gluconeogenesis in the genesis of DKA.

12. Kreisburg RA. Diabetic ketoacidosis: new concepts and trends in pathogenesis and treatment. *Annals of Internal Medicine*, 1978; **88**: 681–95. Review of DKA – pathogenesis and treatment.

13. Exton JH. Mechanisms of hormonal regulation of hepatic glucose metabolism. *Diabetes/Metabolism Reviews*, 1987; **3**: 163–83. Hormonal regulation of hepatic glucose metabolism.

14. Meyer C, Stumvoll M, Nadkarni V, Dostou J, Mitrakou A, Gerich J. Abnormal renal and hepatic glucose metabolism in type 2 diabetes mellitus. *Journal of Clinical Investigation*, 1998; **102**: 619–24. Role of hepatic and renal glucose metabolism in type 2 diabetes.

15. Jensen MD, Caruso M, Heiling V. Insulin regulation of lipolysis in nondiabetic and IDDM subjects. *Diabetes*, 1989; **38**: 1595–601. Insulin regulation of lipolysis.

16. Nurjhan N, Consoli A, Gerich J. Increased lipolysis and its consequences on gluconeogenesis in non-insulin-dependent diabetes mellitus. *Journal of Clinical Investigation*, 1992; **89**: 169–75. Effect of lipolysis on gluconeogenesis in type 2 diabetes.

17. McGarry JD, Woeltje KF, Kuwajima M, Foster DW. Regulation of ketogenesis and the renaissance of camitine palmitoyl transferase. *Diabetes/Metabolism Reviews*, 1989; **5**: 271–84. Review of biochemical pathway of ketogenesis.

18. Reichard GA Jr, Scutches CL, Hoeldtke RD, Owen OE. Acetone metabolism in humans during diabetic ketoacidosis. *Diabetes*, 1986; **35**: 688–74. Acetone metabolism in DKA.

19. Balasse EO, Fery F. Ketone body production and disposal: effects of fasting, diabetes, and exercise. *Diabetes/Metabolism Reviews*, 1989; **5**: 247–70. Ketone body production in various stages.

20. Nosadini R, Avogaro A, Doria A, Fioretto P, Trevisan R, Morocutti A. Ketone body metabolism: a physiological and clinical overview. *Diabetes/Metabolism Reviews*, 1989; **5**: 299–319. Review of ketone body metabolism.

21. Moeller N, Schmitz O, Moeller J, Porksen N, Jorgensen JOL. Dose–response studies on metabolic effects of a growth hormone pulse in humans. *Metabolism*, 1992; **41**: 172–5. Metabolic effects of growth hormone.

22. Schade DS, Eaton RP. Pathogenesis of diabetic ketoacidosis: a reappraisal. *Diabetes Care*, 1979; **2**: 296–306.
Review of DKA.

23. Waldhausl W, Kleinberger G, Korn A, Dudcza R, Bratusch-Marrain P, Nowatny P. Severe hyperglycaemia: effects of rehydration on endocrine derangements and blood glucose concentration. *Diabetes*, 1979; **28**: 577–84.
Effects of rehydration on severe hyperglycaemia.

24. Kitabchi AE, Fisher JN, Murphy MB, Rumbak MJ. Diabetic ketoacidosis and the hyperglycaemic hyperosmolar nonketotic state. In: Kahn CR, Weir GC, eds. *Joslin's Diabetes Mellitus*, 13th edn. Philadelphia: Lea and Febiger, 1994: 738–70.
Review of DKA and HONK.

25. Chupin M, Charbonnel B, Chupin F. C-peptide blood levels in ketoacidosis and in hyperosmolar non-ketotic diabetic coma. *Acta Diabetologica*, 1981; **18**: 123–8.
Contrasting hormonal profiles in DKA versus HHS.

26. Schade DS, Eaton RP. Dose response to insulin in man: differential effects on glucose and ketone body regulation. *Journal of Clinical Endocrinology and Metabolism*, 1977; **44**: 1038–53.
Insulin effects on glucose and ketone body metabolism.

27. Ennis ED, Stahl EJVB, Kreisberg RA. The hyperosmolar hyperglycaemic syndrome. *Diabetes Review*, 1994; **2**: 115.
Review of HHS.

28. Marshall SM, Walker M, Alberti KGMM. Diabetic ketoacidosis and hyperglycaemic non-ketotic coma. In: Alberti KGMM, Zimmet P, DeFronzo RA, eds. *International Textbook of Diabetes Mellitus*, 2nd edn. New York: John Wiley, 1997: 1215–29.
Review of DKA and HONK.

29. Carroll P, Matz R. Uncontrolled diabetes mellitus in adults: experience in treating diabetic ketoacidosis and hyperosmolar coma with low-dose insulin and uniform treatment regimen. *Diabetes Care*, 1983; **6**: 579–85.
Review of uniform treatment regimens for DKA and HHS.

30. Ennis ED, Stahl EJ, Kreisberg RA. Diabetic ketoacidosis. In: Porte D Jr, Sherwin RS, eds. *Diabetes Mellitus*, 5th edn. Amsterdam: Elsevier, 1997: 827–44.
Review DKA.

31. Hillman K. Fluid resuscitation in diabetic emergencies: a reappraisal. *Intensive Care Medicine*, 1987; **13**: 4–8.
Rationale for the use of various fluid regimens in the treatment of diabetic emergencies.

32. Fein IA, Rackow EC, Sprung CL, Grodman R. Relation of colloid osmotic pressure to arterial hypoxemia and cerebral edema during crystalloid volume loading of patients with diabetic ketoacidosis. *Annals of Internal Medicine*, 1982; **96**: 570–5.
Review of various fluid regimens and their effect on cerebral oedema in DKA.

33. Arieff AL, Carrol H. Nonketotic hyperosmolar coma with hyperglycaemia: clinical features, pathophysiology, renal function, acid-base balance, plasma-cerebrospinal fluid equilibria, and the effects of therapy in 37 cases. *Medicine*, 1972; **51**: 73–94.
Review of the treatment of 37 cases of HONK.

34. Wachtel TJ, Silliman RA, Lamberton P. Predisposing factors for the diabetic hyperosmolar state. *Archives of Internal Medicine*, 1987; **147**: 499–501.
Precipitants in the development of HONK.

35. Howard RL, Bichet DO, Shrier RW. Hypernatremic and polyuric states. In: Seldin D, Giebisch O, eds. *The Kidney: Physiology and Pathophysiology*. New York: Raven, 1992: 1578.
Review of fluid and electrolyte balance in hypernatremic and polyuric states.

36. Castellino P, Luzi L, Haymond M, Simonson D, DeFronzo RA. Effect of insulin and plasma amino acid concentrations on leucine turnover in man. *Journal of Clinical Investigation*, 1987; **80**: 1784–93.
Role of insulin in protein metabolism.

37. Kitabchi AE, Fisher IN. Insulin therapy of diabetic ketoacidosis: physiologic versus pharmacologic doses of insulin and their routes of administration. In: Brownlee M, ed. *Handbook of Diabetes Mellitus*. New York: Garland ATPM Press, 1981: 95–149.
Review of low dose insulin therapy regimens in the treatment of DKA.

38. American Diabetes Association Position Statement. Hyperglycemic crises in patients with diabetes mellitus. *Clinical Diabetes*, 2001; **19**: 82–90.

39. Rumbak MJ, Hughes TA, Kitabchi AE. Pseudonormoglycaemia in diabetic ketoacidosis with elevated triglycerides. *American Journal of Emergency Medicine*, 1991; **9**: 61–3.
Effect of hypertriglyceridemia on laboratory values in DKA.

40. Kaminska ES, Pourmotabbed G. Spurious laboratory values in diabetic ketoacidosis and hyperlipidaemia. *American Journal of Emergency Medicine*, 1993; **11**: 77–80.
Effect of hypertriglyceridemia on laboratory values in DKA.

41. Winter MD, Pearson R, Gabow PA, Schultz AL, Lepoff RB. The fall of the serum anion gap. *Archives of Internal Medicine*, 1990; **150**: 311–3.
Effect of new laboratory techniques on anion gap values.

42. Sadjadi SA. Letter to the editor: a new range for the anion gap. *Annals of Internal Medicine*, 1995; **123**: 807.
New range for the anion gap.

43. Assadi FK *et al*. Falsely elevated serum creatinine concentration in ketoacidosis. *Journal of Pediatrics*, 1985; **107**: 562–4.
Effect of acetoacetate levels on serum creatinine levels.

44. Gerard SK, Khayam-Bashi H. Characterization of creatinine error in ketotic patients: a prospective comparison of alkaline picrate methods with an enzymatic method. *American Journal of Clinical Pathology*, 1985; **84**: 659–61.
Effect of acetoacetate levels on serum creatinine levels.

45. Bratusch-Marrain PR, Komajati M, Waldhausal W. The effect of hyperosmolarity on glucose metabolism. *Practical Cardiology*, 1985; **11**: 153–63.
Hyperosmolarity and glucose metabolism.

46. Kitabchi AE, Sacks HS, Young RT, Morris L. Diabetic ketoacidosis: reappraisal of therapeutic approach. *Annual Review of Medicine*, 1979; **30**: 339–57.
Review of various protocols in the treatment of DKA.

47. Sonksen PH, Srivastava MC, Tompkins CV, Nabarro JDN. Growth hormone and cortisol responses to insulin infusion in patients with diabetes mellitus. *Lancet*, 1972; **2**: 155–60.
Classic study of low dose insulin therapy in DKA.

48. Alberti KGGM, Hockaday TDR, Turner RC. Small doses of intramuscular insulin in the treatment of diabetic 'coma'. *Lancet*, 1973; **5**: 515–22.
Classic study of low dose insulin therapy in DKA.

49. Jervell J. Insulin 1996 – 75 years after its discovery. *Diabetic Medicine*, 1996; **13**: 847–9.

50. Kitabchi AE, Ayyagari V, Guerra SMO. Medical House Staff. The efficacy of low dose versus conventional therapy of insulin for treatment of diabetic ketoacidosis. *Annals of Internal Medicine*, 1976; **84**: 633–8.
Classic study of low dose insulin therapy in DKA.

51. Beigelman PM. Severe diabetic ketoacidosis (diabetic coma): 482 episodes in 257 patients; experience of three years. *Diabetes*, 1971; **20**: 490–500.
Review of experience of treatment of large cohort of patients with severe DKA.

52. Abranison E, Arky R. Diabetic acidosis with initial hypokalemia; therapeutic implications. *Journal of the American Medical Association*, 1966; **196**: 401–3.
Hypokalemia in DKA.

53. **Barnes HV, Cohen RD, Kitabchi AE, Murphy MB**. When is bicarbonate appropriate in treating metabolic acidosis including diabetic ketoacidosis? In: Gitnick O, Barnes HV, Duffy TP, eds. *Debates in Medicine*. Chicago: Yearbook Medical Publishers, 1990: 200–27.
Debate on bicarbonate use in DKA.

54. **Morris LR, Murphy MB, Kitabchi AE**. Bicarbonate therapy in severe diabetic ketoacidosis. *Annals of Internal Medicine*, 1986; **105**: 836–40.
Prospective randomized study on the use of bicarbonate in severe DKA.

55. **Fisher IN, Kitabchi AE**. A randomized study of phosphate therapy in the treatment of diabetic ketoacidosis. *Journal of Clinical Endocrinology and Metabolism*, 1983; **57**: 177–80.
Prospective randomized study of phosphate therapy and clinical outcomes in DKA.

56. **Wilson HK, Keuer SP, Lea AS, Boyd AE, Eknoyan O**. Phosphate therapy in diabetic ketoacidosis. *Archives of Internal Medicine*, 1982; **142**: 517–20.
Phosphate therapy in the treatment of DKA.

57. **Kreisberg RA**. Phosphorus deficiency and hypophosphatemia. *Hospital Practice*, 1977; **12**: 121–8.
Review of hypophosphatemia.

58. **Gibby OM, Veale KEA, Hayes TM, Jones JO, Wardrop CM**. Oxygen availability from the blood and the effect of phosphate replacement on erythrocyte 2–3 diphosphoglycerate and hemoglobin-oxygen affinity in diabetic ketoacidosis. *Diabetologia*, 1978; **15**: 381.
Phosphate therapy in DKA.

59. **Arieff AL**. Cerebral edema complicating nonketotic hyperosmolar coma. *Mineral and Electrolyte Metabolism*, 1986; **12**: 383–9.
Review on cerebral oedema and HONK.

3.1 Abnormalities of the microvasculature

K.L. Goh and John Tooke

Introduction

Diabetes mellitus is a metabolic disorder characterized by chronic hyperglycaemia resulting in progressive long-term damage and failure of various organs. These long-term sequelae include cardiovascular morbidity and mortality and microvascular complications involving the eyes, kidney, nervous system, and the foot.

The first description of diabetic retinopathy was documented in 1855 in a 22 year old man with disease duration of four years. In 1890, Hirschberg stated that diabetic retinopathy was specific and distinct from albuminuric (hypertensive) retinopathy. In 1921, de Schweinitz noted that the occurrence of retinopathy was duration-related and hence it was a rare entity prior to the pre-insulin era, during which the outlook for the juvenile form of diabetes was poor and diabetes of long duration was uncommon.[1]

With regard to diabetic nephropathy, the link between diabetes and albuminuria was noted in the early 1800s and by the end of the nineteenth century, the prognostic implications of albuminuria were well-recognized. Kimmelstiel and Wilson described typical histological changes in the glomeruli in diabetic patients (glomerular sclerosis) and noted that coexisting hypertension was often a feature. For a period of time, it was considered that high blood pressure was necessary to perfuse the kidneys of such diabetic patients and not until the 1970s did it become apparent that hypertension is detrimental to diabetic renal disease.[2]

The clinical significance of diabetic microangiopathy became more obvious after the advent of insulin treatment in 1922. This improved the survival of diabetic patients but the associated 'triopathy' of retinopathy, nephropathy, and neuropathy became more apparent.

Microvascular abnormalities have been observed in other conditions such as essential hypertension and Raynaud's disease. However, the triad of microvascular complications of retinopathy, nephropathy, and neuropathy is specific to diabetes. In fact, the likelihood of developing microvascular complications has influenced the diagnostic criteria for diabetes.[3] The 1985 WHO diagnostic criteria (Fasting: whole blood glucose greater than or equal to 6.7 mmol/l or plasma glucose greater than or equal to 7.8 mmol/l and two hour post-oral glucose tolerance test (OGTT): whole blood glucose greater than or equal to 10.0 mmol/l or plasma glucose greater than or equal to 11.1 mmol/l) were chosen on the basis of epidemiological data which revealed that individuals with such glucose levels were at increased risk of developing retinopathy.

Scope of the text

This chapter will review the current concepts relating to the ways diabetes can disturb human microvascular function, the stages in this process and the variety of expression between different vascular beds and different types of diabetes. The cellular and molecular basis underlying the pathogenesis of microangiopathy will also be explored. Finally, therapeutic intervention for prevention and treatment for microangiopathy will also be considered.

Stages

The temporal sequence of microvascular damage develops in a similar manner to atherosclerosis in the large blood vessels, in that there is an initial clinically silent phase before overt vascular disease is apparent.

In the large vessels, injury induced by factors such as oxidized low-density lipoprotein (LDL) and hypertension lead to changes in endothelial function. The production of vasodilating and anti-aggregating substances such as prostacyclin and nitric oxide (NO) are affected, encouraging adherence of macrophages and lymphocytes to the cells. The atheromatous process involves various stages, with formation of fatty streak, fibro-fatty streak and eventually a fibrous plaque, which represent irreversible structural changes. The terminal event occurs with the formation of platelet mural thrombi on the surface of ruptured plaques at thrombogenic sites, such as branches or bifurcation of arteries.[4]

Similarly, there is a functional reversible phase in the development of microangiopathy, where endothelial function is impaired as a consequence of metabolic and haemodynamic insults. This leads to structural adaptation with increased capillary permeability, basement membrane thickening and luminal narrowing. These changes eventually culminate in the terminal event with complete microvascular obstruction. Depending on the site of microvascular damage, response to permanent injury may elicit reparative mechanisms. For example, neovascularization occurs in the retina in response to tissue

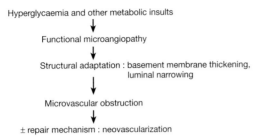

Fig. 1 Stages in development of diabetic microangiopathy.

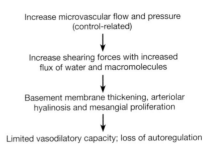

Fig. 2 The haemodynamic hypothesis.

ischaemia. However, as these new vessels differ somewhat in structure, function and support to normal blood vessels, they are more permeable to macromolecules and prone to leakage and haemorrhage[5] (Fig. 1).

Type 1 diabetes

Parving first put forward the haemodynamic hypothesis to link preclinical changes in blood flow to clinical microangiopathy.[6] The hypothesis states that increased blood flow and pressure in the microcirculation early in the disease induce an injury response involving the endothelium. This increase in flow and pressure is related to the degree of glycaemic control and results in an increase in flux of water and other molecules and stimulates increased production of perivascular matrix and basement membrane thickening, with development of arteriolar hyalinosis and mesangial proliferation. This limits the maximal vasodilatory capacity and impairs regulatory function (autoregulation) (Fig. 2).

Indirect clinical evidence for the hypothesis is provided by anecdotal observations of apparent protection against the development of ipsilateral retinopathy and nephropathy in those with unilateral carotid stenosis and renal artery stenosis. The fact that increased basement membrane thickness is observed in subjects with congestive cardiac failure, who are exposed to high venous pressure and probably also elevated capillary pressure, supports the concept that high hydrostatic capillary pressure is instrumental in the development of capillary basement membrane thickening.

In health, organ blood flow at rest should be the minimum required to sustain the tissues; but in the event of an injurious insult or following a period of flow cessation, blood flow should increase in response. In type 1 diabetes, there is considerable direct evidence in support of paradoxical increase in blood flow in the early stage of the disease. Although microvascular hyperperfusion is characteristic under resting conditions, limitation of maximal blood flow in response to stimuli later in the course of the disease is apparent. Reduction of skin maximal vasodilatory response to heat, minor skin trauma (pinprick), arterial occlusion and pharmacological agents have been demonstrated in patients with type 1 disease several years after the initial diagnosis. Microcirculatory autoregulation has also been shown to be impaired in type 1 disease and the degree of impairment correlates with the degree of arteriolar hyalinosis, in support of the hypothesis that a build up of extravascular proteins may be contributory to limited vasodilation.[7]

The quest for direct evidence of capillary hypertension in diabetes in man was hampered by the technical difficulty of studying blood pressure in the microcirculation. With the advent of the technique of cannulating finger skin nailfold capillaries and continuous electronic measurement of capillary pressure, elevated capillary pressure was demonstrated in patients with type 1 disease of less than two years' duration, especially in those with poor glycaemic control. This increase in capillary pressure can respond to improvement in glycaemic control in those with short disease duration and minimal complications. Those with incipient nephropathy, defined as an overnight albumin excretion rate of 20–200 µg/min, had elevated capillary pressure in contrast to healthy controls and also patients with no clinical complications despite similar disease duration and glycaemic control. These data suggest that capillary hypertension is pivotal in the development of microangiopathy.[7]

Early changes in microvascular permeability may act in concert with haemodynamic changes in diabetes in the genesis of microangiopathy. Certainly an increase in microvascular fluid permeability has been demonstrated in the forearm tissues of young patients with short duration of type 1 disease and reasonable glycaemic control, suggesting a primary change in microvascular permeability, at least in a subset of patients, perhaps those that are nephropathy-prone. However, other permeability changes such as the increase in transcapillary escape rate of albumin appear to be related to glycaemic control, although once more, the changes are more obvious in those with microalbuminuria.

Can the model of haemodynamic and permeability changes observed in skin microvasculature be extrapolated to other microvascular beds?

In experiments in diabetic rats, raised intraglomerular capillary pressure is associated with glomerular sclerosis and the appearance of albuminuria. There is also indirect evidence of increased intraglomerular hydrostatic pressure and permeability to macromolecules in early stage of type 1 disease in man. Loss of autoregulation of glomerular filtration rate is seen in those with advanced nephropathy.[8]

Increased retinal blood flow is observed in early diabetic retinopathy and there is further augmentation of blood flow with progression of proliferative changes in the retina. Glycaemic control appears to be an important determinant of retinal blood flow. Several studies indicate that autoregulation of retinal blood flow is impaired in diabetes. It has been demonstrated in patients with type 1 disease that when their blood glucose level is less than 10 mmol/l, autoregulatory control mechanisms break down when mean arterial blood pressure rises by 30 per cent. At a higher level of blood glucose concentration, it was found that autoregulation was absent at 15 per cent rise in mean arterial pressure in the same subjects.[9]

Thus cumulative evidence gathered from studies in different microvascular beds support the role of haemodynamic changes in the pathogenesis of diabetic microangiopathy. However, local mechanisms may play an important role in governing and modifying vascular function in specific vascular beds. For example, natriuretic factors are thought to be important in the renal vascular bed whereas loss of pericyte control may be of key importance to the development of retinopathy.

Are all patients with type 1 disease at equal risk of developing clinical manifestation of microangiopathic complications? Retinopathy appears to affect most patients after a long duration of type 1 disease but this does not appear to be the case for diabetic nephropathy. There is a decline in annual incidence of nephropathy after 20 years of diabetes duration. This suggests the presence of a sub-population of patients with type 1 disease who may not be susceptible to the development of renal disease. Indeed three major studies have shown that diabetic nephropathy coincides among siblings with diabetes, indicating a likely genetic component in the development of diabetic nephropathy. Krolewski *et al.* proposed that a genetic predisposition in addition to environmental factors such as blood glucose level, may be responsible for the onset of microalbuminuria or the risk of progression from microalbuminuria to overt nephropathy.[10]

Type 2 diabetes

Although patients with type 1 and type 2 diabetes are both prone to developing microvascular complications, there are distinct differences in the expression of microangiopathy between the two groups. Firstly, a high prevalence of vascular complications is noted at the time of diagnosis of type 2 diabetes and hypertension commonly coexists. In type 1 disease, diabetic complications usually emerge 10–20 years after initial diagnosis and the prevalence of hypertension in the absence of nephropathy approximates to that of the normal population. Visual loss in type 1 disease is predominantly due to proliferative retinopathy whereas maculopathy is more common in type 2 disease. In type 1 diabetes, renal complications manifest as a typical albuminuric syndrome. However, in type 2 diabetes, the cause of nephropathy is complex, often caused by, or coexisting with arteriolar disease or other renal pathology[11] (Table 1). Functional changes observed in the microcirculation prior to the onset of microangiopathy are also different in type 2 disease. In contrast to type 1 disease, capillary pressure is not elevated in normotensive patients with early type 2 disease. Data on capillary permeability are inconsistent but forearm capillary filtration coefficient is not elevated in normotensive type 2 diabetic patients in comparison to type 1 diabetic patients. However, profound impairment of microvascular vasodilatory capacity is observed in type 2 disease at diagnosis, similar to that seen in patients with long duration of type 1 disease. These differences in microangiopathic disease expression and functional microcirculatory changes suggest a different pathophysiology for microangiopathy in type 2 disease[7] (Table 2).

Although the mechanisms underlying reduced microvascular vasodilatory capacity in type 2 disease are unclear, there is evidence suggestive of abnormalities involving both endothelium-dependent and endothelium-independent pathways. High prevalence of hypertension and microvascular complications at the time of diagnosis of type 2 disease could represent a long duration of occult disease

Table 1 Differences in expression of angiopathy in type 1 and type 2 diabetes

Vascular complication	Type 1	Type 2
Common cause of visual loss	Proliferative retinopathy	Maculopathy
Aetiology of nephropathy	Microvascular disease	Often complicated by arteriolar disease/other renal pathology
Prevalence of hypertension	Present in those with incipient and overt nephropathy; prevalence otherwise equates to normal population	40%; often present at the time of diagnosis

Table 2 Comparison of microvascular function in type 1 and type 2 diabetes

	Type 1	Type 2
Resting blood flow	Increased	Increased
Vasodilatory response	Later reduction	Early reduction
Capillary pressure	Increased	Normal (in early disease)
Fluid permeability	Increased	Relatively normal (in early disease)

preceding diagnosis. The alternative explanation is the influence of prediabetic/insulin-resistant state on the vasculature, increasing precapillary resistance. This would limit vasodilation and result in a high prevalence of hypertension, preventing an early rise of capillary pressure and filtration as opposed to that observed in type 1 disease. In support of this modification of the Haemodynamic hypothesis, impaired maximal vasodilatory response has been demonstrated in the prediabetic phase in subjects with impaired fasting glucose. Abnormalities in vasodilatory function have also been noted in individuals who are insulin-resistant or prone to developing type 2 diabetes such as acromegalic patients who are normoglycaemic, normoglycaemic women with past history of gestational diabetes and normoglycaemic individuals with a first-degree family history of diabetes. This argues strongly for the case that microvascular abnormalities precede the onset of type 2 diabetes.[12]

Other types of diabetes

Maturity onset diabetes of the young (MODY) is a rare form of diabetes, which is characterized by early onset of non-insulin dependent diabetes. In the subtype of MODY with glucokinase gene mutation, patients have an altered pancreatic glucose-sensing setpoint. Such patients have mild fasting hyperglycaemia (6–9 mmol/l), with little deterioration of glucose tolerance with age. In this group of patients, microvascular complications are relatively rare. However, in MODY 1 and 3, with mutations in hepatic nuclear factor (HNF)-4α and -1α respectively, there is progressive deterioration of glycaemic level and higher prevalence of microvascular complications. Certainly, maximum microvascular hyperaemic response is shown to be reduced in MODY 3 subjects and the response was found to correlate negatively with duration of diabetes.[13]

Patients with β-cell destruction secondary to chronic pancreatitis or pancreatic tumours have been reported to be less prone to microvascular complications. This may be related in part to the late age of onset of diabetes in this group of patients and also a limited survival rate. The frequency of diabetic complications seems to increase when there is a family history of diabetes in patients whose pancreatitis is simultaneous with, or precedes the onset of diabetes. Presence of microangiopathy in patients with pancreatic diabetes without a family history of diabetes mellitus, suggests that they may have primary diabetes unmasked by the pancreatitis.[14] Microangiopathy has also been reported in young patients with cystic fibrosis who develop diabetes mellitus and the risk of complications is related to disease duration and glycaemic control. To date, the literature with regards to the microcirculation in patients with diabetes secondary to pancreatic insufficiency is limited.

Cellular and molecular mechanisms

The development of diabetic angiopathy is closely associated with poor glycaemic control, a point reinforced by both the diabetes control and complications trial (DCCT) and United Kingdom prospective diabetes study (UKPDS) studies. Hence, it follows that hyperglycaemia and its biochemical consequences in concert with related metabolic disturbance and hyperinsulinaemia are likely to contribute to the deterioration in microvasular function in diabetes. In particular, microangiopathy is most prominent in cells and tissues where glucose utilization is largely independent of insulin action and hence exposed to glucose levels equivalent to the blood glucose concentration.

Hyperglycaemia exerts a direct and acute toxic effect on the endothelium, as observed in both *in vivo* and *in vitro* models. Prolonged exposure to hyperglycaemia can adversely affect the vasculature via other mechanisms, with a third of the glucose metabolism channeled to the polyol pathway, catalysed by aldose reductase to form sorbitol. Increased accumulation of intracellular sorbitol may cause osmotic damage, a decrease in myoinositol levels and/or alter cellular redox status resulting in hyperglycaemic pseudohypoxia. However, the role of aldose reductase/sorbitol pathway in vascular cells is unclear and some studies have shown that both aldose reductase and sorbitol are only

present in low concentration in such cells. Experimental data on the use of aldose reductase inhibitors to minimise or reverse microvascular damage resulting from the polyol pathway have also been conflicting.[15]

Non-enzymic glycosylation and cross-linking of plasma and cell membrane proteins leading to the formation of advanced glycation products (AGE) can also result from prolonged hyperglycaemic conditions. AGE products can exert a direct toxic effect on the cells by modulating the physico-biochemical properties of the proteins, altering cell wall rigidity, decreasing the susceptibility of the proteins to enzymic breakdown. These properties give rise to increased thickening and rigidity in connective tissues and extracellular matrix collagen seen in diabetes. The crosslinking of these AGE products on cell surfaces also trap plasma proteins such as immunoglobulins and lipoproteins. Studies also suggest that through the glycation process involved in AGE production, reactive oxygen species are formed, which can quench NO and damage DNA. AGE can also bind to receptors on endothelial cells, smooth muscle cells, lymphocytes and monocytes, activating the cells and inducing the production of interleukin, vascular adhesion molecules and tissue factor. These can alter cell permeability, cellular signalling, production of transcription factors and gene expression. Co-localization of AGE and RAGE (a receptor for AGE) have been found in tissues subject to microvascular injury such as retina and glomerulus in animal studies. Aminoguanidine treatment, an inhibitor of advanced glycosylation, has been shown to attenuate these microvascular lesions.[16]

Hyperglycaemia stimulates *de novo* synthesis of diacylglycerol thereby causing sustained activation of the protein kinase C (PKC) pathway. Protein kinase C is a family of isoforms of serine and threonine kinases, several forms of which are expressed in vascular tissues. It is an important regulator of many important vascular functions, enzymatic activities and gene expression involved in the production of extracellular matrix and contractile proteins. The consequences of increased PKC activity are numerous, including increased blood flow in retinal and renal circulations and also abnormalities of permeability, flow, contractility, coagulation changes, basement thickening, cell growth and neovascularization.[17] In the ischaemic retina, level of hypoxia inducible factor-1 is increased and correlates with the increased expression of vascular endothelial growth factor (VEGF), which is an important cytokine that induces angiogenesis and increases vascular permeability. VEGF appears to mediate its mitogenic effects and ocular neovascularization predominantly via the PKC pathway and a PKC isoform beta-selective inhibitor has been shown to inhibit such mitogenic activities (Fig. 3).

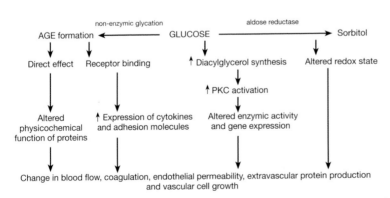

Fig. 3 Impact of biochemical factors on microvascular function.

Oxidative stress has also been implicated in the genesis and progression of endothelial dysfunction in diabetes. This can arise from elevated free radical generation, decreased levels of endogenous antioxidants and/or impaired regeneration of reduced forms of antioxidants. Oxygen-derived free radicals can be generated from glucose auto-oxidation and also from enzymic and non-enzymic pathways such as those involving PKC and AGE. NO, which is an important mediator of vascular function, has a propensity to be quenched by superoxide anion to form the highly toxic peroxynitrite. Toxic free radicals cause damage to macromolecules and DNA through oxidation, fragmentation and cross-linking. Indeed elevated levels of oxygen-derived free radicals are found in red blood cells, plasma and retina of diabetic animals and patients and correlate with the metabolic control, while endogenous antioxidants are found to be decreased in diabetic tissues and blood. Treatment with different antioxidants may also improve many of the metabolic abnormalities and endothelial function in diabetic patients although the precise doses required and the therapeutic potential of this approach remains to be clearly defined (Fig. 4).

Hyperinsulinaemia and decreased insulin sensitivity have been identified as independent risk factors for cardiovascular disease. *In vitro* studies have demonstrated that insulin can exhibit both atherogenic and anti-atherogenic effects on the large blood vessels.[18] The array of tissue effects include an increase in vascular smooth muscle proliferation, synthesis of extracellular matrix and lipids, plasminogen activator factor levels, anti-aggregating effects of platelets, intracellular calcium and nitric oxide availability. The anti-atherogenic effects of insulin may be attenuated in insulin-resistant and diabetic states, resulting in impaired endothelium-dependent vasodilation and increase platelet and blood viscosity.

The microvascular endothelium appears to be more susceptible to the metabolic and mitogenic effects of insulin in comparison to the large-vessel endothelium. Insulin at physiological and supraphysiological levels has been shown to stimulate capillary endothelial cells, pericytes and vascular smooth muscle cells to proliferate. In the same study, large vessel endothelium was found to be unresponsive to insulin. Insulin may also enhance synthesis of type IV collagen and reduce heparan sulphate production, which is an important determinant of charge barrier and hence vascular permeability. Hence it is conceivable that hyperinsulinaemia, especially in the context of type 2 diabetes, may have an important role in cell proliferation and permeability in the microcirculation although the UKPDS study has revealed that any such theoretical negative impact of insulin is more than compensated for by the benefit accrued from better glycaemic control.

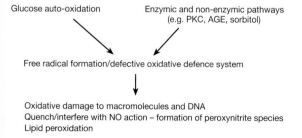

Fig. 4 Role of oxidative stress in diabetic angiopathy.

Metabolic: haemodynamic synergy and its therapeutic implications

There is a wealth of evidence linking hyperglycaemia to the pathogenesis of diabetic microangiopathy. The DCCT has shown that intensive glycaemic control delays the onset and slows the progression of diabetic retinopathy, nephropathy and neuropathy in patients with type 1 diabetes.[19] In the primary prevention cohort, the risk for development of retinopathy and microalbuminuria were reduced by 76 and 39 per cent respectively in those with tight glycaemic control. In the secondary intervention cohort, intensive therapy reduced the risk of progression of retinopathy and development of severe non-proliferative and proliferative retinopathy by 54 and 47 per cent respectively. The risk of progression to albuminuria was reduced by 54 per cent and clinical neuropathy was reduced by 60 per cent. The UKPDS has also shown that tight glycaemic control (HbA$_{1c}$ = 7.0 per cent) over a course of 10 years resulted in a 12 per cent risk reduction for any diabetes-related endpoint, 10 per cent reduction for any diabetes-related death and 6 per cent reduction in all-cause mortality.[20] Most of the risk reduction in the aggregate diabetes-related endpoint were due to a substantial 25 per cent risk reduction in microvascular endpoints. There was no difference in any of the aggregate endpoints with the choice of intensive agents (chlorpropamide, glibenclamide or insulin) used in the study.

Hypertension is associated with endothelial dysfunction and increased systemic capillary permeability in non-diabetic individuals. As hypertension commonly coexists in diabetic patients and is one of the key features of the insulin resistance syndrome, it is important to consider the impact of hypertension in concert with the hyperglycaemic milieu in the genesis and progression of microangiopathy (Fig. 5). High pressure in conjunction with hyperglycaemia have been shown to have distinctive effects on endothelial cell function and vascular permeability in *in vitro* studies. The UKPDS has also shown that tight blood pressure control in patients with type 2 diabetes and hypertension achieved a clinically important reduction in the risk of deaths related to diabetes, diabetes-related complications, progression of diabetic retinopathy and deterioration in visual acuity.[21] In type 1 patients, aggressive blood pressure treatment is also associated with retardation of the decline in renal function in incipient and overt nephropathy. In contrast to other antihypertensive agents, ACE inhibitors are thought to have specific reno-protective effects in addition to blood pressure-lowering benefits. The UKPDS however has shown that in type 2 diabetes, ACE inhibitors and β-blockers are equally effective in the reduction of diabetic endpoints, suggesting that blood pressure-lowering *per se* may be more important than choice of treatment used to achieve it.

Better understanding of the biochemical and molecular pathways in the pathogenesis of diabetic microangiopathy has led to research and development of pharmacological agents that may interfere with or impede the development of microvascular complications. Perhaps these compounds may eventually be used as an alternative or an adjunctive therapy in combination with tight metabolic and haemodynamic control to reduce the occurence of diabetic complications.

Aldose reductase inhibitors (ARIs) are compounds, which inhibit the rate-limiting enzyme of the polyol pathway responsible for catalyzing the reduction of hexoses. The ARIs are divided into carboxylic acids, hydantoin, flavanoids and other compounds. They

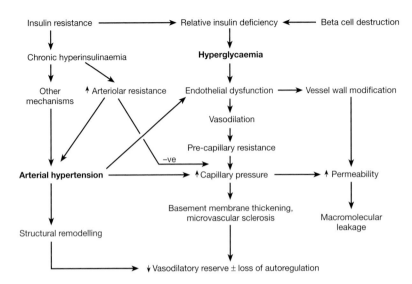

Fig. 5 Combined impact of pressure and hyperglycaemia on the genesis of microangiopathy.

have not been proven to have definite benefits for diabetic patients, as studies involving the use of ARIs in microvascular complications have shown conflicting results. It has been argued that the poor efficacy seen in some studies may be due to the lack of potency of the drugs tested. It has also been suggested that ARIs may be a preventative rather than a curative drug and they should be used in the early phases of the development of diabetic complications.

Aminoguanidine (AG) is a small hydrazine compound which acts as a potent inhibitor of AGE formation in both *in vivo* and *in vitro* settings. AG has been shown to inhibit the cross-linking of proteins, the formation of AGE structures and its pathological sequelae. However, there are concerns regarding the potential side-effects of long-term AG treatment and the theoretical possibility of inducing tumour development. Hence the search is on for more specific AGE-inhibitor drugs with minimal side-effects.

Isoform-specific PKC inhibitors are another class of drugs that may have potential benefits in prevention of microangiopathy. LY290181 has been found to inhibit transcription factor binding to specific PKC-regulated genes involved in vascular function and may therefore inhibit diabetes-induced vascular dysfunction. Another PKC inhibitor, LY333531, was found to ameliorate the glomerular filtration rate, albumin excretion rate and retinal microcirculation in diabetic rats in a dose-responsive manner.

Reduced serum anti-oxidant status has been demonstrated in diabetic patients and has been linked to increased risk of atherosclerosis and microangiopathy. Dietary anti-oxidant supplementation may have a beneficial effect in preventing cellular damage in diabetes. Vitamin E has been shown to improve endothelial function in diabetic rats but other studies have reported a deleterious response to vitamin E supplementation. Vitamin C has been found to improve endothelial function in patients with type 2 diabetes but to date, there are no reports on its long-term effects on vascular function in diabetes.

Insulin resistance is a major abnormality underlying the development of type 2 diabetes and impaired insulin action has been proposed to have a deleterious effect on the vasculature in addition to its effects on glucose metabolism. Insulin sensitizers such as the thiazolidinediones have been shown to improve glucose metabolism and also cardiovascular risk factors and it is plausible that insulin sensitizers may also have a role in reduction of microvascular complications.

Conclusion

The mechanisms underlying microvascular abnormalities in diabetes are indeed complex and the type of diabetes may have a significant bearing on the expression of microangiopathy. At present, the control of glycaemia, hypertension, and early identification of those vulnerable individuals who are most susceptible to developing microangiopathy is a vital step in the prevention and/or retardation of diabetic microvascular complications while awaiting future development of mechanism-specific therapy.

References

1. **Tattersall RB**. The quest for normoglycaemia: a historical perspective. *Diabetic Medicine*, 1994; **11**: 618–35.
2. **Mogensen CE**. Diabetic renal disease: the quest for normotension – and beyond. *Diabetic Medicine*, 1995; **12**(9): 756–69.
3. National Diabetes Data Group. Classification and diagnosis of diabetes and other categories of glucose intolerance. *Diabetes*, 1979; **28**: 1039–57.
4. **Ross R**. The pathogenesis of atherosclerosis: a perspective for the 1990s. *Nature*, 1993; **362**: 801–9.
5. **Zatz R, Brenner BM**. Pathogenesis of diabetic microangiopathy. The hemodynamic view. *American Journal of Medicine*, 1986; **80**(3): 443–53.
6. **Parving HH, Viberti GC, Keen H, Christiansen JS, Lassen NA**. Hemodynamic factors in the genesis of diabetic microangiopathy. *Metabolism*, 1983; **32**: 943–9.
7. **Tooke JE**. Microvascular function in human diabetes – a physiological perspective. *Diabetes*, 1995; **44**: 721–6.
8. **Hostetter TH, Troy JL, Brenner BM**. Glomerular haemodynamics in experimental diabetes. *Kidney International*, 1981; **19**: 410.
9. **Rassam SMB, Patel V, Kohner EM**. The effect of experimental hypertension on retinal autoregulation in humans: a mechanism for progression of diabetic retinopathy. *Experimental Physiology*, 1995; **80**: 53–68.

10. Quinn M, Angelico MC, Warram JH, Krolewski AS. Familial factors determine the development of diabetic nephropathy in patients with IDDM. *Diabetologia*, 1996; **39**: 940–5.

11. Fioretto P *et al.* Heterogeneous nature of microalbuminuria in NIDDM: studies of endothelial function and renal structure. *Diabetologia*, 1998; **41**: 233–6.

12. Tooke JE, Goh KL. Endotheliopathy precedes type 2 diabetes. *Diabetes Care*, 1998; **21**: 2047–9.

13. Hattersley AT. Maturity-onset diabetes of the young: clinical heterogeneity explained by genetic heterogeneity. *Diabetic Medicine*, 1998; **15**: 15–24.

14. Verdonk CA, Palumbo PJ, Gharib H, Bartholomew LG. Diabetic microangiopathy in patients with pancreatic diabetes mellitus. *Diabetologia*, 1975; **11**(5): 394–400.

15. Boel E, Selmer J, Flodgaard HJ, Jensen T. Diabetic late complications: will aldose reductase inhibitors or inhibitors of advanced glycosylation endproduct formation hold promise? *Journal of Diabetes and its Complications*, 1995; **9**: 104–29.

16. Vlassara H. Recent progress in advanced glycation endproducts and diabetic complications. *Diabetes*, 1997; **46**(suppl. 2): S19–25.

17. King GL, Kunisaki M, Nishio Y, Inoguchi T, Shiba T, Xia P. Biochemical and molecular mechanisms in the development of diabetic vascular complications. *Diabetes*, 1996; **45**(suppl. 3): S105–8.

18. Feener EP, King GL. Vascular dysfunction in diabetes mellitus. *Lancet*, 1997; **350**: SI9–13.

19. The Diabetes Control and Complications Trial Research Group. The effect of intensive treatment of diabetes on the development and progression of long-term complications in insulin-dependent diabetes mellitus. *New England Journal of Medicine*, 1993; **329**: 978–86.

20. UKPDS Group. Intensive blood glucose control with sulphonylureas or insulin compared with conventional treatment and risk of complications in patients with type 2 diabetes (UKPDS 33). *Lancet*, 1998; **352**: 837–53.

21. UKPDS Group. Tight blood pressure control and risk of macrovascular and microvascular complications in type 2 diabetes: UKPDS 38. *British Medical Journal*, 1998; **317**: 703–13.

3.2 Vascular complications: the molecular basis of vascular disease

Angela M. Carter and P.J. Grant

Introduction

Diabetes mellitus is characterized by a range of complications related to the duration of the disease. These complications can roughly be divided into microvascular and macrovascular disorders. The microvascular complications are specific to diabetes, and include retinopathy, nephropathy, and neuropathy. The macrovascular complications, including coronary artery disease, peripheral vascular disease and stroke, occur in the non-diabetic population also but appear at an earlier age and more frequently in people with diabetes.

Microvascular complications occur in subjects with both type 1 and type 2 diabetes in a duration-dependent manner. Studies to determine factors related to the development of microvascular complications have predominantly been carried out in people with type 1 diabetes although it is likely that similar mechanisms contribute to the pathogenesis of these disorders in all forms of diabetes mellitus. Thus no particular delineation between the different forms of the disease will be presented in relation to these complications in subsequent sections of this chapter. Retinopathy occurs in over 90 per cent of people with diabetes, given a sufficient duration of the disease. Similarly, some degree of neuropathy occurs in the majority of subjects with diabetes. In contrast, however, nephropathy occurs in only 35–45 per cent of those with type 1 and in less than 20 per cent of people with type 2 diabetes.

The underlying mechanisms for the development of macrovascular complications in subjects with diabetes are likely to be similar to that of non-diabetic people. However the severity of the metabolic disturbance associated with diabetes exaggerates and accelerates the development and progression of these complications. For instance, the Framingham study indicated that for coronary artery disease the increased risk for those with diabetes is 3–5-fold compared to that of people without diabetes. In particular, the protective effect of female sex apparent in those without diabetes is lost in diabetic women, in whom the incidence of macrovascular disease is similar to that of men with diabetes.

Factors contributing to the development of long-term diabetic complications

Hyperglycaemia is common to both type 1 and type 2 diabetes and there is a substantial body of evidence implicating hyperglycaemia in the development of the microvascular complications of diabetes. The original definition of diabetes was based on the plasma concentration of glucose that was thought to be associated with risk of developing retinopathy. Additionally, epidemiological studies indicate that small increases in blood glucose, within what was thought to be the 'normal' range, are associated with a marked increase in macrovascular disorders.

The benefits of good glycaemic control in preventing the development, or slowing the progression of, microvascular and also to some extent macrovascular complications has been demonstrated in type 1 diabetes in the Diabetes Control and Complications Trial (**DCCT**)[1] and for type 2 diabetes in the recently reported UK Prospective Diabetes Study (UKPDS).[2] Despite convincing evidence for a direct association between hyperglycaemia and microvascular and macrovascular complications, the mechanisms by which poor metabolic control is translated into vascular damage remain unclear.

In people with type 1 and type 2 diabetes, cardiovascular complications are the most common cause of death, in particular, the presence of nephropathy is associated with a considerable increase in risk for death by 30–40-fold. Thus, common mechanisms may contribute to the development of nephropathy and cardiovascular disease. Given the limited incidence of nephropathy, this points to the possibility of shared genetic factors related to the pathogenesis of these disorders.

Evidence for the contribution of genetic factors to the pathogenesis of long-term diabetic complications

DCCT and familial clustering of microvascular complications

In the DCCT, 241 diabetic relatives of 217 DCCT patients were investigated for correlations with the presence and severity of retinopathy and nephropathy.[3] In the primary prevention group, there was no difference in the incidence of retinopathy in relatives of those DCCT subjects who developed retinopathy, compared with those without retinopathy, but there was a significant difference in the secondary prevention group. In the conventional treatment group, there was a significant correlation of severity of retinopathy between relatives and DCCT subjects, whereas this was not found in the intensive treatment group.

There was a five-fold increase of nephropathy in relatives of DCCT subjects with nephropathy compared to those without. The association was observed in both the conventional and intensive treatment groups, with the odds ratio greater in the conventional treatment group, but no correlation between the severity of nephropathy between affected relatives was observed.

This study provided firm evidence for a role for familial factors rela-ted to the progression of retinopathy and the development of nephrop-athy. Familial association may be related to a combination of shared genetic and environmental factors, however, a genetic contribution to the development or progression of these disorders is supported by the epidemiology of these complications. Retinopathy occurs in virtually all people with diabetes given sufficient duration of disease, although not all go on to develop more severe forms of the disease. Thus it appears that genetic factors are likely to influence the progression but not the development of retinopathy. In contrast, nephropathy occurs in a minority of those with diabetes and clusters

in families, lending greater support for a genetic predisposition to its development.

Familial clustering of macrovascular complications

Coronary artery disease is a complex polygenic disorder characterized by the long-term development of atheroma with superimposed plaque rupture and thrombosis leading to the syndrome of acute myocardial infarction (AMI). Although there have been no studies specifically addressing the issue of hereditability of coronary artery disease and AMI in diabetic subjects, family studies indicate a seven-fold risk in an individual with a first degree relative who suffered a premature fatal AMI. Clinical studies indicate that there are a wide variety of 'classic' risk factors for coronary artery disease and AMI including smoking, dyslipidaemia, hypertension, and abnormalities in glucose metabolism. Case-control studies have implicated a number of candidate genes for atheroma formation and thrombosis (Table 1) and there is evidence that complex gene-environment interactions play a role in this disorder.

Disorders of glucose metabolism

Complications arising from hyperglycaemia are most notable in tissues where glucose uptake is independent of insulin action. The

Table 1 Polymorphisms identified within the genes encoding some of the factors related to an increased risk of atherothrombotic vascular disease

Gene	Polymorphism	Associations with cardiovascular disease
Angiotensin-converting enzyme (ACE)	ID	D allele associated with increased serum ACE and also associated with myocardial infaction (MI), particularly in subjects otherwise considered to be at low risk
ApoE	E2, E3, E4	E4 allele associated with increased levels of serum cholesterol and also associated with ischaemic heart disease (IHD)
Paraoxonase	Met45Leu	Leu45 associated with elevated paraoxonase plasma concentration. Leu45 associated with IHD
PAI-1	4G/5G	4G allele associated with increased levels of plasma PAI-1 and also associated with IHD
Fibrinogen	−455 G/A	A allele associated with elevated fibrinogen levels. Inconsistent results in relation to IHD
Factor VII	Arg353Glu	Arg allele associated with elevated plasma factor VII. One study found association with MI in subjects with a family history of MI
Factor XIII	Val34Leu	Leu allele found to be protective for MI and deep venous thrombosis (DVT) but possibly risk factor for intracerebral haemorrhage
Factor V	Arg506Gln (factor V Leiden)	Gln allele is associated with resistance of factor V to activated protein C and related to DVT. Also reported to be associated with IHD especially in the presence of other risk factors
Prothrombin	G20210A	A allele associated with increased levels of prothrombin and related to DVT. Also reports of associations with IHD especially in the presence of other risk factors
Platelet glycoprotein IIIa	Leu33Pro	Pro allele associated with premature MI, premature ischaemic stroke and coronary stent thrombosis

polyol pathway of intracellular glucose metabolism and the pathway of non-enzymatic glycation of proteins have been extensively studied in relation to hyperglycaemia. Evidence exists to implicate both systems in the pathogenesis of diabetic complications[4] and the genes coding for proteins involved in these pathways are clearly candidates for these complications.

Polyol pathway

The polyol pathway and the consequences of its overactivity in the presence of hyperglycaemia are summarized below. Nishimura has provided a comprehensive review of this pathway in relation to the development of diabetic complications.[5]

When glucose accumulates intracellularly, it is either phosphorylated to glucose-6-phosphate by the enzyme hexokinase or it is reduced to sorbitol by the enzyme aldose reductase. The affinity of aldose reductase for glucose being low, the majority of intracellular glucose is transformed to glucose-6-phosphate. However, during hyperglycaemic episodes the hexokinase/glucose-6-phosphate pathway becomes saturated, giving rise to an increased flux through the polyol pathway, leading to an increase in intracellular sorbitol accumulation. Intracellular sorbitol is converted to fructose by the action of sorbitol dehydrogenase.

Sorbitol does not diffuse out of cells efficiently and accumulates in the retina, lens, arterial wall, and Schwann cells of peripheral nerves. These closely mirror the sites associated with the development of the long-term complications of diabetes suggesting a causative role. Increased aldose reductase activity and increased intracellular sorbitol accumulation may contribute to cellular dysfunction via a number of mechanisms.

The osmotic stress associated with the intracellular accumulation of sorbitol may cause cellular dysfunction, in part, via a decrease in intracellular myoinositol. Increased flux through the polyol pathway gives rise to a reduction in the cofactor NADPH via increased activity of aldose reductase. Since NADPH is essential for catalysing normal cellular processes, reduction in the available NADPH is thought to influence a number of cellular functions including decreased glutathione reductase and decreased constitutive nitric oxide synthase activity. A reduction in glutathione reductase would lead to decreased inactivation of free radicals and consequent oxidative stress and cellular damage. A decrease in nitric oxide synthase activity would lead to decreased constitutive nitric oxide production with consequent effects on vascular tone.

Increased flux through the polyol pathway also gives rise to increased intracellular fructose accumulation via the action of sorbitol dehydrogenase. Fructose is a more effective glycating agent than glucose so increased traffic through sorbitol dehydrogenase is likely to contribute to the pathogenesis of diabetic complications via the production of intracellular advanced glycation end products (AGEs). This increased activity also gives rise to an increase in the $NADH/NAD^+$ ratio and this has been associated with an increased production of diacylglycerol, increased protein kinase C, and decreased Na^+,K^+-ATPase activity, leading to perturbation of intracellular ionic balance and detrimental effects on nerve conduction. The intracellular metabolic consequences of hyperglycaemia have been extensively described by Williamson and Ido.[6]

Animal studies have confirmed the link between aldose reductase activity, sorbitol accumulation, and microvascular complications. In animal models, over-expression of human aldose reductase gives rise to increased intracellular sorbitol with the subsequent development of nephropathy, retinopathy, and neuropathy. More importantly, the development and progression of these complications is prevented or delayed by administration of aldose reductase inhibitors. In human trials little benefit of aldose reductase inhibitors has been demonstrated. It is possible that the agents used have poor cellular uptake or the duration of treatment may have been insufficient to demonstrate significant benefit.

Despite the lack of efficacy of aldose reductase inhibitors in humans,[7] in those with type 2 diabetes erythrocyte aldose reductase levels have been shown to be significantly higher in people with retinopathy or nephropathy compared to those without complications. This association was independent of glycaemic control, duration of diabetes or age, indicating that elevated levels are not solely dependent on hyperglycaemia. In addition, there is considerable inter-individual variation in the activity of aldose reductase purified from erythrocytes. Aldose reductase activity correlates with the level of aldose reductase determined by immunoassay, indicating that the increased activity reflects increased cellular expression rather than inter-individual variation in the affinity of aldose reductase for its substrate. Since levels of erythrocyte aldose reductase have been shown to be stable over time, the observed large inter-individual variation in levels may be due to genetic factors. In support of this, linkage analyses of sib-pairs among diabetic Pima Indians have demonstrated linkage of genetic markers close to the aldose reductase gene locus with nephropathy.[8]

Aldose reductase polymorphism

A CA dinucleotide repeat polymorphism occurs 2.1 kb upstream of the aldose reductase gene transcription start site, and the association of this polymorphism with diabetic microvascular complications has been investigated. In Chinese people with type 2 diabetes, 7 alleles were identified, $Z-6, Z-4, Z-2, Z, Z+2, Z+4$ and $Z+6$.[9] In this study, the $Z-2$ allele was significantly associated with early-onset retinopathy for it was present in 59 per cent of people with early onset retinopathy (most of these presented with proliferative retinopathy at diagnosis of diabetes), whereas only nine per cent of people with no evidence of retinopathy after a mean of 15 years duration of diabetes possessed this allele. Subsequently, in a larger study of Caucasians with type 1 diabetes, an increased incidence of the $Z-2$ allele, accompanied by a decreased incidence of the $Z+2$ allele, was found in those with nephropathy compared with those free from complications after 20 years duration.[10]

Maeda et al.[11] found no association of the dinucleotide repeat polymorphism with erythrocyte aldose reductase level suggesting that this polymorphism is not functional but acting as a marker for a functional polymorphism elsewhere in the aldose reductase gene. Since an increase in aldose reductase level has been related to microvascular complications it is possible that genetic variation within the aldose reductase gene, particularly within the gene regulatory regions, may give rise to an increased expression of aldose reductase thereby leading to an increased flux through the polyol pathway with consequent detrimental effects on cellular function. In support of this, a common −106 C/T polymorphism has been identified, with the T allele significantly associated with nephropathy.[12] The relationship of the −106 C/T polymorphism with erythrocyte aldose reductase is at present unknown.

Non-enzymatic glycation

A detailed review of non-enzymatic glycation and its relationship to diabetic complications is given by Chappey et al.[13] and summarized below.

Prolonged hyperglycaemia results in the production of AGEs. Proteins with a long half-life initially undergo reversible glycosylation resulting in the formation of Schiff bases and Amadori products (for example the glycated haemoglobin HbA_{1c}) and subsequently irreversible glycation gives rise to AGEs. Direct effects of AGEs include cross-linking of proteins and generation of reactive oxygen intermediates with consequent oxidative stress and production of oxidised low-density lipoprotein (LDL), which has known atherogenic properties. Additional effects of AGEs are mediated via interaction with cellular receptors of which RAGE (the receptor for AGE) is the most extensively characterized. RAGE is expressed by a number of different cell types including endothelial cells, monocytes and macrophages, smooth muscle cells and neurones. The consequences of AGE formation and AGE/RAGE interaction are summarized in Fig. 1.

AGE interaction with endothelial cell RAGE results in the induction of vascular cell adhesion molecule-1 (VCAM-1) expression on the cell surface. This gives rise to increased monocyte adhesion and extravasation resulting in extravascular accumulation of monocytes and monocyte-derived macrophages. AGE/RAGE interaction also facilitates the accumulation of AGEs within the extracellular matrix where they are involved in cross-linking extracellular matrix proteins. This results in modification of protein structure and function, leading to a decrease in their degradation and contributes to the extracellular matrix accumulation. In addition, monocytes and macrophages express RAGE which facilitates their migration towards, and accumulation within, areas of AGE deposition.

AGE interaction with endothelial cell RAGE also leads to the synthesis and expression of tissue factor giving rise to a pro-coagulant state, which is enhanced by the concomitant down-regulation of endothelial cell thrombomodulin. Furthermore, AGE/RAGE interaction induces the expression of endothelin-1, a potent vasoconstrictor, and inhibits the production of the potent vasodilators nitric oxide and prostacyclin, leading to vasoconstriction, which may contribute to hypertension in diabetes. AGEs present in the cell membranes of red blood cells and platelets may give rise to a decrease in membrane fluidity, which has been associated with an increased risk of vascular complications. AGEs also promote the increased adhesion of these cells to the endothelium and may give rise to altered platelet function.

Animal studies have provided evidence that AGE formation is intimately involved in the development and progression of long-term diabetic complications. Injection of AGEs results in vascular AGE deposition with increased endothelial cell permeability, extra-vascular monocyte accumulation and a reduction in endothelium dependent vasodilatation. Prolonged administration results in demonstrable deposition in the eyes and aorta and the most profound effects in the kidneys. These effects are inhibited by the concurrent administration of aminoguanidine which prevents AGE-dependent protein cross-linking. It is interesting to note the similarities that aminoguanidine has with metformin which was reported in UKPDS as being particularly beneficial in the prevention of AMI. The formation of AGE proteins and their interaction with RAGE expressed by various cell types is likely to be a major mechanism for the development of both micro- and macro-vascular complications associated with diabetes. Evidence to support this comes from a study in which injection of soluble RAGE into atherosclerosis prone rodents was associated with a decreased development of atheroma.

There are a number of polymorphisms of the gene encoding RAGE and one in particular, Gly82Ser, present in approximately 10 per cent of the population, occurs within the AGE binding site of this receptor.[14] No association of this polymorphism with macrovascular disease in those with type 2 diabetes was found.

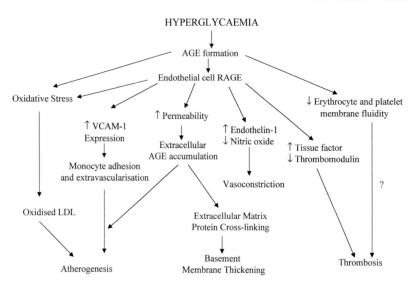

Fig. 1 Hyperglycaemia and non-enzymatic glycation. Prolonged hyperglycaemia results in the formation of AGEs. AGEs either act directly to cause protein cross-linking or they interact with cellular receptors including RAGE. AGE/RAGE interaction gives rise to numerous effects including increased endothelial cell permeability with consequent extravascular accumulation of AGE, and increased expression of endothelin-1 and VCAM-1 and decreased expression of nitric oxide and thrombomodulin which have profound effects on endothelial cell function.

Similarly, in Chinese people with type 2 diabetes there was no significant association of Gly82Ser with nephropathy or retinopathy.[15] Interestingly Ser82 was present in approximately 45 per cent of these people, both with and without diabetes, which differs significantly from the 10 per cent incidence reported by Hudson et al.[14] in Europeans, Asians, and Pima Indians. Further studies in this area are awaited with interest.

Nerve conduction and osmotic balance

Na$^+$,K$^+$-ATPase

The Na$^+$,K$^+$-ATPase is a membrane-bound sodium pump which maintains high intracellular K$^+$ and low extracellular Na$^+$ and regulates normal osmotic balance, resting membrane potential and muscle and nerve excitation. Maintenance of the Na$^+$ gradient mediates the cellular transportation of numerous ions including Ca^{2+}, Cl$^-$ and also glucose and amino acids. In the kidney it is the predominant regulator of Na$^+$ and water reabsorption.[16] The Na$^+$,K$^+$-ATPase comprises two major subunits, α and β, and a minor γ subunit. The α subunit contains the catalytic site whilst the β subunit is involved in directing the complex to the cellular membrane and is also essential for enzyme activity. Na$^+$,K$^+$-ATPase is expressed as several different isozymes, with at least four different α subunits (α_1, α_2, α_3 and α_4) and three different β subunits (β_1, β_2 and β_3), which display tissue specific distributions.[16]

Na$^+$,K$^+$-ATPase activity is important in membrane potential generation and nerve conduction and erythrocyte Na$^+$,K$^+$-ATPase has been correlated with sciatic nerve activity. Erythrocyte Na$^+$,K$^+$-ATPase activity in subjects with type 1 and type 2 diabetes is reduced. This observed reduction in erythrocyte Na$^+$,K$^+$-ATPase activity is greater in ethnic compared with white populations, reflecting an increased incidence of neuropathy in ethnic groups. Thus, there may be genetic factors influencing Na$^+$,K$^+$-ATPase activity and predisposing to diabetic neuropathy.

Na$^+$,K$^+$-ATPase polymorphism

A polymorphism of the α_1 subunit has been identified, located within the first intron of the gene, which was associated with reduced erythrocyte Na$^+$,K$^+$-ATPase activity in those with type 1 diabetes, but not in non-diabetic people.[17] The polymorphism was significantly associated with the presence of neuropathy, with 10 per cent of those with no neuropathy possessing the polymorphic site compared with 73 per cent of those with mild neuropathy and 81 per cent of those with severe neuropathy. Weak associations with retinopathy and nephropathy were observed although these disappeared after accounting for the presence of neuropathy. To date no further studies have confirmed or refuted these findings and since this polymorphism occurs within the 1st intron of the gene it is possible that it acts as a marker for a functional polymorphism elsewhere in the Na$^+$,K$^+$-ATPase gene locus.

As mentioned earlier, increased flux through the polyol pathway gives rise to decreased Na$^+$,K$^+$-ATPase activity. This leads to the interesting possibility of interactions between polymorphisms of aldose reductase and Na$^+$,K$^+$-ATPase that may enhance the development of diabetic complications, in general, and in particular neuropathy.

Genetic factors and hypertension

Renin–angiotensin system

The renin–angiotensin system has an important role in many aspects of vascular homeostasis (Fig. 2). Renin cleaves angiotensinogen to form angiotensin I, which is converted to the active peptide angiotensin II by the action of angiotensin-converting enzyme (ACE). Angiotensin II regulates renal Na$^+$ and water reabsorption, is a potent vasoconstrictor and has effects on smooth muscle cells, cardiac myocytes, and cardiac fibroblasts. In addition, angiotensin-converting enzyme inactivates bradykinin (a potent vasodilator and inhibitor of smooth muscle cell proliferation), thereby compounding the pressor effects of angiotensin II. The majority of the effects of angiotensin II are mediated via interaction with the angiotensin II receptor subtype 1 (AT1). These effects include stimulation of vascular smooth muscle cells leading to proliferation, migration, and hypertrophy, with similar effects on cardiac myocytes. Angiotensin II also stimulates cardiac fibroblasts to increase extracellular matrix production. Thus, in addition to renal influences, the renin–angiotensin system is likely to have significant effects on the heart.[18]

Variation in the production of angiotensin II or interactions with AT1 may give rise to effects on the vasculature and the heart. A number of polymorphisms of the components of the renin–angiotensin system have been described and have been investigated in relation to their association with hypertension, cardiovascular disorders and with the microvascular complications of diabetes.

Angiotensin-converting enzyme polymorphism

Macrovascular disorders

A 287 bp insertion/deletion (I/D) polymorphism within the 16th intron of the ACE gene has been identified which is associated with differences in serum and cellular levels of angiotensin-converting enzyme. The highest levels of angiotensin-converting enzyme are present in those of DD genotype and the lowest levels in those of II genotype, with ID genotype associated with intermediate levels. The polymorphism accounts for approximately 50 per cent of the variation in circulating angiotensin-converting enzyme levels. The DD genotype confers an increased risk for myocardial infarction compared with the II genotype, with associations found particularly in those who would otherwise be considered low risk for myocardial infarction.[19] Studies in relation to the extent or severity of coronary artery disease, although contradictory, tend to indicate no significant association, suggesting that it is related to the acute occlusive event as opposed to atherosclerotic plaque development. The angiotensin-converting enzyme I/D polymorphism has also been reported to be a risk factor for AMI in people with type 2 diabetes. In contrast to what might have been expected however, no convincing association of the angiotensin-converting enzyme I/D polymorphism with either hypertension or stroke has been shown. However, the study of the angiotensin-converting enzyme I/D polymorphism highlights the problems of a candidate gene approach to case–control studies. Although there are positive associations reported with AMI, there are an equal number of negative reports and probably a number that remain unpublished. Meta-analysis does indicate a small but significant excess risk of AMI in people with the DD genotype, although these results have to be viewed with the inherent bias of meta-analysis in mind, most notably publication bias.

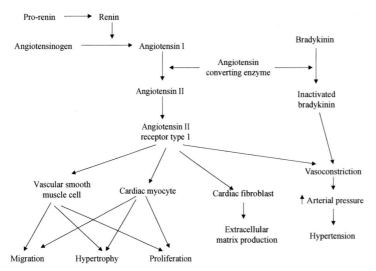

Fig. 2 The renin–angiotensin system. The renin–angiotensin system is essential for the control of arterial blood pressure. Angiotensin-converting enzyme converts angiotensin I to the active peptide angiotensin II which mediates its effects via interaction with cellular receptors giving rise to significant effects on the heart and vasculature.

Microvascular disorders

The potential role of angiotensin II in the pathogenesis of diabetic nephropathy has prompted a number of investigators to determine the association of the angiotensin-converting enzyme I/D polymorphism with the microvascular complications of diabetes. Several of these studies have been the subject of a meta-analysis which included in excess of 5000 subjects in total.[20] Overall, there was a significant association of the I/D polymorphism with nephropathy but not retinopathy. Possession of the D allele was associated with nephropathy in a dominant manner (that is, DD + ID versus II) in both type 1 and type 2 diabetes and in different racial sub-groups with similar odds ratios of approximately 1.3. The lack of association with retinopathy indicates that although genetic factors modulate the risk of microvascular disorders, the specific genetic factors may differ between the different subtypes of disease.

The role of the renin–angiotensin system in the pathogenesis of diabetic nephropathy is supported by the clinical efficacy of angiotensin-converting enzyme inhibitors in slowing the progression of nephropathy. Comparison has shown that for a similar lowering of blood pressure the benefits of angiotensin-converting enzyme inhibitors in relation to microalbuminuria far outweigh that of other anti-hypertensive agents, suggesting that the effects of the renin–angiotensin system on renal function may be independent of local pressor effects.

As mentioned previously, diabetic nephropathy is associated with considerable morbidity and mortality which is usually related to increased cardiovascular risk. The angiotensin-converting enzyme I/D polymorphism is associated with both cardiovascular disease and with diabetic nephropathy, suggesting that the D allele of the angiotensin-converting enzyme I/D polymorphism may represent a common risk factor. It is likely that associations are related to differences in serum and/or cellular angiotensin-converting enzyme levels, giving rise to increased angiotensin II formation. The issues relating to angiotensin-converting enzyme inhibition and diabetic nephropathy and hypertension, and the possibility of genotype-dependent benefits have been covered in detail.[18,21]

Angiotensinogen polymorphisms

A number of variants of the angiotensinogen gene have been identified, including the coding polymorphisms Met235Thr and Thr174Met, which account for approximately 10 per cent of the variation in circulating angiotensinogen levels. Several studies have determined the association of these polymorphisms with hypertension, cardiovascular disease, and microvascular complications in diabetes. The results in relation to cardiovascular disease and hypertension have been largely contradictory and have therefore not been discussed in this chapter.

In relation to microvascular diabetic complications, the Met235Thr polymorphism has been associated with albuminuria in Chinese people with type 2 diabetes, related to an increased incidence of the T allele in those with proteinuria compared to those free from complications. The T allele is present in a minority of white people whereas 70 per cent of Chinese people possess this allele. The incidence of albuminuria is also significantly higher in Chinese populations compared with Caucasian populations suggesting that the increased incidence of Thr235 may in part explain the increased risk in these people.[22] Two studies, one a family study and one a case–control study, have indicated a gender-specific association of Thr235 with nephropathy, with a significant association of the T allele with nephropathy found only in men. In addition, one study has found a significant interaction of Met235Thr and the angiotensin-converting enzyme I/D polymorphism in which there was a greater proportion of people with nephropathy in those possessing Thr235 and the angiotensin-converting enzyme D allele compared with those possessing Met235 and angiotensin-converting enzyme II genotype.[23] A similar trend was observed in the Chinese studied by Young et al.[22] It is interesting to speculate that the observed interaction between these two polymorphisms is due to an additive increase in angiotensin II and its sequelae.

Angiotensin II receptor

Polymorphisms of the AT1 receptor include T573C, a silent polymorphism within the coding region, and A1166C which occurs within the 3′-untranslated region of the gene. Reported associations of the C allele of A1166C with hypertension have been inconsistent. However, an interaction of the angiotensin-converting enzyme I/D polymorphism and A1166C has been reported in relation to myocardial infarction (MI), with an association of DD with MI only observed in those possessing C1166.[19] In people with type 1 diabetes, the C1166 allele was associated with nephropathy, but only in those with poor glycaemic control.[24] Further studies will be required to confirm these associations. Due to the location of *A1166C* within the 3′-untranslated region of the gene this polymorphism may influence the stability of the transcribed mRNA, thereby leading to an increase in receptor number. Thus, as with the interaction between Thr235 and angiotensin-converting enzyme D allele, the possibility arises that if C1166 gives rise to increased cellular expression of AT1, a potentiation of effect with elevated levels of angiotensin II might be expected.

Genetic factors and dyslipidaemia

Dyslipidaemia is a general term used to describe a variety of lipid and lipoprotein abnormalities which are associated with atherosclerosis. The efficacy of lipid lowering agents in the prevention of atherothrombotic disorders clearly demonstrates the importance of these abnormalities in the pathogenesis of atherosclerosis.

The major lipids in the circulation are cholesterol and triglycerides and elevated levels of both are associated with an increased risk of cardiovascular disease. In relation to triglycerides, the strongest and most consistent associations with cardiovascular disease have been described in people with type 2 diabetes in whom a classic pattern of low high-density lipoprotein (HDL) and raised LDL cholesterol with increased triglyceride in association with insulin resistance is most commonly observed. These lipids are insoluble in plasma and are therefore transported in lipoproteins, which consist of a lipid core of cholesterol ester and triglyceride surrounded by various members of the apolipoprotein family. The apolipoproteins stabilize the lipid core and act as ligands for receptors involved in lipid clearance as well as regulating the activity of a number of enzymes involved in lipid metabolism and clearance. A variety of lipoproteins exist including chylomicrons, LDL and HDL which all serve differing functions. Elevated LDL is associated with atherosclerosis whereas HDL is associated with protection from atherosclerosis.

A comprehensive review of lipid abnormalities and their management in subjects with diabetes is to be found in Betteridge.[25]

Genetic variation within the genes encoding any of the factors related to lipid production, transport, hydrolysis, or clearance are obvious candidate genes for the development of vascular disease and many rare mutations have been identified which give rise to familial hyperlipidaemia. Franceschini[26] has reviewed these mutations and how they have helped in the understanding of lipid structure and function. In addition, a number of common polymorphisms have been identified which may be related to an increased risk for the development of atherosclerotic disorders. These have been reviewed by Semenkovich and Heinecke[27] and are described briefly below.

ApolipoproteinE polymorphism

ApoE is an integral component of the majority of lipoproteins and is essential for their normal clearance from the circulation in a receptor dependent manner. Thus ApoE plays a protective role in relation to the pathogenesis of atherosclerosis. Animal studies confirm this since ApoE knockout mice have hyperlipidaemia and extensive atherosclerosis, whereas animals over-expressing ApoE are protected from the development of atherosclerosis.

A common polymorphism of ApoE exists which is characterized by three common alleles: E2, which is the least common, E3, which is the most common, and E4. These alleles are defined by two polymorphic sites, Cys112Arg and Arg158Cys. E2 is defined by Cys112 : Cys158, E3 by Cys112 : Arg158 and E4 by Arg112 : Arg158. Possession of the E4 allele is associated with elevated LDL and triglycerides and the E4 allele has been associated with an increased risk for cardiovascular disease in those with type 1 and type 2 diabetes as well as in non-diabetic subjects. In addition, in type 1 diabetes, subjects possessing the E4 allele demonstrate a greater fall in LDL in response to a low cholesterol diet compared to subjects possessing the E3 allele.[28]

Lipoprotein lipase polymorphisms

Lipoprotein lipase is the enzyme involved in clearance of triglyceride-rich lipoproteins and is therefore thought to be anti-atherogenic. Lipoprotein lipase is stimulated by insulin and insulin insufficiency is related to decreased lipoprotein lipase activity and increased triglyceride levels. A number of polymorphisms of the gene encoding lipoprotein lipase have been described including Asn291Ser which has been associated with a decrease in plasma HDL and an increased risk for premature atherosclerosis. It appears that this polymorphism is related to the development of atherosclerosis in non-diabetics and diabetics.[29] In people with diabetes these polymorphisms may interact with metabolic disturbances characteristic of diabetes to give rise to early and extensive atherosclerosis, although this has not been investigated.

ApolipoproteinC-III polymorphism

ApoC-III inhibits lipoprotein lipase and over-expression of human ApoC-III in mice gives rise to elevated triglyceride levels, which is associated with the development of atherosclerosis. ApoC-III expression is suppressed by insulin, and insulin deficiency would be expected to be associated with decreased lipoprotein lipase activity and elevated triglyceride levels, suggesting a mechanism for the development of lipid abnormalities in subjects with diabetes. There are a number of polymorphisms in the promoter and 3′-untranslated region of the gene encoding lipoprotein lipase, which have been related to differences in triglyceride level and with insensitivity to insulin action. The association of these polymorphisms with the development of cardiovascular disease in those with diabetes is at present unknown; however the apoC III S2 allele is associated with severe hypertriglyceridaemia in people with type 2 diabetes.[29]

Paraoxonase polymorphisms

The enzyme paraoxonase is bound exclusively to HDL and paraoxonase purified from HDL is capable of protecting LDL from oxidative modification, suggesting that the apparent protective effect of HDL may be related, in part, to paraoxonase activity. In addition, paraoxonase activity is reduced in people with diabetes, with the lowest levels in those with diabetic nephropathy.[30] There is considerable inter-individual variation in paraoxonase activity towards paroxon as substrate suggesting a potential genetic influence.

Two polymorphisms of the paraoxonase gene, Gln192Arg and Met55Leu, have been studied in relation to paraoxonase activity and diabetic macrovascular disease. In those with type 2 diabetes, Arg192 and Leu55 have been associated with the presence of ischaemic heart disease. Gln192Arg and Met55Leu are in linkage disequilibrium, with Leu54 occurring more frequently with Arg192. Differences in the association of both of these polymorphisms with paraoxonase activity exist when either paroxon or phenylacetate are used as substrates.[30] However, a recent study has shown that HDLs containing Arg192 or Leu55 paraoxonase are less effective at protecting LDL from oxidative modification compared with Gln192 or Met55 paraoxonase.[31] Hence the association of Arg192 and Leu55 with ischaemic heart disease may be due to defective protection from lipid peroxidation leading to predisposition to atherosclerosis.

Genetic factors and haemostasis

The haemostatic system maintains a delicate balance between coagulation, anticoagulation, platelet activation/inhibition and fibrinolysis in order to maintain vascular patency (Fig. 3). Apart from being present in plasma, a number of haemostatic factors are found as components of the normal and diseased vessel wall, including fibrinogen, von-Willebrand factor, tissue plasminogen activator, and plasminogen activator inhibitor-1 (**PAI-1**). In contrast, tissue factor is only found in the vessel wall. It is a potent activator of the coagulation cascade upon exposure to circulating factor VIIa and is abundant in atherosclerotic plaques. The ultimate result of activation of the coagulation cascade, either by exposure of subendothelial tissue factor or by contact activation, is thrombin generation. Thrombin cleaves fibrinogen to form soluble fibrin and activates factor XIII which is then capable of cross-linking soluble fibrin thereby consolidating the fibrin clot. Thrombin is also a potent platelet activating agent, inducing a conformational change in platelet glycoprotein IIb/IIIa leading to platelet deposition and aggregation.

Aberration of any haemostatic factor may in the end lead to the development of atherosclerosis. In support of this, a number of large prospective studies and case–control studies have identified significant associations of a number of haemostatic factors, in particular fibrinogen, with cardiovascular disease. In addition, considerable effort has been directed towards identifying common genetic variants of the genes encoding the various haemostatic factors and the determination of their association with cardiovascular disease (Table 1). In people with type 1 and type 2 diabetes a number of haemostatic abnormalities are present in those with and without diabetic complications. These include elevated levels of PAI-1, fibrinogen and factor VII; these abnormalities and the contribution of genetic factors have been extensively reviewed elsewhere[32] and are summarized below.

Plasminogen activator inhibitor-1

PAI-1 is the major inhibitor of tissue-type plasminogen activator in the circulation and as such is the primary regulator of intra-vascular fibrinolysis. Although there are inconsistent reports of the relationship of PAI-1 to diabetic complications in people with type 1 diabetes, in those with type 2 diabetes there is a consistent and marked increase in plasma PAI-1. In these people PAI-1 clearly clusters with features of the insulin resistance syndrome, particularly with triglycerides. Polymorphisms of the *PAI-1* gene include a CA dinucleotide repeat, and a common single nucleotide I/D polymorphism in the promoter (4G/5G) at position −675, see Fig. 4.

The 4G/5G polymorphism is associated with plasma PAI-1 levels, the highest levels in those homozygous for the 4G allele and lowest levels in those homozygous for the 5G allele. This has been attributed to a difference in transcription factor binding, with both the 4G and 5G alleles binding an activator whereas only the 5G allele additionally binds a repressor leading to decreased *PAI-1* gene transcription relative to the 4G allele (Fig. 4). In those with type 2 diabetes and in non-diabetics, homozygosity for the 4G allele is associated with ischaemic heart disease and it is likely that this is due to suppression of fibrinolysis resulting from the increase in PAI-1. There is a significant

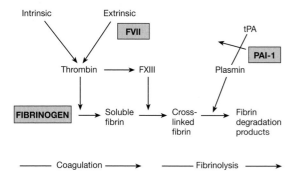

Fig. 3 Simplified cartoon of the haemostatic mechanisms involved in the regulation of thrombin and fibrin formation and fibrin degradation. With the exception of tissue factor, coagulation factors circulate in the inactive form and are activated in the coagulation cascade resulting in thrombin generation. The activation of the coagulation cascade leads to fibrin formation, whilst the fibrinolytic system is involved in clot remodelling and fibrin breakdown. Factors discussed in the text are boxed.

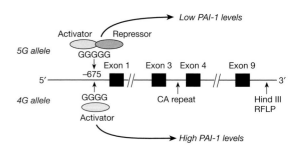

Fig. 4 Polymorphisms of the *PAI-1* gene. The 4G/5G polymorphism at position − 675 of the *PAI-1* gene is associated with plasma PAI-1, with the lowest levels in those homozygous for the 5G allele. This is related to differences in transcription factor binding, both alleles bind an activation factor at this site whereas the 5G allele additionally binds a repressor leading to decreased transcription and consequently lower levels of PAI-1 relative to the 4G allele.

interaction of 4G/5G with serum triglyceride in relation to PAI-1 level, in those homozygous for the 4G allele there is a significantly greater increase in plasma PAI-1 with increasing triglyceride compared with those homozygous for the 5G allele. Thus, the risk associated with possession of the 4G/4G genotype in people with type 2 diabetes is likely to be exacerbated by elevated plasma triglycerides. In addition to cardiovascular disease, the 4G allele has also been associated with diabetic retinopathy in Pima Indians with type 2 diabetes, although no association with plasma PAI-1 and retinopathy was observed.[33] This finding remains to be confirmed in further studies.

Fibrinogen

A number of prospective studies have found fibrinogen to be an independent risk factor for cardiovascular disease. Most studies have demonstrated elevated levels of fibrinogen in people with diabetes in whom there is a weak correlation of fibrinogen with some features of the insulin resistance syndrome. Fibrinogen is a complex glycoprotein comprising pairs of three non-identical polypeptides ($\alpha_2\beta_2\gamma_2$), encoded by separate genes. There are a number of polymorphisms of these genes, including several in the β-fibrinogen gene promoter, which are of particular importance since the synthesis of the β-fibrinogen chain is thought to be the rate limiting step in the secretion of fibrinogen.

The −455 G/A promoter polymorphism has been the most extensively studied of the β-fibrinogen polymorphisms and is related to differences in plasma fibrinogen, with the highest levels in those possessing the A allele. A number of studies have investigated the association of −455 G/A with cardiovascular disease in people with and without diabetes, although the results have been inconsistent. In one study, there was an association of the −455 G/A polymorphism with coronary artery disease in subjects with type 2 diabetes, which was independent of plasma fibrinogen, indicating that the −455 G/A polymorphism may be acting as a marker for a functional polymorphism elsewhere in the fibrinogen gene locus.[34]

Factor VII

Associations of plasma factor VII levels with cardiovascular disease have been confused by the apparent association with fatal myocardial infarction. Despite this, elevated levels of factor VII have been reported in people with diabetes, with the highest levels in those with microalbuminuria. In a similar manner to PAI-1, in those with type 2 diabetes factor VII appears to cluster with features of the insulin resistance syndrome, in particular triglycerides. Polymorphisms of the factor VII gene include a decanucleotide insertion at position −323 of the promoter and a coding region Arg353Gln polymorphism, with Gln353 and the 10 bp insertion associated with the lowest plasma factor VII level. The association of these polymorphisms with cardiovascular disease in non-diabetics also remains controversial and no studies have reported significant associations of these polymorphisms with diabetic complications.

Conclusions

Despite a significant flurry of activity in relation to the genetics of the vascular complications of diabetes, at present there is no coherent strategy to clarify this issue. The inconsistencies in reported genotype : disease associations highlight the problems associated with case–control studies and, in particular, the crucial importance of a clearly defined phenotype.

An important consideration when carrying out genetic association studies is the multifactorial nature of vascular diseases, which involve complicated interactions between different genetic factors and also between genetic and environmental factors. The potential for gene–gene interactions was highlighted earlier in this chapter in relation to polymorphisms of the renin–angiotensin system. It is also impossible to make clear distinctions between genes and environment in relation to vascular disease and we ignore environmental issues at our peril. The epidemiology of cardiovascular disease demonstrates a massive increase in AMI after the Great War that cannot be explained solely by enhanced diagnostic acumen. It is clearly not feasible that this is due to genetic influences *per se* and it is intellectually more coherent to view this as being due to environmental influences, for instance changes in diet and activity levels in this century, interacting with established genetic variants. In population terms there is considerable weight to the view that environmental influences underlie the association of insulin resistance with atherothrombotic risk. A similar argument can be constructed in relation to microvascular complications which are unequivocally related to the environment of hyperglycaemia.

Important advances will be made in the next decade, however, and there are three areas worthy of consideration. First, the completion of the human genome project will take us into a new era of functional analysis of gene transcription and protein activity. Identification of cis- and trans-acting factors which modulate promoter function and gene expression and the study of coding polymorphisms that alter protein structure and activity will allow future studies to be designed on a more rational basis. Second, it is hoped that studies of quantitative trait analysis such as the San Antonio Study based in Texas will provide us with important candidates for study in relation to different vascular phenotypes. Third, there is a need to move away from simple case–control studies to affected sib-pair studies which are more powerful tools for association studies of candidate genes and which, if large enough, can themselves be used for linkage studies.

In the present millennium, advances in genetic techniques will foster more efficient analyses of data and more powerful studies. The genetic basis of any polygenic disorder, such as vascular disease, has to be integrated into a rational pathophysiological basis of disease that takes due account of environmental risk in the broadest sense. The elucidation of these relationships will ultimately give us a true perspective on the genetic basis of vascular disorders in both diabetic and non-diabetic populations.

References

1. **The Diabetes Control and Complications Trial Research Group**. The effect of intensive treatment of diabetes on the development and progression of long-term complications in insulin-dependent diabetes mellitus. *New England Journal of Medicine*, 1993; **329**: 977–86.

2. **UK Prospective Diabetes Study (UKPDS) Group**. Intensive blood-glucose control with sulphonylureas or insulin compared with conventional treatment and risk of complications in patients with type 2 diabetes (UKPDS 33). *Lancet*, 1998; **352**: 837–53.

3. **The Diabetes Control and Complications Trial Research Group**. Clustering of long-term complications in families with diabetes in the diabetes control and complications trial. *Diabetes*, 1997; **46**: 1829–39.

4. Nathan, DM. The pathophysiology of diabetic complications: how much does the glucose hypothesis explain. *Annals of Internal Medicine*, 1996; **124**: 86–9.

5. Nishimura C. Aldose reductase in glucose toxicity: a potential target for the prevention of diabetic complications. *Pharmacological Reviews*, 1998; **50**: 21–33.

6. Williamson JR, Ido Y. The vascular cellular consequences of hyperglycaemia. In: Tooke JE, ed. *Diabetic Angiopathy*. London: Arnold, 1999: 161–86.

7. Airey M, Bennett C, Nicolucci A, Williams R. Aldose reductase inhibitors for the prevention and treatment of diabetic peripheral neuropathy. *Cochrane Database of Systematic Reviews*, 2000; CD002182.

8. Imperatore G, Hanson RL, Pettitt DJ, Kobes S, Bennett PH, Knowler WC. Sib-pair linkage analysis for susceptibility genes for microvascular complications among Pima Indians with type 2 diabetes. *Diabetes*, 1998; **47**: 821–30.

9. Ko BC-B, Lam KS-L, Wat NM-S, Chung SS-M. An (AC)n dinucleotide repeat polymorphic marker at the 5′ end of the aldose reductase gene is associated with early-onset diabetic retinopathy in NIDDM patients. *Diabetes*, 1995; **44**: 727–32.

10. Heesom AE, Millward A, Demaine AG. Susceptibility to diabetic neuropathy in patients with insulin dependent diabetes mellitus is associated with a polymorphism at the 5′ end of the aldose reductase gene. *Journal of Neurology, Neurosurgery and Psychiatry*, 1998; **64**: 213–6.

11. Maeda S *et al.* Diabetic nephropathy is not associated with the decanucleotide repeat polymorphism upstream of the aldose reductase (ALR2) gene but with erythrocyte aldose reductase content in Japanese subjects with type 2 diabetes. *Diabetes*, 1999; **48**: 420–2.

12. Moczulski DK *et al.* Aldose reductase gene polymorphisms and susceptibility to diabetic nephropathy in type 1 diabetes mellitus. *Diabetic Medicine*, 2000; **17**: 111–18.

13. Chappey O, Dosquet C, Wautier M-P, Wautier J-L. Advanced glycation end products, oxidant stress and vascular lesions. *European Journal of Clinical Investigation*, 1997; **27**: 97–108.

14. Hudson BI, Stickland MH, Grant PJ. Identification of polymorphisms in the receptor for advanced glycosylation end products (RAGE) gene: prevalence in type 2 diabetes and ethnic groups. *Diabetes*, 1998; **47**: 1155–7.

15. Liu L, Xiang K. RAGE Gly82Ser polymorphism in diabetic microangiopathy. *Diabetes Care*, 1999; **22**: 646.

16. Blanco G, Mercer RW. Isozymes of the Na-K-ATPase: heterogeneity in structure, diversity in function. *American Journal of Physiology*, 1998; **275**: F633–50.

17. Vague P, Dufayet D, Coste T, Moriscot C, Jannot MF, Raccah D. Association of diabetic neuropathy with Na/K ATPase gene polymorphism. *Diabetologia*, 1997; **40**: 506–11.

18. Morgan T, Brunner HR. The renin–angiotensin system and the heart: beyond 2000. *Heart*, 1996; **76**(3S): 98–103.

19. Cambien F, Evans A. Angiotensin I converting enzyme gene polymorphism and coronary heart disease. *European Heart Journal*, 1995; **16**(suppl. K): 13–22.

20. Fujisawa T *et al.* Meta-analysis of association of insertion/deletion polymorphism of angiotensin I-converting enzyme gene with diabetic nephropathy and retinopathy. *Diabetologia*, 1998; **41**: 47–53.

21. Cooper ME. Pathogenesis, prevention, and treatment of diabetic nephropathy. *Lancet*, 1998; **352**: 213–9.

22. Young RP, Chan JCN, Critchley JAJH, Poon E, Nicholls G, Cockram CS. Angiotensinogen T235 and ACE insertion/deletion polymorphisms associated with albuminuria in Chinese type 2 diabetic patients. *Diabetes Care*, 1998; **21**: 431–7.

23. Marre M *et al.* Contribution of genetic polymorphism in the renin–angiotensin system to the development of renal complications in insulin-dependent diabetes. Genetique de la Nephropathie Diabetique (GENEDIAB) Study Group. *Journal of Clinical Investigation*, 1997; **99**: 1585–95.

24. Doria A, Onuma T, Warram JH, Krolewski AS. Synergistic effect of angiotensin II type 1 receptor genotype and poor glycaemic control on risk of nephropathy in IDDM. *Diabetologia*, 1997; **40**: 1293–9.

25. Betteridge DJ. Risk factors for arterial disease in diabetes: dyslipidaemia. In: Tooke JE, ed. *Diabetic Angiopathy*. London: Arnold, 1999: 65–92.

26. Franceschini G. Apolipoprotein function in health and disease: insights from natural mutations. *European Journal of Clinical Investigation*, 1996; **26**: 733–46.

27. Semenkovich CF, Heinecke JW. The mystery of diabetes and atherosclerosis. Time for a new plot. *Diabetes*, 1997; **46**: 327–34.

28. Blaauwwiekel EE, Beusekamp BJ, Sluiter WJ, Hoogenberg K, Dullaart RPF. Apolipoprotein E genotype is a determinant of low-density lipoprotein cholesterol and of its response to a low-cholesterol diet in type 1 diabetic patients with elevated urinary albumin excretion. *Diabetic Medicine*, 1998; **15**: 1031–5.

29. Marcais C *et al.* Severe hypertriglyceridaemia in Type II diabetes: involvement of apoC-III Sst-I polymorphism, LPL mutations and apo E3 deficiency. *Diabetologia*, 2000; **43**: 1346–52.

30. Ruiz J. Diabetes mellitus and the late complications: influence of the genetic factors. *Diabetes and Metabolism*, 1997; **23**: 57–63.

31. Mackness B, Mackness MI, Arrol S, Turkie W, Durrington PN. Effect of the human serum paraoxonase 55 and 192 genetic polymorphisms on the protection by high density lipoprotein against low density lipoprotein oxidative modification. *FEBS Letters*, 1998; **423**: 57–60.

32. Grant PJ. Risk factors for arterial disease in diabetes: coagulopathy. In: Tooke JE, ed. *Diabetic Angiopathy*. London: Arnold, 1999: 93–112.

33. Nagi DK, McCormack LJ, Mohamed-Ali V, Yudkin JS, Knowler WC, Grant PJ. Diabetic retinopathy, promoter (4G/5G) polymorphism of *PAI-1* gene, and *PAI-1* activity in Pima Indians with type 2 diabetes. *Diabetes Care*, 1997; **20**: 1304–9.

34. Carter AM, Mansfield MW, Stickland MH, Grant PJ. Fibrinogen β gene −455 G/A polymorphism and fibrinogen levels: risk factors for coronary artery disease in subjects with non-insulin-dependent diabetes mellitus. *Diabetes Care*, 1996; **19**: 1267–70.

4 Diabetic retinopathy

Jane R. MacKinnon and John V. Forrester

Introduction

Approximately 2 per cent of people with diabetes will become legally blind as a result of diabetic retinopathy, and a larger number will have significantly impaired vision affecting their daily lives. They may have concerns ranging from difficulty reading the telephone directory to loss of their driving license, and hence restricted independence. The main issues in diabetic retinopathy are identification of those at risk of visually threatening eye disease and institution of appropriate and adequate treatment. All diabetic patients should have access to an effective screening programme. Laser photocoagulation of the retina remains the cornerstone of treatment of sight threatening diabetic retinopathy and internationally agreed guidelines are available concerning its use.[1] This chapter will discuss the epidemiology of diabetic retinopathy, the characteristic clinical features, current ideas on pathogenesis and will give an outline of practical management.

Epidemiology

A diabetic person is 10–20 times more likely to become blind than a non-diabetic. Diabetes is the commonest cause of blindness in the working age population of the western world. It has been estimated that approximately 25 per cent of the diabetic population have some form of diabetic retinopathy. The prevalence of diabetic retinopathy increases with duration of diabetes. Diabetic retinopathy of any degree is more prevalent in the younger onset insulin dependent patient. The prevalence of more severe diabetic eye disease in the form of proliferative retinopathy is also higher in those with type 1 diabetes.

Wisconsin Epidemiologic Study of Diabetic Retinopathy

The Wisconsin Epidemiologic Study of Diabetic Retinopathy (WESDR)[2–6] is to date the most comprehensive epidemiological study of diabetic retinopathy with the longest follow up period. Our understanding of the incidence and progression of diabetic retinopathy is largely based on the very large database produced by this important study. The WESDR population of 2361 was defined in 1979–80 and consisted of 'younger onset' and 'older onset' persons with diabetes who lived and received their primary medical care in an 11-county area of southern Wisconsin, USA. All younger onset insulin dependent patients who had been diagnosed before the age of

30 years were included in the study (*n*=996), and were compared with a probability sample of older onset patients taking insulin (*n*=637) and not taking insulin (*n*=692). The study population had a baseline examination in 1980–82 and 4, 10 and 14 years later.[2–5] Masked grading of stereoscopic colour fundus photographs was used to determine the presence and severity of retinopathy objectively. Grading of photographs utilized modifications of the Early Treatment Diabetic Retinopathy Study (ETDRS) adaptation of the modified Airlie House classification of diabetic retinopathy.[7]

Prevalence of retinopathy

Data from baseline examination in the WESDR confirmed that the younger onset insulin dependent group had the highest prevalence of any degree of retinopathy or of severe retinopathy, while those in the older onset non-insulin dependent group had the lowest rates. The prevalence of retinopathy increases with the duration of diabetes (Fig. 1).

A steep increase in the prevalence of any degree of retinopathy exists in those with younger onset diabetes, starting at 2 per cent in those with less than two years diabetes to 98 per cent in those who have had diabetes for 15 or more years. The prevalence of proliferative disease in the same group increases from 0 per cent in those with less than five years of disease to 26 per cent after 15–16 years duration, and 56 per cent in those 20 years following diagnosis.

By contrast the subjects in the older onset groups had higher initial rates of any form of retinopathy. This undoubtedly reflects the subacute onset of diabetes in these patients and inaccuracy in establishing the precise timing of the hyperglycaemic state. The United Kingdom Prospective Diabetes Study (UKPDS)[8] reported retinopathy of any degree present in at least one eye of 39 per cent of men and 35 per cent of women on diagnosis of non-insulin dependent diabetes. Figures from the WESDR differ in that 23 per cent of the older onset insulin dependent diabetics within two years of diagnosis were found to have retinopathy along with 20 per cent of non-insulin dependent diabetics. The rates of retinopathy including proliferative retinopathy remain higher in the insulin-taking patients in the years following diagnosis (Fig. 1).

Duration of diabetes remains a significant factor in the prevalence of diabetic maculopathy. In the WESDR, assessment of patients with diabetes onset before the age of 30 revealed clinically significant macular oedema (see page 54) varying from 0 per cent in those who had diabetes for less than five years to 29 per cent in those whose

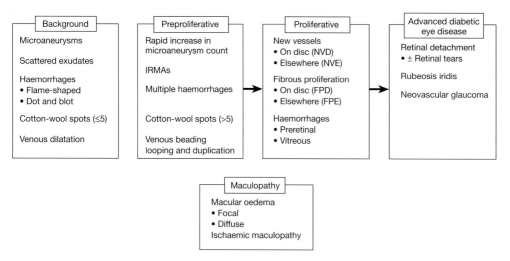

Fig. 1 Stages of diabetic retinopathy. Background and pre-proliferative retinopathy are alternatively classified as mild, moderate, severe or very severe non-proliferative retinopathy. (With permission from Dowler JGF, Hamilton AMP. Clinical features of diabetic eye disease. In: Pickup JC, Williams G, eds. *Textbook of Diabetes*. 2nd edn. Oxford: Blackwell Science, 1997: 46.3.)[71]

duration of diabetes was 20 or more years.[2] Macular oedema in this group was associated with longer duration of diabetes, proteinuria, diuretic use, male gender and higher glycosylated haemoglobin. In the older onset group, prevalence rates of macular oedema varied from 3 per cent in those who had diabetes for less than five years to 28 per cent in those whose duration of diabetes was 20 or more years.[3] Similarly, presence of oedema in the older group was associated with duration of diabetes, proteinuria and higher glycosylated haemoglobin. However in addition there was a definite association with insulin use and higher systolic blood pressure.

Clinically significant macular oedema is more likely to present in older onset patients within the first few years of diagnosis and when established tends to cause a more significant reduction in visual acuity.

Progression of retinopathy

In the seventeenth WESDR[5] report published in 1998, the 14-year incidence and progression of diabetic retinopathy and associated risk factors in type 1 diabetes are given (see Fig. 1). 634 of the original younger onset cohort participated at the 14-year assessment. A high rate of progression of retinopathy of 86 per cent at 14 years is reported. Progression of retinopathy was associated with less severe retinopathy, being male, higher glycosylated haemoglobin levels or raised diastolic blood pressure at baseline. 37 per cent of the cohort progressed to proliferative disease and 26 per cent developed macular oedema. Proliferative retinopathy was associated with a higher initial and subsequent rise in glycosylated haemoglobin, more severe retinopathy at baseline and the presence of hypertension. Development of macular oedema was also associated with high and increasing glycosylated haemoglobin levels, more severe retinopathy at baseline, but additionally was related to the presence of gross proteinuria at the initial assessment.

Racial differences in risk of retinopathy

Several studies have indicated a difference in the incidence of retinopathy among different ethnic groups and races. Harris *et al*.[9] examined 105 type 2 patients who had no evidence of retinopathy at baseline examination. After an average of four years follow-up using non-mydriatic fundus photography a significant difference was found in the incidence of retinopathy between black and white participants, such that 50 per cent of black compared to 19 per cent of white subjects developed retinopathy of any type. These findings could not be explained by differences in risk factors for retinopathy or potential confounders after adjustment for systolic blood pressure, glycosylated haemoglobin, sex and type of diabetes treatment. Differences in the genetic susceptibility to the adverse effects of hyperglycaemia are likely to be present but the aetiology of these differences is currently unknown.

Epidemiological implications

The incidence of diabetes is increasing in both developing and developed countries around the world, implying an increase in the prevalence of diabetic eye disease. Extrapolation of data from the 10-year WESDR[4] report suggest that of the 5.8 million Americans with known diabetes, approximately 900 000 will develop proliferative retinopathy. On further analysis of the 14-year WESDR[5] report, the, the authors estimate that of the 500 000 Americans with IDDM, 185 000 would develop proliferative retinopathy and 85 000 develop clinically significant macular oedema over a 14-year period.

Classification and pathogenesis

The pathogenesis of diabetic retinopathy is not fully understood but essentially consists of a microangiopathy affecting both retinal and choroidal vessels (Fig. 2).

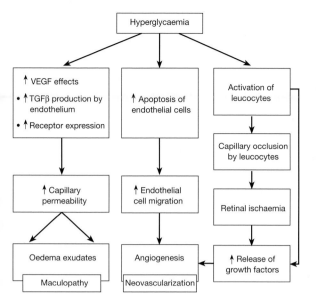

Fig. 2 Pathogenesis of the 2 sight-threatening features of diabetic retinopathy – maculopathy and neovascularization. VEGF: vascular endothelial growth factor, TGF-β: transforming growth factor β. (With permission from Forrester JV, Knott RM. Diabetic retinopathy: what goes wrong in the retina? In: Williams G, ed. *Horizons in Medicine*, No. 10. London, Royal College of Physicians of London, 1998: 227.)[72]

Degeneration of pericytes, the contractile supporting cells which encircle the capillary endothelial cells, is the earliest finding along with thickening of the basement membrane and the formation of microaneurysms. Circulating leukocytes are abnormal in diabetes, exhibiting altered rheological properties such as reduced deformability and increased activation. These changes result in them sticking to the vascular endothelium and occluding ocular capillaries. Retinal ischaemia is the consequence, and areas of vascular leakage occur where the blood retinal barrier has been broken down. These pathological features provide the basis for the classification of diabetic retinopathy.

Diabetic retinopathy encompasses a spectrum of signs which can be broadly divided into three categories:

(1) Non-proliferative diabetic retinopathy (NPDR)

(2) Proliferative diabetic retinopathy (PDR)

(3) Diabetic maculopathy

An alternative simple broad categorization is:

(1) Non-sight threatening (90%)

(2) Sight threatening, that is, exudative maculopathy, proliferative retinopathy or retinal ischaemia (10 per cent)

The presence of a single microaneurysm in the fundus is enough to diagnose background retinopathy, but hunting for solitary lesions by direct ophthalmoscopy is beyond the scope of most clinicians involved in diabetic screening. Most of the larger published series have used multiple photographic fundal fields to grade retinopathy.

A number of grading systems are used for research. The Airlie House classification was the cornerstone in grading when first published in the1960s and has been used in various revised forms by investigative groups since then. The Modified Airlie House classification was used by the WESDR study,[7] and was further revised for use in the EURODIAB study,[10] while further extension of the scale became the ETDRS retinopathy severity scale.[11]

No clinically detectable diabetic retinopathy

Before retinopathy can be identified clinically, a number of pathological changes are detectable including alterations in blood flow and loss of pericytes. Pericytes are responsible for vascular tone and therefore loss of their function may result in an increase in retinal blood flow. Thickening and altered composition of the basement membrane occurs along with breakdown of the blood retinal barrier, which is manifest as increased vascular permeability. Diabetic patients with no retinopathy exhibit subtle changes in visual function, such as reduced contrast sensitivity and impaired colour vision (particularly along the blue-yellow colour axis).[12] Isocapnic hyperoxia reverses the early contrast sensitivity defects found in those with minimal retinopathy, highlighting the importance of tissue hypoxia in the pathogenesis of retinopathy.[13]

Non-proliferative diabetic retinopathy (NPDR)

Most clinicians will be familiar with grouping of NPDR into background diabetic retinopathy (BDR) and pre-proliferative diabetic retinopathy (PPDR) (Fig. 1). The following classification is however increasingly used; it allows a more accurate grading and assessment of whether the retinopathy is 'low risk' or 'high risk'.

Mild

The first manifestation of diabetic retinopathy is the appearance of one or more microaneurysms in the fundus which are visualised as small red dots. Small retinal haemorrhages become apparent later and together constitute the 'dot and blot' appearance. MacKenzie and Nettleship described retinal microaneurysms in 1879 and we now know that these are not static lesions but have an unexpectedly high turnover rate. Although the net count of microaneurysms may remain unchanged around half of those present on initial examination may disappear over a two-year period with new microaneurysms forming in other locations.[14]

Stitt *et al.* have described four distinct types of microaneurysms relating to their histological features.[15] All types are associated with loss of pericytes and later endothelial cells from the capillaries. They are also associated with accumulation in the lumen of polymorphonuclear cells (type 1), red blood cells (type 2), red cell breakdown products (type 3) or fibrosis and lipid infiltration (type 4). Current knowledge does not explain how microaneurysms form, although it is unlikely that they are solely related to loss of pericytes. They probably arise from abortive attempts to revascularize areas of ischaemic retina. Endothelial cell proliferation may be stimulated by growth factors released by platelets and leucocytes attracted to areas of endothelial damage where adhesion molecules and procoagulant products are expressed.

Hard exudates are extracellular accumulations of lipid and protein from leakage of serum through abnormal vessel walls. They appear as waxy yellow deposits with discrete edges. Some are observed around leaking microaneurysms in circinate patterns. As the retinal vessels become increasingly more permeable to various plasma constituents, these are initially absorbed by the retinal cells but ultimately begin to accumulate, contributing to basement membrane thickening and forming extravascular deposits. Macrophages are attracted to sites of leakage to remove these deposits and degenerating cells. Dying lipid-filled macrophages and fibrinoid material compose the clinically visible hard exudate.

Data from the ETDRS[17] suggests that elevated serum lipid levels are associated with an increased risk of retinal hard exudates in subjects with diabetic retinopathy, with an accompanying increased risk of visual impairment.

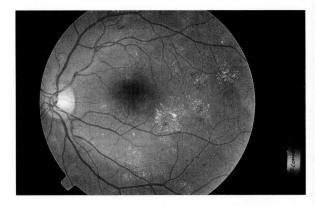

Fig. 3 Severe non-proliferative retinopathy.

Moderate

Moderate NPDR consists of severe retinal haemorrhages in at least one quadrant, or the presence of cotton wool spots, venous beading or intraretinal microvascular abnormalities (IRMA).

Cotton wool spots appear as fluffy white lesions in the posterior pole of the fundus. They represent localized infarcts of the nerve fibre layer of the retina and therefore are most likely to be found on viewing the posterior retina where the nerve fibre layer is at its thickest. The interruption of axoplasmic flow caused by ischaemia and subsequent build up of transported material within the nerve axons is responsible for the opaque white appearance of these lesions. It has been shown that cotton wool spots correspond to localized non-arcuate scotomata in the visual field.[18] Cotton wool spots may appear suddenly during periods of changing glucose regulation and may be more prevalent with coexisting hypertension. A single cotton wool spot has little predictive power for the subsequent development of proliferative retinopathy, but multiple (five or more) cotton wool spots are associated with a doubling of the risk of progression to proliferative disease within one year.[19]

As a response to increased retinal ischaemia IRMA appear. These are defective dilated capillaries lying flat within the retina and are most frequently seen adjacent to areas of capillary closure. Clinically they differ from retinal neovascularization by their intraretinal location, absence of profuse leakage on fluorescein angiography and failure to cross over major blood vessels. With the appearance of increasingly widespread IRMAs, indicating extensive capillary non-perfusion, the risk of developing proliferative retinopathy within one year increases four-fold.[19]

Severe

Any one of severe retinal haemorrhages in four quadrants, or venous beading in two quadrants or extensive IRMA in one quadrant is consistent with severe NPDR. Venous calibre may be generally increased in early diabetic retinopathy, but localized venous changes serve as an indicator of severe capillary non-perfusion. A range of venous abnormalities are observed in both the large and small retinal vessels including dilatation, formation of saccular dilated areas or beads, venous looping and reduplication of veins. The presence of venous beading is a more powerful predictor of subsequent neovascularization than any other single abnormality.[19] Larger dark blot

haemorrhages represent haemorrhagic retinal infarcts. They are another indicator of adjacent areas of capillary non-perfusion (Fig. 3).

Very severe

Any two of the features of severe NPDR listed above, that is, severe retinal haemorrhages in four quadrants, venous beading in two quadrants or extensive IRMA in one quadrant constitute very severe NPDR.

Proliferative diabetic retinopathy

NVD and NVE

New vessels form as a response to retinal ischaemia and represent an attempt to re-establish a blood supply to unhealthy areas of retina. Neovascularization is described clinically as 'new vessels at the disc' (NVD) (Fig. 4) or 'new vessels elsewhere' (NVE) (Fig. 5). It has been estimated that non-perfusion of over a quarter of the retina must be present before NVD appear. NVE are most frequently found along the major temporal arcades above and below the macula. New vessels look unusual in that they tend to form loops or arcades, often criss-crossing adjacent vessels randomly instead of the dichotomous branching pattern of normal vessels. The Diabetic Retinopathy Study Research Group predicted that between 20 and 30 per cent of patients with NVE will progress to optic disc neovascularization within one year.[20] The risk of severe visual loss is increased if the NVE are associated with preretinal or vitreous haemorrhage. They initially develop in the potential space between the vitreous and retina, originating from veins and passing through gaps in the internal limiting membrane. The internal limiting membrane is absent at the disc and may in part explain the predilection for neovascularization here.

The fibrovascular network of new vessels becomes adherent to the collagen and hyaluronate matrix of the posterior vitreous and leaks plasma. Migration and growth of activated vascular endothelial cells eventually promotes contracture of the vitreous gel. The vitreous contracts anteriorly due to the strong attachment of the vitreous base to the pars plana area. Usually this 'posterior vitreous detachment' is incomplete because of strong adhesion to the new vessels. If vitreous separation is complete this may result in regression of new vessels

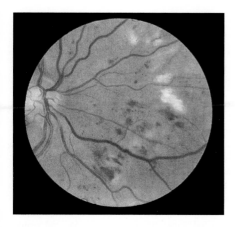

Fig. 4 Proliferative retinopathy – new vessels at the disc.

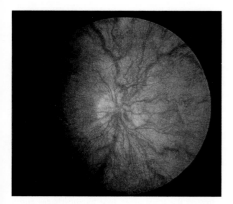

Fig. 5 Proliferative retinopathy – new vessels elsewhere.

because of loss of contact with the vitreous framework to support further growth. However posterior vitreous detachment is more likely to be incomplete, causing elevation of new vessels from the plane of the retina initially then allowing them to further proliferate over the posterior hyaloid face.

Further separation of the posterior vitreous face from the retina pulls on these fragile new vessels, tearing them and resulting in haemorrhage either into the pre-retinal space or the vitreous gel itself. Visual loss is sudden, painless and may be profound depending on the density of blood. Pre-retinal haemorrhage displays itself as a relatively well demarcated crescentic shape with a level superior border conforming to the limits of the detached posterior vitreous. Vitreous haemorrhage results in partial or complete loss of the red reflex with loss of retinal detail on ophthalmoscopy.

Retinal ischaemia is a prerequisite for proliferative retinopathy and develops as a result of capillary occlusion. Intravascular coagulation occurs as a result of a number of rheological alterations associated with diabetes. Platelets exhibit increased stickiness,[21] leucocytes

become activated[22] and less deformable,[23] and the vascular endothelium shows increased expression of adhesion molecules.[24] It is suggested that trapped leucocytes may increase vascular permeability by damaging the blood-retinal barrier. Endothelial dysfunction or damage induced by release of proteolytic enzymes and oxygen free radicals from these leucocytes will result in flow disturbances and capillary non-perfusion. Alterations in retinal,[25] choroidal[26] and central retinal artery[72] blood flow velocity have been documented in patients with diabetic retinopathy using several techniques. These events are likely to occur even before retinopathy is clinically detectable, becoming progressively more widespread and pathogenic with deteriorating retinopathy. Circulating levels of various adhesion molecules are raised in those with progressively worsening retinopathy as a result of shedding from both activated leucocytes and abnormal endothelium.[27] In the diabetic rat model, leucocytes have been shown histologically to occlude retinal capillaries, proliferating locally, releasing growth factors and presumably initiating new vessel formation.[22]

Tractional retinal detachment

Strong attachments between proliferating fibrovascular tissue originating from the retina and extending over the posterior vitreous surface exert tractional forces on the retina as these neovascular sheets contract. The tractional vector may be tangential, anteroposterior or bridging in orientation. Elevation of the retina may be localised and static or may progress to involve the macula, or occasionally result in retinal hole formation and rhegmatogenous detachment requiring urgent surgery. Retinal detachment appears as a greyish elevation of the retina, having a concave shape if tractional but becoming convex if a tear is present, allowing fluid to accumulate beneath it.

Rubeosis iridis

The neovascular response seen in PDR is not confined to the retina but may also involve the anterior segment of the eye with new vessels growing over the plane of the iris. New vessel growth is thought to be stimulated by the high levels of growth factors known to accumulate in the vitreous cavity in proliferative diabetic retinopathy. The iris becomes exposed to these growth factors during anterograde flow from the vitreous to the anterior chamber and drainage angle. It has been shown experimentally that vascular endothelial growth factor (VEGF), which occurs at high levels in the vitreous in PDR, is a potent stimulator of iris new vessel formation. Rubeotic or neovascular glaucoma may result as a consequence of new vessel formation within the irido-corneal angle. Neovascular glaucoma frequently presents acutely with the raised pressure causing cornea oedema, ocular pain and abrupt deterioration in vision.

Diabetic papillopathy

Disc swelling in diabetes in the absence of intra-cranial pathology, has been characterized as a syndrome of transient oedema of the optic disc with minimal impairment of optic nerve function. It presents infrequently, is likely to be a local disc vasculopathy, and has been reported in both type 1 and 2 diabetics with any degree of retinopathy. It generally resolves without treatment (within 3.7 months)[28] with good vision maintained unless associated with persistent macular oedema or the complications of proliferative retinopathy.[28,29]

Diabetic maculopathy

Diabetic maculopathy may occur in association with non-proliferative or proliferative retinopathy. It is the major cause of visual loss in diabetic patients. Diabetic maculopathy can be divided into the following groups:

(1) Focal oedema

(2) Diffuse oedema

(3) Ischaemic maculopathy

(4) Mixed maculopathy

Macular oedema

Retinal oedema is defined as any increase in water in retinal tissue resulting in an increase in its volume. The intracellular volume is increased as a result of cytotoxic oedema, whilst extracellular oedema occurs due to vasogenic factors. A diabetic retinal pigment epitheliopathy may also contribute to oedema by leakage of fluid through the retinal pigment epithelial cells.[30] Macular oedema *per se* is defined as the presence of retinal thickening or hard exudates within one disc diameter (1500 μm) of the centre of the fovea. Diffuse macular oedema is probably due to widespread breakdown of the blood-retinal barrier secondary to glucose induced microvascular damage. Glucose toxicity induces specific morphological changes in the retinal vessels: the tight junctions may remain intact, but the vessels develop fenestrations similar to those found in the naturally permeable choroidal vessels.[31] Focal oedema is more common than diffusely oedematous maculopathy, which constituted only 8.6 per cent of cases in a recent audit by the Royal College of Ophthalmologists.[32] Focal oedema is observed as localised areas of retinal thickening usually in association with leaking microaneurysms which may be surrounded by a complete (circinate) or incomplete ring of hard exudates (Fig. 6).

The ETDRS first defined the concept of clinically significant macular oedema (CSMO) to identify sight-threatening disease. CSMO is defined as the presence of one or more of the following:

(1) Retinal oedema within 500 μm of the centre of the fovea.

(2) Hard exudates within 500 μm of the fovea if associated with adjacent retinal thickening (which may be outside the 500 μm limit).

(3) Retinal oedema of one disc area or larger any part of which is within one disc diameter (1500 μm) of the centre of the fovea.

Macular oedema is extremely difficult to detect with the direct ophthalmoscope because of the two-dimentionality of the view obtained. Oedema is more readily detected by binocular stereoscopic slit lamp examination.

The vitreomacular interface is likely to play a role in the pathogenesis of macular oedema and indeed spontaneous resolution of oedema occurs as a consequence of vitreomacular separation.[33] Changes in hydrostatic pressure within the vasculature as described by Starling's law may also contribute. Kristinsson *et al.* noted that a significant dilatation and elongation of retinal arterioles and venules could be identified prior to the onset of macular oedema.[34]

Macular ischaemia

A consistent finding in diabetic retinopathy is enlargement of the foveal avascular zone. The foveal avascular zone (FAZ) was measured angiographically in 144 subjects with retinopathy and 27 controls by Mansour *et al.*[35] The FAZ was significantly smaller in control eyes (0.405 mm^2) than in eyes with diabetic retinopathy, and smaller in eyes with background diabetic retinopathy (0.737 mm^2) than in eyes with proliferative retinopathy (0.866 mm^2) and preproliferative retinopathy (1.001 mm^2). Irregularity of the contour of the FAZ was also found in those with diabetic retinopathy. Arend *et al.* report similar findings but additionally find that there is a significant increase in both FAZ size and perifoveal intercapillary area in diabetic patients with reduced visual acuity matched with those with normal vision.[36] Macular ischaemia is usually diagnosed using fluorescein angiography to map the area of capillary non-perfusion. It is suggested clinically by the presence of small white vessels around the fovea, deep blot haemorrhages and a featureless appearance.

Mixed maculopathy

Many patients present with a mixed picture of macular oedema and ischaemia and with time either characteristic may predominate. From both a therapeutic and prognostic point of view it is useful to assess the relative components of the maculopathy present (see page 59).

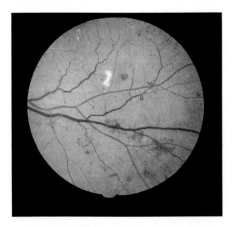

Fig. 6 Mild background diabetic retinopathy with a circinate exudate.

Box 1   Risk factors for diabetic retinopathy

- Duration of diabetes
- Poor glycaemic control
- Hypertension
- Pregnancy
- Puberty
- Nephropathy/proteinuria
- Hyperlipidaemia
- Anaemia

Risk factors

Several risk factors are known to enhance the risk of development and progression of diabetic retinopathy and are listed in Box 1.

Duration of diabetes

Duration of diabetes is the strongest factor affecting the development of retinopathy in both type 1 and type 2 diabetes (WESDR) (see page 49).

Glycaemic control

The Diabetic Control and Complications Trial (DCCT) published its results in 1993,[37] confirming that tight glycaemic control in people with type 1 diabetes leads to a significant decrease in the incidence and progression of diabetic retinopathy. It also demonstrated that an intensive regime of tight diabetic control reduces the incidence of PDR and macular oedema, lowers the need for retinal laser treatment, and most importantly reduces the risk of visual loss. Over the nine-year period of the trial the incidence of diabetic retinopathy was reduced by 76 per cent in the intensively treated group. 'Early worsening' of diabetic retinopathy within 12 months of institution of intensive insulin therapy was observed in 13.1 per cent compared to 7.6 per cent on conventional treatment.[38] The most important risk factors for early worsening were higher haemoglobin A_{1c} at screening and reduction of this in the first six months of the trial. Chantelau provides evidence that upregulation of serum insulin-like growth factor-I concentration triggers acceleration of diabetic retinopathy.[39] Reducing hyperglycaemia over a five month period from greater than 16 mmol/l to less than 10 mmol/l increased serum insulin-like growth factor-I levels by 70–220 per cent in four patients with type 1 diabetes. While proteinuria and symptomatic neuropathy regressed, all had progression of retinopathy with the onset of macular oedema requiring laser treatment.

The United Kingdom Prospective Diabetes Study (UKPDS) investigated the role of blood glucose control in NIDDM over a 20-year period.[40] Over 5000 patients with newly diagnosed type 2 diabetes took part in a randomized intervention trial of intensive treatment with insulin or sulphonylurea compared to a conventional treatment group (diet control). The study reported a 25 per cent reduction in microvascular endpoints in the intensive treatment group over a mean of 10 years follow up, including a significant reduction in the progression of retinopathy, reduced risk of requiring laser treatment and fewer cataract extractions. Improved control reduced the risk of serious deterioration of vision by nearly one half.

Hypertension

A number of recent studies have investigated the role of hypertension and blood pressure control in the risk of diabetic complications (ABCD and Facet trials, Hypertension Optimal Treatment (HOT) study, EUCLID and UKPDS 38). The UKPDS divided their cohort of type 2 diabetics into 2 groups: the 'tight control' group (blood pressure less than 150/85) and the 'less tight control' group (blood pressure less than 180/105).[41] The tight control group were randomised to either Atenolol or Captopril while the less tight control group were treated with other antihypertensive agents, avoiding β-blockers and angiotensin-converting enzyme inhibitors. Overall the tight blood pressure group had a 37 per cent reduction in microvascular disease, compared to the less tight group – a more dramatic reduction than with tight glycaemic control. This result was predominantly due to a reduction in the development or progression of retinopathy, the tight control group having a 34 per cent reduction in risk of laser treatment, and a 47 per cent lower risk of loss of visual acuity. Atenolol and Captopril were equally effective.

Blood pressure modification with an angiotensin-converting enzyme inhibitor in type 1 patients was investigated by the EUCLID study group; its findings in relation to diabetic retinopathy were reported in 1998.[42] The patients were non-hypertensive and mostly normoalbuminuric. A 50 per cent reduction in the progression of retinopathy by at least one level was found; retinopathy was classified from photographs on a five level scale from none to proliferative.

A recent WESDR report[73] has suggested that increased pulse rate may be a clinical indicator of overall risk of diabetic retinopathy, but is not an independent variable.

Pregnancy

Klein *et al.* report that current pregnancy is significantly associated with progression of any retinopathy.[43] The increased risk may either be due to suboptimal control itself or to the rapid improvement in metabolic control which often is observed in early pregnancy.[44] Microaneurysm counts during pregnancy and postpartum suggest that there is continuous turnover of microaneurysms during pregnancy, and that the microaneurysm count increases to its highest level at three months postpartum.[45] Excellent metabolic control before conception is suggested to reduce the risk of microvascular progression.

Puberty

Both the prepubertal and pubertal duration of diabetes as well as the duration of diabetes appear to be of great importance in the development of retinopathy. Holl *et al.* examined 441 children or adolescents divided into two subject groups with a prepubertal onset of diabetes or onset of diabetes during puberty.[46] In children with a prepubertal onset of diabetes, retinopathy occurred after a pubertal duration of 10.9 years, compared to 15.1 years in children with onset of diabetes in puberty, suggesting an additional risk conveyed by prepubertal years of diabetes. They also showed that long-term metabolic control had a significant influence on the prevalence of retinopathy in both groups. Patients with haemoglobin A_{1c} levels above or equal to 7.5 per cent showed signs of retinopathy after a mean of 15.5 years, while those with glycosylated haemoglobin levels below this developed retinopathy after 18.3 years.

Renal disease

The 14-year report from the WESDR demonstrated that the risk of macular oedema in those with gross proteinuria at baseline was increased by 95 per cent in type 1 patients.[5] After controlling for other risk variables, the relationship between gross proteinuria and proliferative retinopathy was of borderline significance ($p = 0.052$). Improvement in renal function by dialysis or transplantation often results in resolution of macular oedema.[47]

The complex pathogenic mechanisms involved in diabetic retinopathy and nephropathy are unlikely to be identical. Cross sectional studies have shown that 35 per cent of patients with proliferative retinopathy do not show signs of diabetic nephropathy. A recent paper followed up a subgroup of patients with proliferative disease and no evidence of nephropathy. None of the 24 patients identified developed persistent microalbuminuria during the 10-year follow up period.[48] It is therefore unsafe to assume that diabetics who are normoalbuminuric are not at risk of sight threatening retinopathy.

Hyperlipidaemia

Interesting data from the ETDRS group demonstrates an increased risk of retinal hard exudates in association with elevated serum lipid levels.[17] Patients with raised total serum cholesterol levels or low-density lipoprotein cholesterol levels at baseline were twice as likely to have retinal hard exudates as patients with normal levels. The risk of visual acuity loss was independently associated with the extent of hard exudate, even after adjusting for the extent of macular oedema. It is therefore suggested that lipid lowering therapy in diabetics with raised serum lipid levels may be beneficial from a visual point of view as well as reducing cardiovascular mortality.

The EURODIAB IDDM Complications Study has suggested a possible relationship between serum triglyceride levels and diabetic retinopathy. Elevated serum triglycerides in this large study of 3250 insulin-dependent patients were associated with both moderate to severe NPDR and proliferative disease.[10] Serum lipid modification therefore appears to be a useful strategy in the prevention and slowing of retinopathy.

Anaemia

The relationship between haemoglobin levels and diabetic retinopathy has been addressed by a study from Finland.[49] Haemoglobin levels from 1691 subjects attending a diabetic clinic were measured. Using multiple logistic regression analyses to control for confounders they showed that the odds ratio of having any retinopathy was 2.0 among subjects with a haemoglobin level of less than 12 g/dl. Those with diabetic retinopathy and reduced haemoglobin also had an increased risk of developing more severe retinopathy (odds ratio 5.3).

Management

The management of diabetic retinopathy can be divided into systemic measures and those involving the eye. As detailed previously there are a number of modifiable risk factors for the incidence and progression of retinopathy including glycaemic control, hypertension, anaemia, hyperlipidaemia and renal disease. It is important to consider these factors in the management of a patient with retinopathy, as they may often be more readily manipulated than the ocular treatment options available.

The findings of the EUCLID Study Group outlining the effect of lisinopril, an angiotensin-converting enzyme inhibitor, on the progression of retinopathy in normotensive people with type 1 diabetes are preliminary but exciting.[42] They suggest a protective effect on the progression of retinopathy in insulin dependent diabetics with normal blood pressure and little or no nephropathy over a two-year period. A 50 per cent reduction in progression of retinopathy by one level compared to placebo is reported; patients were graded photographically using a five-level scale of none to proliferative. Report 39 of the UKPDS group also indicates a role for angiotensin-converting enzyme inhibitors in the prevention of both macro- and micro-vascular complications by tight blood pressure

control in type 2 diabetics.[50] However no specific beneficial effect of angiotensin-converting enzyme inhibitors was found over β-blockers. This suggests that blood pressure control in itself may be of more significance than the agent used.

Worsening of diabetic retinopathy with the institution of tight diabetic control has been identified as a particular problem in patients with long-standing poor glycaemic control. The frequency of 'early worsening' of retinopathy in the DCCT's cohort of type 1 diabetics in the first 12 months following commencement of intensive insulin therapy has recently been published.[38] Significant progression of retinopathy was recorded in 13.1 per cent of those assigned to intensive insulin treatment at their 6 and/or 12 month review. Higher HbA_{1c} levels at onset of better glycaemic control were associated with early progression. They found no evidence to support the suggestion that more gradual reduction of glycaemia might be associated with less risk of early worsening. The DCCT data certainly indicates that the long-term benefits of intensive insulin therapy greatly outweigh the risks of early worsening. In patients with a high HbA_{1c} and tending towards high-risk proliferative retinopathy, it would therefore seem prudent to delay tightening of control until after adequate retinal laser has been applied.

Screening for diabetic retinopathy

Screening for diabetic retinopathy should be performed for two main reasons: firstly the detection of any form of retinopathy and secondly the identification of disease of sufficient severity to require treatment. Screening for retinopathy clearly fulfils the precepts required for screening of any human disease. As well as being asymptomatic early in the disease, treatment is effective when required and is cost effective. The value of screening for the diabetic population is undisputed and has led to the following recommendation for implementation (European Consensus Document):[51]

- All patients aged over 12 years and/or entering puberty should be screened.

- Screening should be performed annually and should include measurement of visual acuity along with dilated fundoscopy.

- Screening should be performed appropriately and comprehensively involving a combination of diabetologists, optometrists, general practitioners and photographic screening.

No matter which screening modality is employed in a retinopathy screening programme, its effectiveness should be audited and validated. A disturbing paper from New York[52] studied the claims data from 4410 diabetics (age 31–64) eligible for retinopathy screening over a two-year period. Only 34 per cent of patients were screened for retinopathy over the period of a year, and only 16 per cent received an annual screen in two consecutive years. Obviously this has worrying health and economic implications. A number of groups have compared the effectiveness of retinal photography in comparison with ophthalmoscopy in the screening of retinopathy. Fundal photographs require to be evaluated by a trained observer; the results of screening are comparable to ophthalmoscopy.[53] The British Diabetic Association Mobile Screening Group published details from 64 905 screening episodes in 1996.[54] Of those screened, 5.6 per cent were referred to an

Ophthalmology department and 1.2 per cent required laser treatment. Importantly, where sequential data was available, a year by year fall in the incidence of sight threatening retinopathy was demonstrated. This was as a result of the screening programmes detecting incipient problems in the initial cycles of screening.

Ocular history

All diabetic patients must be screened for diabetic retinopathy on an annual basis particularly because visually threatening retinopathy may remain completely asymptomatic even in the presence of profuse neovascular proliferation. Specific symptoms may alert the clinician to specific ocular problems. Blurring of vision is a relatively common complaint and can on occasions be the first symptom of diabetes. Poor glycaemic control is often associated with transient visual blurring due to changes in the refractive index of the lens. The osmotic effect of hyperglycaemia alters the shape and focusing power of the lens. Patients may describe difficulty reading and find viewing objects in the distance easier with their reading glasses on. Difficulty reading small print may also indicate the onset of diabetic maculopathy or pre-senile cataract (observed as an opacity within the red reflex).

Sudden painless loss of vision in one eye is most commonly due to haemorrhage from new vessels into the vitreous gel. Vitreous haemorrhage may result as a consequence of sudden contraction of the vitreous detaching itself from its retinal adhesions as it shrinks. Sudden escape of blood into the vitreous gel often results in rapid dispersion of haemorrhage and profound loss of vision. Patients will describe, 'everything becoming black' while some may be aware of a red streak appearing initially at the onset of leakage. Retinal detachment may occur simultaneously with vitreous haemorrhage or in isolation. The commonest symptoms heralding a retinal detachment are a sudden shower of floaters, photopsia (pin-point flashes of light most likely noticed on eye closure or dim lighting) and an enlarging visual field defect. The presence of vitreous haemorrhage often precludes an adequate view of the fundus and therefore B-scan ultrasound is indispensable in allowing the retinal position to be checked.

The only painful presentation of diabetic related eye disease is rubeotic glaucoma. Vascular proliferation over the surface of the iris with occlusion of the drainage angle of the eye results in elevation of the intra-ocular pressure. The eye becomes tense, inflamed and chronically painful with poor vision as a consequence of corneal oedema.

Ocular examination

Visual acuity

Recording visual acuity is fundamental to any visual assessment. A Snellen chart is most commonly used in the UK although other distance acuity charts can be employed, some of which use a more regular step-wise decrease in letter size. Distance glasses should be worn if available but refractive errors can simply be overcome by asking the patients to look through a pin-hole at the chart. Testing reading vision is of particular importance as a measure of macular function and is performed with the patient's reading glasses on a standard reading chart.

Dilated fundoscopy

All patients should have their pupils dilated prior to fundoscopy. Struggling to observe the macula through undilated pupils is frustrating for the clinician and inadequate for screening. Pupils are dilated with a combination of tropicamide 1 per cent and phenylephrine 2.5 or 10 per cent drops (systemic absorption of phenylephrine can cause transient elevation of blood pressure). Full pupillary dilation takes around 30 min. The presence of diabetic autonomic neuropathy may require additional drop instillation because of poor pupil dilatation. Dilation with mydriatics is a safe activity and very unlikely to precipitate acute angle closure glaucoma. Patients on current topical treatment for chronic glaucoma can be safely dilated.

Fundoscopy with a direct ophthalmoscope has the capacity to identify abnormalities or absence of the red reflex, lens opacities, and numerous retinal signs. New vessels most frequently originate at the optic disc or in the vicinity of the major vascular arcades. The presence of haemorrhages and exudates at the macula are signs to alert the examiner of significant retinopathy here. Macular oedema is extremely difficult to detect with the direct ophthalmoscope and if suspected should be referred to an ophthalmologist for examination using a hand held lens which allows a magnified stereoscopic view of the fundus.

Further investigations

Referral to ophthalmologist

Direct ophthalmoscopy is an adequate screening tool for diabetic retinopathy. However, the two-dimentionality and restricted view of the peripheral fundus can be overcome by the use of binocular indirect ophthalmoscopy, diagnostic contact lenses and hand-held lenses used in conjunction with the slit-lamp microscope. Referral for examination by an ophthalmologist is indicated in a variety of situations and with varying degrees of urgency. The Royal College of Ophthalmologists published their indications for referral to an ophthalmologist in 1997[1] (Box 2).

Fluorescein angiography

The management of diabetic maculopathy in particular relies heavily on fundus fluorescein angiography (FFA). It aids differentiation of ischaemic from exudative maculopathy and can also be used to confirm early proliferative disease. A 5 ml solution of sodium fluorescein is injected into an antecubital vein following which a series of retinal photographs are taken as the dye transits through the circulation. The retinal vasculature is outlined with areas of oedema identified by progressive leakage of dye. Ischaemia is manifest by loss of capillary perfusion by the fluorescent dye.

B-Scan ultrasonography

Inability to obtain an adequate view of the fundus in a diabetic, whether due to dense cataract formation or vitreous haemorrhage is an indication for B-scan ultrasound examination. In the hands of an experienced operator this technique can give valuable information about the status of the vitreous and retina. In particular it is essential in determining whether a retinal detachment requiring surgery is present.

Visual fields

The main role for visual fields in the management of diabetic retinopathy lies not in routine monitoring but in assessment of the peripheral visual field for driving purposes.[55] Retinal laser photocoagulation has damaging effects on the peripheral visual field. In the attempt to prevent blindness, a visual field within legal limits for

Box 2 Indications for referral to an ophthalmologist *(adapted from Reference (1))*

- ◆ Urgent referral
  - (1) New vessels on the disc or elsewhere
  - (2) Preretinal or vitreous haemorrhage
  - (3) Rubeosis iridis
  - (4) Retinal detachment
    ((2) and (4) should be seen on the same day, the others within 2–3 days)
- ◆ Early referral
  - (1) Pre-proliferative (that is, severe or very severe retinopathy)
  - (2) Non-proliferative retinopathy with macular involvement
  - (3) Haemorrhages or hard exudates within one disc diameter of the centre of the fovea
  - (4) Reduced visual acuity not corrected by pinhole (Patients should be seen within 3–4 weeks)
- ◆ Routine referral
  - (1) Non-proliferative retinopathy with circinate or plaque exudate within the major temporal arcades but not threatening the macula
  - (2) Retinal findings that are not characteristic of diabetic retinopathy
  - (3) Reduced vision of unknown cause

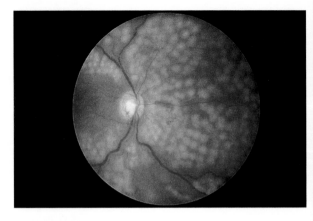

Fig. 7 Panretinal photocoagulation.

Box 3 High risk characteristics in eyes with proliferative retinopathy

- ◆ NVD of at least one quarter disc area
- ◆ NVD with any vitreous or preretinal haemorrhage
- ◆ NVE more than or equal to a half disc area with any vitreous or preretinal haemorrhage

driving may be sacrificed. Enlargement of the blind spot in association with diabetic papillopathy is a rare finding on visual field testing.

Treatment of diabetic retinopathy

Laser photocoagulation

The cornerstone of treatment of both proliferative retinopathy and exudative maculopathy remains laser photocoagulation of the retina.[56] The exact mechanism of action is not precisely known although it is thought that by destruction of ischaemic retinal tissue the stimulus to neovascularization is reduced. Aqueous samples taken from diabetic subjects following panretinal laser for proliferative retinopathy show reduced levels of VEGF associated with more complete photocoagulation.[57]

Laser treatment is applied using a slit lamp with magnifying contact lens or indirect ophthalmoscope delivery system. Laser power, wavelength and burn size can be varied depending on the areas of the retina being treated and the individual response of the eye. Panretinal photocoagulation is applied in a regular pattern with one burn diameter between each spot, covering the pre- and post-equatorial regions outside the vascular arcades, avoiding the macula (Fig. 7).

Complications as a result of laser application include worsening or onset of maculopathy, vitreous haemorrhage or tractional retinal detachment. As elevated new vessels regress they separate from the posterior hyaloid face infrequently resulting in vitreous or subhyaloid haemorrhage. While the vessels are regressing, the fibrous component of a neovascular network may increase, avulsing the vessels themselves and producing tractional forces on the retina. Full panretinal photocoagulation reduces the visual field by around 40–50 per cent and may fall below DVLA standards for driving.[58] It is essential that patients should be informed of this risk.

The Diabetic Retinopathy Study (DRS) was a prospective multi-centre clinical trial, which when published in 1978 demonstrated conclusively that panretinal photocoagulation reduces the risk of visual loss in proliferative retinopathy.[56] The risk of severe visual loss is reduced by at least 50 per cent at two and five years in those with high risk characteristics (Box 3) by this therapy and by up to 70 per cent in moderate risk patients compared to untreated control eyes. The DRS identified three high-risk characteristics for severe visual loss (defined as a visual acuity of 1/60 or worse). Unless the criteria in Box 3 are met, treatment is usually withheld and the patient followed up at three monthly intervals.

Management of proliferative retinopathy

New vessels on the disc

Early neovascularization at the disc, seen as flat new vessels, usually responds well to basic panretinal laser comprising around 1500–2000 burns. Established new vessels and florid new vessels which appear to proliferate aggressively in younger patients, require more extensive therapy (around 5000 burns) usually performed over two or more sittings. Further laser is applied at weekly intervals until regression of new vessels is achieved. Patients who are intolerant of laser may find the procedure easier with local anaesthesia in the form of a retro-bulbar injection. In some cases general anaesthesia may be the only solution, particularly if high risk characteristics are present requiring extensive treatment.

New vessels elsewhere

New vessels occurring beyond one disc diameter of the optic nerve are particularly associated with tractional retinal detachment, emphasizing the importance of timely detection and treatment. NVE are treated by panretinal photocoagulation in the same way as NVD, however the effectiveness of treatment may be increased by targeting the more ischaemic areas of the retina as seen clinically or on fluorescein angiography.

Management of diabetic maculopathy

The ETDRS and British Multicentre Photocoagulation Study showed that appropriate macular photocoagulation was effective in preventing central visual loss due to macular oedema, in many cases up to seven years. The main objectives in the management of exudative diabetic maculopathy are early detection of clinically significant maculopathy (see page 54) and treatment with laser before the fovea becomes involved. Visual acuity rarely improves following laser – the aim of treatment is prevention of future deterioration. Focal maculopathy, usually identifiable as a circinate area of exudates, can be treated in the absence of a FFA by direct application of laser to the centre of the circinate where a cluster of microaneurysms are often visible. More generalised oedema requires a FFA prior to treatment to adequately assess the extent of vascular leakage and ischaemia.

The EDTRS validated the use of grid laser therapy for diffuse macu-lopathy.[59] Results are often disappointing, with many not responding even to repeated applications of laser particularly if the oedema has been long-standing. Generalized breakdown of the blood retinal barrier with retinal pigment epithelial damage is likely to contribute to the poor prognosis for maculopathy. Grid laser photocoagulation consists of 100–200 laser burns of low intensity scattered across the macula, avoiding the area within 300 μm of the fovea and being cautious in the area of the papillomacular bundle (Fig. 8). Ischaemic maculopathy does not respond to laser treatment and may deteriorate if it is given.

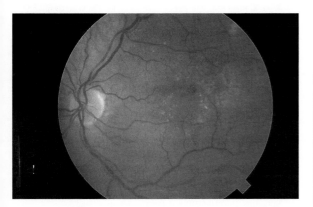

Fig. 8 Macular grid.

Vitreo-retinal surgery

Vitrectomy

Surgical removal of the vitreous gel eliminates both the scaffolding along which fibrovascular tissue can proliferate, and the excessive growth factors which are harboured within the vitreous. Numerous studies have shown increased levels of growth factors such as VEGF, basic fibroblast growth factor, insulin-like growth factor-I and epidermal growth factor in the vitreous of those with proliferative retinopathy. Boulton et al. have demonstrated that there is a correla-tion between intravitreal growth factor levels with both disease state (whether active or fibrotic) and method of glycaemic management (insulin or non-insulin treated).[60]

ETDRS report 17 states that the five-year cumulative rate of pars plana vitrectomy (performed via microsurgical instruments inserted into the eye through the area of the pars plana posterior to the lens) was 5.3 per cent in their cohort despite timely laser photocoagula-tion.[61] The ETDRS enrolled 3711 patients with mild to severe non-proliferative or early proliferative retinopathy in both eyes and randomized one eye of each patient to early photocoagulation or deferral of laser. Some patients, particularly younger type 1 patients, continue to exhibit progression of their proliferative disease in spite of multiple sessions of laser photocoagulation. Fortunately, pars plana vitrectomy has improved the visual prognosis for patients such as these, with 48 per cent having an acuity of 20/100 or better at one year post surgery, half of whom were able to achieve 20/40 or better.[61] The indications for vitrectomy are listed in Box 4.

The most common indication for vitrectomy is persistence of a dense vitreous haemorrhage. The stage at which surgery should be performed varies depending on whether the patient has type 1 or 2 diabetes. Vitrectomy should be considered at around three months in a type 1 diabetic and six months in a type 2 diabetic. Clearing the vitreous haemorrhage allows laser to be applied intra-operatively using an endolaser probe.

Cataract surgery

Around 15 per cent of all cataract surgery performed is on diabetic patients.[62] In those with cataract advanced to such a degree that it is impossible to visualise the fundus or perform laser treatment, surgery should be expedited. Panretinal photocoagulation can be performed preoperatively or immediately postoperatively. Those with better vision undergoing cataract surgery should be counselled on the possibility of worsening of their retinopathy. The results of surgery

---

Box 4 Indications for vitrectomy *(adapted from Reference (1))*

- ◆ Severe non-clearing vitreous haemorrhage
- ◆ Dense pre-macular haemorrhage
- ◆ Tractional macular detachment
- ◆ Combined tractional/rhegmatogenous retinal detachment
- ◆ Severe widespread fibrovascular proliferation
- ◆ Iris neovascularization with vitreous haemorrhage

are best in eyes with no retinopathy and worst in those with active proliferative retinopathy.[63] Postoperative complications include severe anterior uveitis, the development or progression of rubeosis and the onset or worsening of maculopathy. A recent paper[64] assessed the changing pattern of macular oedema following cataract surgery in diabetics. They found that clinically significant macular oedema at the time of surgery is unlikely to resolve spontaneously, but similar oedema arising after surgery commonly resolves within one year, particularly if retinopathy is mild.

Support services for visual handicap

The psychological impact of loss of vision is huge and often provokes a grieving reaction, particularly in younger patients with rapid visual loss. Patients who have lost sight due to diabetes have particular practical difficulties to adjust to. Daily management of glycaemia is possible for the visually handicapped using various techniques including high visibility or 'speaking' blood glucose meters, 'click-count' or preset syringes along with 'pill organizers' for oral medication. Patients who have been taught to manage their own diabetes successfully are more likely to regain their independence and to retain their self-esteem. Early registration with Social Services triggers vital financial, practical and emotional support. Ophthalmologists have a duty to ensure that those eligible are promptly added to the Blind or Partially Sighted Register.

Current controversies in diabetic retinopathy

Vitrectomy for macular oedema

A number of papers have recently highlighted the possible visual benefits of pars plana vitrectomy for diabetic macular oedema. In a small series of 10 patients, Harbour et al. have indicated that acuity may improve up to six lines following surgical removal of a thickened taut membrane on the posterior aspect of the vitreous face.[65] Several Japanese groups have studied the relationship between the vitreo-macular interface and macular oedema. Spontaneous vitreomacular separation may promote resolution of diabetic macular oedema and consequently improve visual acuity.[33] Vitrectomy for diffuse or cystoid macular oedema has been advocated for those without posterior vitreous detachment[66] even if there is no clinical evidence of traction from a thickened posterior hyaloid membrane. Perifoveal microcirculation has been reported to improve following vitrectomy in these patients.[74] The service implications for this are substantial should this treatment option become accepted practise.

Macular laser when visual acuity is normal

Controversy exists as to whether laser photocoagulation should be applied to eyes with clinically significant macular oedema and a normal visual acuity, as recommended by the ETDRS group.[67] Side effects of macular photocoagulation include loss of central visual function and scotoma formation. Patients with normal acuity are far more likely to be aware of these effects following laser than those who are already visually impaired. The ETDRS data suggests that macular laser reduces the risk of 'moderate visual loss' by about 50 per cent, however the absolute risk is lower for eyes with good vision (20/20 or better) at baseline. Recent reassessment of the EDTRS data by Ferris and Davis suggests that there is little to gain from early intervention in eyes where oedema does not involve or imminently threaten the centre of the macula, and vision remains good.[67] Clinical judgement and recognition of other factors such as the status of the fellow eye, systemic risk factors and ability to maintain follow up should all be assessed.

Novel therapies for diabetic retinopathy

Inappropriate activation of protein kinase C (PKC) has been implicated in the pathophysiology of diabetic retinopathy and nephropathy. Activation of PKC, particularly the β-isoforms, results in modulation of various vascular functions including changes in retinal blood flow along with alteration in vascular contractility, permeability and proliferation.[68] Oral administration of a specific PKC β-inhibitor (LY333531) has been shown to ameliorate the abnormal retinal haemodynamic changes seen in diabetic patients in a phase 1 trial.[69] Other abnormalities of vascular physiology in diabetic retinopathy such as nitric oxide (NO) deficiency, leucocyte activation and increased production of superoxide and endothelin may also become the focus of treatment with specific oral agents in the future.[70]

References

1. **The Royal College of Ophthalmologists**. *Guidelines for Diabetic Retinopathy* 1997. The Royal College of Ophthalmologists, 17 Cornwall Terrace, London.

2. **Klein R, Klein BE, Moss SE, Cruickshanks KJ**. The Wisconsin Epidemiologic Study of diabetic retinopathy: IX. Four-year incidence and progression of diabetic retinopathy when age at diagnosis is less than 30 years. *Archives of Ophthalmology*, 1989; **107**: 237–43.

3. **Klein R, Klein BE, Moss SE, Cruickshanks KJ**. The Wisconsin Epidemiologic Study of diabetic retinopathy: X. Four-year incidence and progression of diabetic retinopathy when age at diagnosis is 30 years or more. *Archives of Ophthalmology*, 1989; **107**: 244–9.

4. **Klein R, Klein BE, Moss SE, Cruickshanks KJ**. The Wisconsin Epidemiologic Study of diabetic retinopathy: XIV. Ten-year incidence and progression of diabetic retinopathy. *Archives of Ophthalmology*, 1994; **112**: 1217–28.

5. **Klein R, Klein BEK, Moss SE, Cruickshanks KJ**. The Wisconsin Epidemiologic Study of diabetic retinopathy: XVII. The 14-year incidence and progression of diabetic retinopathy and associated risk factors in type 1 diabetes. *Ophthalmology*, 1998; **105**: 1801–15.

6. **Klein R, Klein BE, Moss SE, Cruickshanks KJ**. The Wisconsin Epidemiologic Study of diabetic retinopathy: XV. The long-term incidence of macular oedema. *Ophthalmology*, 1995; **102**: 7–16.

7. **Klein R** *et al.* An alternative method of grading diabetic retinopathy. *Ophthalmology*, 1986; **93**: 1183–7.

8. United Kingdom Prospective Diabetes Study, 30. Diabetic retinopathy at diagnosis of non-insulin dependent diabetes mellitus and associated risk factors. *Archives of Ophthalmology*, 1998; **116**: 297–303.

9. **Harris EL, Sherman SH, Georgopoulos A**. Black-white differences in risk of developing retinopathy among individuals with type 2 diabetes. *Diabetes Care*, 1999; **22**: 779–83.

10. **Sjolie AK** *et al.* Retinopathy and vision loss in insulin-dependent diabetes in Europe. The EURODIAB IDDM Complications Study. *Ophthalmology*, 1997; **104**: 252–60.

11. ETDRS Report No. 10. Grading Diabetic retinopathy from stereoscopic colour fundus photographs – an extension of the modified Airlie House classification. *Ophthalmology*, 1991; **98**: 786–806.

12. Ismail GM, Whitaker D. Early detection of changes in visual function in diabetes mellitus. *Ophthalmic Physiology and Optics*, 1998; **18**: 3–12.

13. Harris A, Arend O, Danis RP, Evans D, Wolf S, Martin BJ. Hyperoxia improves contrast sensitivity in early diabetic retinopathy. *British Journal of Ophthalmology*, 1996; **80**: 209–13.

14. Hellstedt T, Immonen I. Disappearance and formation rates of microaneurysms in early diabetic retinopathy. *British Journal of Ophthalmology*, 1996; **80**: 135–9.

15. Stitt AW, Gardiner TA, Archer DB. Histological and ultrastructural investigation of retinal microaneurysm development in diabetic patients. *British Journal of Ophthalmology*, 1995; **79**: 362–7.

16. Chew EY *et al.* Association of elevated serum lipid levels with retinal hard exudate in diabetic retinopathy. Early Treatment Diabetic Retinopathy Study (EDTRS) Report 22. *Archives of Ophthalmology*, 1996; **114**: 1079–84.

17. Bek T, Lund-Anderson H. Cotton-wool spots and retinal light sensitivity in diabetic retinopathy. *British Journal of Ophthalmology*, 1991; **75**: 13–7.

18. Early Treatment Diabetic Retinopathy Study Research Group. Fundus photographic risk factors for the progression of diabetic retinopathy. Report No. 12. *Ophthalmology*, 1991; **98**: 823–33.

19. Diabetic Retinopathy Study Research Group. Photocoagulation treatment of proliferative diabetic retinopathy: clinical application of diabetic retinopathy study (DRS) findings. DRS Report No. 8. *Ophthalmology*, 1981; **88**: 583–600.

20. Collier A, Watson HH, Patrick AW, Ludlam CA, Clarke BF. Effect of glycaemic control, metformin and gliclazide on platelet density and aggregability in recently diagnosed type 2 (non-insulin dependent) diabetic patients. *Diabetes and Metabolism*, 1989; **15**: 420–5.

21. Schroder S, Palinski W, Schmid-Schonbein GW. Activated monocytes and granulocytes, capillary nonperfusion, and neovascularisation in diabetic retinopathy. *American Journal of Pathology*, 1991; **139**: 81–100.

22. Pecsvarady Z *et al.* Decreased polymorphonuclear leukocyte deformability in NIDDM. *Diabetes Care*, 1994; **17**: 57–63.

23. McLeod DS, Lefer DJ, Merges C, Lutty GA. Enhanced expression of intracellular adhesion molecule-1 and p-selectin in the diabetic human retina and choroid. *American Journal of Pathology*, 1995; **147**: 642–53.

24. Grunwald JE, Riva CE, Sinclair SH, Brucker AJ, Petrig BL. Laser Doppler velocimetry study of retinal circulation in diabetes mellitus. *Archives of Ophthalmology*, 1986; **104**: 991–6.

25. MacKinnon JR, O'Brien C, Swa K, Aspinall P, Butt Z, Cameron D. *Acta Ophthalmologica Scandinavica*, 1997; **75**: 661–4.

26. Olson JA, Whitelaw CM, McHardy KC, Pearson DWM, Forrester JV. Soluble leucocyte adhesion molecules in diabetic retinopathy stimulate retinal endothelial cell migration. *Diabetologia*, 1997; **40**: 1166–71.

27. Regillo CD *et al.* Diabetic papillopathy. Patient characteristics and fundus findings. *Archives of Ophthalmology*, 1995; **113**: 889–95.

28. Stransky TJ. Diabetic papillopathy and proliferative retinopathy. *Graefe's Archives for Clinical and Experimental Ophthalmology*, 1986; **224**: 46–50.

29. Weinberger D, Fink-Cohen S, Gaton DD, Priel E, Yassur Y. Non-retinovascular leakage in diabetic maculopathy. *British Journal of Ophthalmology*, 1995; **79**: 727–31.

30. Ishibashi T, Inomata H. Ultrastructure of retinal vessels in diabetic patients. *British Journal of Ophthalmology*, 1993; **77**: 574–8.

31. Bailey CC, Sparrow JM, Grey RH, Cheng H. The National Diabetic Retinopathy Laser Treatment Audit. I. Maculopathy. *Eye*, 1998; **12**: 69–76.

32. Hikichi T, Fujio N, Akiba J, Azuma Y, Takahashi M, Yoshida A. Association between the short-term natural history of diabetic macular edema and the vitreomacular relationship in type II diabetes mellitus. *Ophthalmology*, 1997; **104**: 473–8.

33. Kristinsson JK, Gottfredsdottir MS, Stefansson E. Retinal vessel dilatation and elongation precedes diabetic macular oedema. *British Journal of Ophthalmology*, 1997; **81**: 274–8.

34. Mansour AM, Schachat A, Bodiford G, Haymond R. Foveal avascular zone in diabetes mellitus. *Retina*, 1993; **13**: 125–8.

35. Arend O, Wolf S, Harris A, Reim M. The relationship of macular microcirculation to visual acuity in diabetic patients. *Archives of Ophthalmology*, 1995; **113**: 610–4.

36. DCCT Research Group. The effect of intensive treatment of diabetes on the development and progression of long-term complications in insulin dependent diabetes mellitus. *New England Journal of Medicine*, 1993; **329**: 977–1034.

37. DCCT Research Group. Early worsening of diabetic retinopathy in the Diabetes Control and Complications Trial. *Archives of Ophthalmology*, 1998; **116**: 874–86.

38. Chantelau E. Evidence that upregulation of serum IGF-1 concentration can trigger acceleration of diabetic retinopathy. *British Journal of Ophthalmology*, 1998; **82**: 725–30.

39. UK Prospective Diabetes Study (UKPDS) Group. Intensive blood-glucose control with sulphonylureas or insulin compared with conventional treatment and risk of complications in patients with type 2 diabetes (UKPDS 33). *Lancet*, 1998; **352**: 837–53.

40. UK Prospective Diabetes Study Group. Efficacy of atenolol and captopril in reducing risk of macrovascular and microvascular complications in type 2 diabetes: UKPDS 39. *British Medical Journal*, 1998; **317**: 713–20.

41. Chaturvedi N *et al.* Effect of lisinopril on progression of retinopathy in normotensive people with type 1 diabetes. The EUCLID study group. EURODIAB Controlled Trial of Lisinopril in Insulin-Dependent Diabetes Mellitus. *Lancet*, 1998; **351**: 28–31.

42. Klein BE, Moss SE, Klein R. Effect of pregnancy on progression of diabetic retinopathy. *Diabetes Care*, 1990; **13**: 34–40.

43. Chew EY *et al.* Metabolic control and progression of retinopathy. The Diabetes in Early Pregnancy Study. National Institute of Child Health and Human Development Diabetes in Early Pregnancy Study. *Diabetes Care*, 1995; **18**: 631–7.

44. Hellstedt T, Kaaja R, Teramo K, Immonen I. The effect of pregnancy on mild diabetic retinopathy. *Graefe's Archives for Clinical and Experimental Ophthalmology*, 1997; **235**: 437–41.

45. Holl RW, Lang GE, Grabert M, Heinze E, Lang GK, Debatin KM. Diabetic retinopathy in pediatric patients with type-1 diabetes: effect of diabetes duration, prepubertal and pubertal onset of diabetes, and metabolic control. *Journal of Paediatrics*, 1998; **132**: 790–4.

46. Aiello LM. Diagnosis, management and treatment of nonproliferative diabetic retinopathy and macular edema. In: Albert DM, Jakobiec FA, eds. *Principles and Practice of Ophthalmology: Clinical Practice.* Philadelphia: WB Saunders, 1994: 747–60.

47. Lovestam-Adrian M, Agardh E, Agardh CD. The incidence of nephropathy in type 1 diabetic patients with proliferative retinopathy: a 10-year follow-up study. *Diabetes Research in Clinical Practice*, 1998; **39**: 11–17.

48. Qiao Q, Keinanen-Kiukaanniemi S, Laara E. The relationship between hemoglobin levels and diabetic retinopathy. *Journal of Clinical Epidemiology*, 1997; **50**: 153–8.

49. UK Prospective Diabetes Study Group. Efficacy of atenolol and captopril in reducing risk of macrovascular and microvascular complications in type 2 diabetes: UKPDS 39. *British Medical Journal*, 1998; **317**: 713–20.

50. Retinopathy Working Party. A protocol for screening for diabetic retinopathy. *Diabetic Medicine*, 1991; **8**: 233–7.

51. Mukamel DB, Bresnick GH, Wang Q, Dickey CF. Barriers to compliance with screening guidelines for diabetic retinopathy. *Ophthalmic Epidemiology*, 1999; **6**: 61–72.

52. Lee VS *et al.* The diagnosis of diabetic retinopathy. Ophthalmoscopy versus fundus photography. *Ophthalmology*, 1993; **100**: 1504–12.

53. British Diabetic Association Mobile Retinal Screening Group. Practical community screening for diabetic retinopathy using the mobile retinal camera: report of a 12 centre study. *Diabetic Medicine*, 1996; **13**: 946–52.

54. Williamson TH, George N, Flanagan DW, Norris V, Blamires T. Driving standard visual fields in diabetic patients after panretinal laser photocoagulation. *Vision in Vehicles*, Amsterdam: North Holland, 1991; **111**: 265–72.

55. Diabetic Retinopathy Research Group. Photocoagulation treatment of proliferative diabetic retinopathy: the second report of Diabetic Retinopathy Study findings. *Ophthalmology*, 1978; **85**: 82–106.

56. Uchita M, Wakabayashi T, Shinoda K, Ishida S, Kawashima S, Yamada M. Does panretinal photocoagulation reduce vascular endothelial growth factor and hepatocyte growth factor in eyes with proliferative diabetic retinopathy. trial [ARVO abstract]. *Investigative Ophthalmology and Visual Science*, 1999; **40**: S705. Abstract no. 3725.

57. Buckley SA, Jenkins L, Benjamin L. Fields, DVLC and panretinal photocoagulation. *Eye*, 1992; **6**: 623–5.

58. Early Treatment of Diabetic Retinopathy Study Research Group. Treatment techniques and clinical guidelines for photocoagulation of diabetic macular oedema: ETDRS report no.2. *Ophthalmology*, 1987; **94**: 761–74.

59. Boulton M *et al*. Intravitreal growth factors in proliferative diabetic retinopathy: correlation with neovascular activity and glycaemic management. *British Journal of Ophthalmology*, 1997; **81**: 228–33.

60. Early Treatment of Diabetic Retinopathy Study Research Group. Pars plana vitrectomy in the early treatment diabetic retinopathy study. ETDRS report no. 17. *Ophthalmology*, 1992; **99**: 1351–7.

61. Benson WE, Brown GC, Tasman W, McNamara JA, Vander JF. Extracapsular cataract extraction with placement of posterior chamber lens in patients with diabetic retinopathy. *Ophthalmology*, 1993; **100**: 730–8.

62. Hykin PG, Gregson RMC, Stevens JD, Hamilton PAM. Extracapsular cataract extraction in proliferative diabetic retinopathy. *Ophthalmology*, 1993; **100**: 394–9.

63. Dowler JG, Schmi KS, Hykin PG, Hamilton AM. The natural history of macular edema after cataract surgery in diabetes. *Ophthalmology*, 1999; **106**: 663–8.

64. Harbour JW, Smiddy WE, Flynn HW, Rubsamen PE. Vitrectomy for diabetic macular edema associated with a thickened and taut posterior hyaloid membrane. *American Journal of Ophthalmology*, 1996; **121**: 405–13.

65. Tachi N, Ogino N. Vitrectomy for diffuse macular edema in cases of diabetic retinopathy. *American Journal of Ophthalmology*, 1996; **122**: 258–60.

66. Ferris FL, Davies MD. Treating 20/20 eyes with diabetic macular edema. *Archives of Ophthalmology*, 1999; **117**: 675–6.

67. Ishii H, Koya D, King GL. Protein kinase C activation and its role in the development of vascular complications in diabetes mellitus. *Journal of Molecular Medicine*, 1998; **76**: 21–31.

68. Aiello LP, Bursell SE, Devries T, Alatorre C, King GL, Ways DK. Amelioration of abnormal retinal hemodynamics by a protein kinase C b selective inhibitor (LY333531) in patients with diabetes: results of a phase 1 safety and pharmacodynamic clinical trial [ARVO abstract]. *Investigative Ophthalmology and Visual Science*, 1999; **40**: S192. Abstract no. 1014.

69. McCarthy MF. Nitric oxide deficiency, leukocyte activation, and resultant ischaemia are crucial to the pathogenesis of diabetic retinopathy/neuropathy – preventive potential of antioxidants, essential fatty acids, chromium, ginkgolides, and pentoxifylline. *Medical Hypotheses*, 1998; **50**: 435–49.

70. Dowler JGF, Hamilton AMP. Clinical features of diabetic eye disease. In: Pickup JC, Williams G, eds. *Textbook of Diabetes*. 2nd edn. Oxford: Blackwell Science, 1997: 46.3.

71. Forrester JV, Knott RM. Diabetic retinopathy: what goes wrong in the retina? In: Williams G, ed. *Horizons in Medicine*, No. 10. London, Royal College of Physicians of London, 1998: 227.

72. Mackinnon JR, McKillop G, O'Brien C, Swa K, Butt Z, Nelson P. Colour Doppler imaging of the ocular circulation in diabetic retinopathy. *Acta Ophthalmologica Scandinavica*, 2000; **78**: 386–9.

73. Wong TY, Moss SE, Klein R, Klein BE. Is the pulse rate useful in assessing risk of diabetic retinopathy and macular oedema? The Wisconsin Epidemiological Study of Diabetic Retinopathy. *British Journal of Ophthalmology*, 2001; **85**: 925–7.

74. Kadonosono K, Itoh N, Ohno S. Periforeal micro circulation before and after vitrectomy for diabetic cystoid macular oedema. *American Journal of Ophthalmology*, 2000; **130**: 740–4.

5 Diabetic nephropathy

Roberto Trevisan and Giancarlo Viberti

Introduction

Clinical diabetic nephropathy is defined by the presence of persistent proteinuria (urinary albumin excretion rate greater than 300 mg/day) in sterile urine of diabetic patients with concomitant retinopathy but without other renal disease or heart failure.[1] Once manifest, diabetic nephropathy is characterized by a progressive decline in renal function, resulting in end-stage renal disease. Histological changes of diabetic glomerulopathy are present in over 96 per cent of type 1 diabetic patients with clinical proteinuria and in approximately 85 per cent of type 2 (non-insulin-dependent) diabetic patients who develop proteinuria with concomitant retinopathy. In the absence of retinopathy, 30 per cent of proteinuric type 2 patients have a non-diabetic renal lesion.

Between 25 and 50 per cent of diabetic patients develop kidney disease although a smaller percentage require dialysis or kidney transplantation. The mortality from all causes in diabetic patients with nephropathy is 20–40 times higher than that of peer patients without nephropathy. Diabetic nephropathy is now the single most common cause of renal failure in the Western World and in some countries diabetic patients represent up to 40 per cent of all patients entering renal replacement treatment programmes. Because the prevalence of type 2 diabetes is at least 5–6 fold higher than type 1 diabetes, this form of diabetes now contributes to at least 50 per cent of diabetic patients in end-stage renal disease.

Natural history and clinical course of diabetic nephropathy in type 1 diabetic patients

The evolution of diabetic nephropathy proceeds through several distinct but interconnected phases: an early phase of physiological abnormalities of renal function, a 'micro-albuminuria' phase and a clinical phase with persistent clinical proteinuria progressing to end-stage renal failure (Table 1).[1,2]

Early renal abnormalities

Soon after the diagnosis of type 1 diabetes, several renal abnormalities may be observed. Supranormal values of renal plasma flow (RPF) and glomerular filtration rate (above 135 ml/min/1.73 m^2) are found in approximately 20–40 per cent of patients. Hyperfiltration is partially related to the degree of metabolic control, and intensified insulin therapy with improvement of blood glucose control reduces glomerular filtration rate toward normal. The haemodynamic abnormalities are associated with an increase in kidney size. Nephromegaly is a prerequisite for the occurrence of glomerular hyperfiltration. The prognostic significance of nephromegaly, however, remains unclear. Although elevated glomerular filtration rate has been implicated in the initiation and progression of renal disease, the prognostic significance of glomerular hyperfiltration remains controversial in humans. Two prospective studies, a case control and a cohort study,[3,4] reported a faster rate of decline of glomerular filtration rate in diabetic patients with hyperfiltration, but the long-term significance of the phenomenon remains unclear at present. There is a good correlation between glomerular filtration rate and RPF increases in diabetic patients, but increases in RPF can account only for approximately 60 per cent of the increase in glomerular filtration rate. The remainder of the glomerular filtration rate increase is accounted for by a rise in intraglomerular pressure described below.

Micro-albuminuria

A proportion of diabetic patients exhibits elevated rates of urinary albumin excretion well before clinically persistent proteinuria

Table 1 Phases of diabetic nephropathy

Phase of disease progression	Urinary albumin excretion rate	Glomerular filtration rate	Blood pressure
Normo-albuminuria	<20 µg/min	Normal or elevated	Increasing
Micro-albuminuria	20–200 µg/min	Normal or elevated	Rising further
Overt proteinuria	≥200 µg/min	Decreasing	Elevated
Renal failure	≥200 µg/min	Reduced	Elevated

develops. An increase in albumin excretion rate ranging between 20 and 200 µg/min is defined as micro-albuminuria.[5] Longitudinal studies of cohorts of type 1 diabetic patients have demonstrated that micro-albuminuria is a predictor for the development of clinical diabetic nephropathy and is associated with a 20-fold higher risk of progression to overt renal disease compared to patients with normo-albuminuria. Albumin excretion rates in healthy individuals range between 1.5 and 20 µg/min with a median around 6.5 µg/min. The average day-to-day variation of albumin excretion rate is about 40 per cent and is similar both in normal and diabetic subjects. For this reason, an accurate classification of albumin excretion rate requires multiple measurements (usually three) over a period of a few weeks.

Persistent micro-albuminuria may be found after one year of type 1 diabetes and can be present at diagnosis in type 2 disease. The significance of micro-albuminuria in patients with short-term diabetes is still unclear, but in individuals with five or more years duration of diabetes micro-albuminuria is the consequence of definite, albeit early, renal damage. Morphological studies have showed that structural lesions such as increased mesangial fractional volume and decreased filtration surface area are, on average, more advanced at this stage, confirming that micro-albuminuria is a sign of renal disease. Once micro-albuminuria is established the albumin excretion rate tends to rise with time at an average rate of about 14 per cent per year.

The excess albumin excretion rate in diabetic patients with persistent micro-albuminuria is most likely to be the result of an increased transglomerular flux as a consequence of an increase in transglomerular pressure gradient. A loss of the fixed negative electrical charge on the glomerular membrane may also have a role.

Micro-albuminuria is consistently associated with higher levels of blood pressure, independent of age, sex, duration of diabetes, body mass index and blood glucose control. The magnitude of this blood pressure rise is approximately 10–15 per cent above that of diabetic patients with normal albumin excretion and often occurs within the so-called normal blood pressure range. At this stage of micro-albuminuria, there is no hint of renal failure and glomerular filtration rate can even be supranormal. Studies of transition from normo- to micro-albuminuria have documented that the diabetic patients who progress show increases in blood pressure as the albumin excretion rate rises within the normal range. Similar observations have been made in type 2 diabetes. This raises the possibility that elevated blood pressure levels may be one factor contributing to the initiation of renal damage or, alternatively, that high blood pressure and an increase in urinary albumin excretion may represent concomitant manifestations of a common process responsible for the development of diabetic nephropathy.

Micro-albuminuria is also consistently associated with other cardiovascular risk factors (Box 1). Thus, micro-albuminuria in diabetes can be considered as an early sign of damage not only of the kidney but also of the cardiovascular system.

Overt nephropathy

In diabetic patients who progress to overt, persistent albuminuria (albumin excretion rate above 300 mg/24 h), glomerular filtration rate gradually declines in a linear fashion at a rate ranging, in more recent years, from 1.2 to 22 ml/min/year (average 4.5 ml/min/year).[1] The reason for the differences in the rates of progression are not entirely known, but blood pressure, blood glucose control, the degree of

> **Box 1 Concomitants of micro-albuminuria: the micro-albuminuria syndrome**
>
> - Elevated blood pressure
> - Atherogenic lipid profile (increased VLDL-triglycerides, decreased HDL-cholesterol, increased lipoprotein(a))
> - Elevated plasma fibrinogen and PAI-1 levels
> - Decreased insulin sensitivity
> - Increased total body exchangeable sodium
> - Sodium sensitivity of blood pressure
> - Increased transcapillary escape of albumin
> - Impaired basal endothelium-dependent vasorelaxation
> - Increased left ventricular volume
> - High sodium–lithium countertransport activity
> - Diabetic retinopathy
> - Increased prevalence of diabetic neuropathy
> - Increased prevalence of peripheral vascular disease
> - 'Silent' ischaemic heart disease

proteinuria and, in some cases, hypercholesterolaemia are likely to be promoters of progression. In several studies, the increase in urinary protein excretion correlated with the progression of the renal disease. Recent data suggest that proteins filtered by the glomerulus cause injury of the tubulointerstitium, leading to parenchymal damage and, ultimately, renal scarring and insufficiency.[6] Before the introduction of early, intensive treatment for hypertension in diabetic patients, end-stage renal failure occurred an average of seven years after the onset of proteinuria. Today, the period between onset of overt proteinuria and renal replacement therapy is more than double that which it once was.

Elevation of blood pressure is a feature of about 85 per cent of patients with proteinuria and blood pressure rises about 7 per cent per year in association with progressive renal failure. The excess of arterial hypertension in type 1 diabetes seems to be largely accounted for by patients with overt clinical nephropathy, whereas long-term uncomplicated diabetic patients tend to have lower blood pressure levels than those of age-matched healthy controls.

Diabetic retinopathy and hyperlipidaemia are present in most patients with nephropathy. At this stage, the course of renal failure does not seem to be reversible, but available treatment modalities slow the rate of decline in renal function and delay the need for renal replacement therapy.

Nephropathy in type 2 diabetes

Renal failure in type 2 diabetes develops in a smaller percentage of patients of European origin, but because the incidence of type 2 diabetic patients is much greater, about one half of the diabetic patients in end-stage renal failure (ESRF) belong to this group.[7]

The prevalence of clinical proteinuria ranges between 10 and 40 per cent in type 2 diabetic patients, with large ethnic variations.

Diabetes duration and hypertension are related to the presence of proteinuria. Incidence data show that the cumulative risk of persistent proteinuria varies between 25 and 50 per cent after a diabetes duration of 20 years or more. Recent observational studies of type 2 diabetic patients with nephropathy have demonstrated that the rate of fall in glomerular filtration rate varies considerably from one patient to another. The increase in blood pressure to a hypertensive level is an early feature and accelerates the progression of renal disease in type 2 diabetic patients. ESRF, however, is about 20 times less frequent in European subjects with type 2 diabetes compared to those with type 1 diabetes, because other competing causes of death, especially cardiovascular disease, in the older type 2 diabetic group prevent progression to ESRF. In ethnic groups where ischaemic heart disease is less common and type 2 diabetes develops at a younger age (such as in the Japanese, Asian and Indian American), the frequency of end-stage renal failure is similar to, if not higher than, that in type 1 diabetic patients.

Micro-albuminuria in type 2 diabetic patients appears to be not only a predictor of renal disease but also a powerful marker of cardiovascular mortality.[8] Increased albuminuria is associated with coronary heart disease, cardiac failure and peripheral vascular disease. Several cardiovascular risk factors have been linked with micro-albuminuria in type 2 diabetic patients, such as lipoprotein abnormalities, hyperinsulinaemia, insulin resistance and markers of endothelial dysfunction. None of these, however, can entirely explain the increased cardiovascular mortality in patients with abnormal albumin excretion rate.

Pathogenesis of diabetic kidney disease

There is no doubt that the diabetic milieu is necessary for diabetic glomerular lesions to develop. Both retrospective and prospective studies have suggested a relationship between blood glucose control and risk of diabetic nephropathy. The Diabetes Control and Complication Trial (DCCT Study)[9] and the United Kingdom Prospective Diabetes Study (UKPDS)[10] have now precisely documented that the rate of development and progression of diabetic nephropathy is closely associated with glycaemic control both in type 1 and type 2 diabetic patients. Nevertheless, in many patients no renal disease develops (assessed by levels of urinary albumin excretion rate and level of glomerular filtration rate), despite several years of poor diabetes control. It thus appears that in humans hyperglycaemia is necessary, but not sufficient, to cause renal damage and that other factors are needed for the manifestation of the clinical syndrome.

Several biochemical mechanisms have been advocated to explain the deleterious effects of high glucose concentrations in the kidney (see also Chapter 3.2).

Non-enzymatic glycation

A possible link between hyperglycaemia and diabetic nephropathy resides in non-enzymatic glycosylation of cellular proteins.[11] The exposure of lysine amino terminal groups of circulating or structural protein to increasing amount of glucose would lead, by basic chemical stoichiometry, to increasing covalent binding of glucose to protein. These covalent products can then participate in cross-linking between or within proteins, producing advanced glycosylation end products (**AGE**). The amount of AGE is related to the extent and severity of advanced complications of diabetes. The AGE-products lead to synthesis and secretion of cytokines when bound to a specific AGE-receptor. AGE can induce an excess cross-linking of collagen molecules in the glomerular plasma membrane affecting the assembly and architecture of glomerular basement membrane (GBM) and mesangial matrix and potentially act on mesangial cells via platelet-derived growth factor causing cells to synthesize more extracellular matrix. All these processes may lead to enhanced deposition of extracellular matrix proteins in the mesangium, interfere with the mesangial clearance of macromolecules and alter macrophage function, therefore contributing to mesangial expansion and glomerular occlusion (see also Chapter 3.2).

The polyol pathway

Another possible mechanism of tissue injury involves excessive intracellular production of sorbitol from glucose, a reaction catalysed by aldose reductase. Sorbitol accumulation would cause tissue damage, via a disruption of cellular osmoregulation along with a depletion of myo-inositol. Although some beneficial effect of aldose-reductase inhibition has been reported in diabetic animals, other studies both in rodents and man have given negative results. Renal damage in the diabetic kidney is, therefore, unlikely to occur through a mechanism involving the polyol pathway (see also Chapter 3.2, pp. 40–41).

Glucotoxicity

Glucose itself has a direct toxic effect on the cells. Cultured human endothelial cells chronically exposed to high glucose concentrations show alterations in cell cycle and proliferation and increased gene expression and synthesis of collagen, fibrinonectin and laminin, which may explain the increase in extracellular matrix production observed in the diabetic kidney. Mesangial cells exposed to elevated glucose concentrations synthesize less heparan-sulphate. This could contribute to reduction of the electronegative charge which physiologically restricts the transcapillary flux of circulating albumin, thus giving rise to proteinuria. Moreover, in mesangial cells high glucose levels induce the transcription and secretion of transforming growth factor (TGF)-β1, unique among the cytokines in stimulating matrix synthesis and inhibiting matrix degradation. Considerable evidence has accumulated that high glucose levels lead to sustained activation of protein kinase C in vascular tissues.[12] Glucose-induced protein kinase C activation has been implicated in the development of several haemodynamic and morphological abnormalities associated with diabetic microvascular complications.

Haemodynamic and hypertrophic pathways

Early glomerular haemodynamic disturbances may participate directly in the development of glomerulosclerosis and its attendant proteinuria. In diabetes, transmission of systemic blood pressure to the glomerular capillaries is facilitated by a proportionally greater reduction in afferent versus efferent arteriolar resistance, with a consequent rise of the glomerular capillary hydraulic pressure.[13] Elevated intraglomerular pressure via increased mechanical stress and shear forces may damage the endothelial surface and disrupt the normal structure of the glomerular barrier, eventually leading to mesangial proliferation, increase in extracellular matrix production, and thickening of the glomerular basement membrane. The haemodynamic abnormalities are usually associated with hypertrophic changes in the glomerulus. Marked renal hypertrophy is a very early event and hyperplastic and hypertrophic changes may precede the haemodynamic abnormalities. Distinct sequential molecular steps translate the mechanical stimulus of altered haemodynamics into metabolic and hypertrophic events. They include a sensing mechanism and the translation of the signal to evoke changes in protein expression and enzymatic activity. Laminar shear stress results in generation of active TGF-β1, platelet-derived growth factor (PDGF) and altered extracellular matrix deposition. Application of mechanical stretch induces matrix and TGF-β1 production in human mesangial cells, and also vascular endothelial growth factor (VEGF), one of the most powerful promoters of vascular permeability.

Familial and genetic aspects

The annual incidence of diabetic nephropathy rises rapidly over the first 15–20 years of diabetes, but declines sharply thereafter. This leads to a cumulative incidence that, after approximately 20 years of diabetes, plateaus around 30–35 per cent.[1] This pattern of risk is compatible with an individual susceptibility to renal damage partly independent of the environmental perturbations caused by diabetes, and has stimulated the search for factors, other than glycaemic control, which contribute to it.

That there is an individual predisposition to diabetic nephropathy is supported by the observation that this complication clusters in families. In a large study of families with multiple type 1 diabetic siblings, the cumulative incidence of diabetic nephropathy was 71.5 per cent if the diabetic proband had persistent proteinuria, but only 25.4 per cent if the proband had normo-albuminuria. This difference of almost 50 per cent in risk is consistent with a major gene effect for diabetic kidney disease.[14]

Further information has come from other family studies showing that a family history of cardiovascular disease and essential hypertension greatly increases the risk of nephropathy in diabetes. Furthermore, first degree non-diabetic relatives of type 1 diabetic patients with albuminuria have reduced insulin sensitivity and abnormal lipid profiles. This familial aggregation of renal and cardiovascular disease and their risk factors has led to the suggestion that these disorders may share a common pathogenic basis.

The suggestion that hereditary causes are involved in the liability to diabetic nephropathy has stimulated the search for cell and genetic markers that would allow early diagnosis and identification of patients at risk as well as help clarify the molecular mechanisms of this complication.

Sodium–lithium countertransport

The sodium–lithium countertransporter is a cell membrane cation transport system. An increase in red blood cell sodium–lithium countertransport activity, consistently associated with essential hypertension and its vascular complications, has been reported by several, though not all, authors both in type 1 and type 2 diabetic patients with micro- or macro-albuminuria. The significant correlation between the activity of this transport system in diabetic probands with nephropathy and their parents and the close association of sodium–lithium countertransport activities found in diabetic identical twins strongly suggests heritability of elevated activities in diabetic nephropathy. That an increased sodium–lithium countertransport activity may confer an increased risk for nephropathy and its vascular complications is supported by a clustering of metabolic, haemodynamic and morphological abnormalities (such as poorer metabolic control, reduced insulin sensitivity, a more atherogenic lipid profile, greater proximal tubular reabsorption of sodium, higher glomerular filtration rates, increased left ventricular thickness and larger kidney size) in those patients with a high sodium–lithium countertransport activity, but without overt proteinuria.[15]

Sodium–hydrogen antiporter

As sodium–lithium countertransport does not operate *in vivo*, the relevance of this abnormality to the pathogenesis of diabetic renal disease remains uncertain. A plasma membrane protein which catalyses the electroneutral exchange of extracellular sodium for intracellular hydrogen, the sodium–hydrogen antiport, has recently received attention. The most widely studied sodium–hydrogen isoform, referred to as NHE 1, is ubiquitously expressed and is involved in three important cellular functions: (1) intracellular pH regulation, (2) cell volume control, and (3) stimulus-response coupling and cell proliferation. The activity and expression level of this antiporter can be modulated by a large variety of chemical factors, including growth factors, tumour promoters and hormones, as well as physical factors such as changes in cell volume, extracellular acidification and degree of cell spreading.

An increased sodium–hydrogen antiport activity has been reported in leucocytes and red blood cells of type 1 diabetic patients with nephropathy. More recently, it was shown that this abnormal phenotype is also conserved in skin fibroblasts after several passages and in Epstein-Barr-immortalized lymphoblasts, suggesting that the overactivity of the antiport is intrinsically determined. The elevated maximal velocity of the exchanger was due to increased turnover rate per site. The importance of genetic factors was confirmed by the close association of maximal velocities of antiport activities found in fibroblasts of type 1 diabetic sibling pairs.[16] Of great relevance was the observation that in these same siblings there was close concordance of degree of glomerular lesions.

The kinetic abnormalities of sodium–hydrogen antiport described in cells from type 1 diabetic patients with nephropathy are similar to those reported in cells from patients with essential hypertension, supporting the contention that an inherited predisposition to essential hypertension increases the risk of diabetic nephropathy.

The abnormalities of sodium–hydrogen antiport do not reflect modifications in sodium–hydrogen antiport gene(s) and it seems more likely that some of the regulatory pathways of the sodium–hydrogen exchange may be important for its overactivity in diabetic nephropathy. Inhibition of protein kinase C in lymphocytes of type 1 diabetic patients with albuminuria normalizes the elevated activity of the antiporter. Increased sodium–hydrogen antiport activity is closely associated with abnormal cell proliferation in several cell types both in essential hypertension and in diabetic nephropathy. Extracellular matrix synthesis, in particular collagen production, has also been found to be significantly greater in fibroblasts from patients with nephropathy. Since sodium–hydrogen antiport may be activated by extracellular matrix protein, this coexistence of an altered matrix synthesis with an overactive cation transport system may help to understand the reason for the excessive matrix deposition which lead to glomerular sclerosis in diabetic nephropathy.

This body of data supports the view that the reason for an increased susceptibility to diabetic nephropathy resides in the host cell response to diabetes-induced dysregulation of a number of growth factors and vasoactive compounds whose expression and circulating or tissue levels are increased. Increased concentrations of growth factors and plasma glucose may exert a more profound effect in that subset of diabetic patients characterized by an intrinsic over-activity of Na^+/H^+ antiport activity or predisposed to overreact to any hypertrophic or hyperplastic stimulus.

Candidate genes for diabetic nephropathy

The search for genes potentially involved in susceptibility to the development of diabetic nephropathy has generated intensive research activity and contrasting reports. There are a number of pathways implicated, by clinical and experimental studies, in the predisposition to diabetic nephropathy. Candidate genes have included diabetes susceptibility genes, genes involved in the regulation of blood pressure, glomerular structural genes, genes controlling insulin-mediated glucose metabolism, and genes affecting cardiovascular risk. The most common study design is the examination of a candidate gene by means of association studies comparing allele frequencies between cases with nephropathy and controls with normo-albuminuria.

Polymorphisms in the components of renin-angiotensin system, which play a central role in the regulation of blood pressure, sodium metabolism and glomerular haemodynamics, have been actively investigated. Initially, the insertion (I)/deletion (D) polymorphism of the *angiotensin-converting enzyme* gene, responsible for a large proportion of the genetic variation in serum angiotensin-converting enzyme levels, was found to be associated with diabetic nephropathy in two small studies, but other case–control studies were unable to confirm this, although they did show a relationship with the cardiovascular complications of diabetic nephropathy. A recent multicentre study in type 1 patients with nephropathy and proliferative retinopathy showed that the severity of renal involvement was dependent on angiotensin-converting enzyme I/D polymorphism, with a dominant effect of angiotensin-converting enzyme D allele [adjusted odds ratio for renal involvement attributable to D allele 1.9]. Although in this study there was no independent effect of AGT, or AT1R polymorphisms on the risk for nephropathy, a significant interaction between angiotensin-converting enzyme I/D and AGT M235T polymorphisms was observed, suggesting the possibility that genetically determined AGT levels can affect risk for diabetic nephropathy through angiotensin I generation.[17] Recent meta-analyses of published data have suggested a weak association of the D allele with nephropathy; the association seems to be stronger in Japanese populations with a much smaller effect of D allele in Caucasians.[18] Thus, within the limitations of available data, the angiotensin-converting enzyme/ID polymorphism does not appear to play a major role in the initiation of diabetic nephropathy in Caucasian diabetic patients. Interestingly angiotensin-converting enzyme I/D polymorphism seems to affect the rate of glomerular filtration rate decline, once diabetic nephropathy is established. It has been suggested that angiotensin-converting enzyme inhibition may be less effective in preventing the glomerular filtration rate decline or in decreasing micro-albuminuria in type 1 diabetic patients with DD genotype (see also Chapter 3.2, pp. 43–44).

The candidate gene approach may not represent the best strategy to identify susceptibility genes for diabetic renal disease. Linkage analysis using concordant or discordant sib-pairs is another possible approach. In Caucasian type 2 diabetic sib-pairs with nephropathy, linkage has been demonstrated to markers on chromosome 12 and 20, although the number of sib-pairs in this study was small.[19] In a total genome screening of 98 Pima Indians sib-pairs with nephropathy, linkage with four regions has been demonstrated, on chromosomes 7, 3, 9 and 20. By applying the discordant sib-pairs strategy to test for linkage between diabetic nephropathy and chromosomal regions containing loci that encode for proteins of the renin-angiotensin system, a major susceptibility locus was found in the region 3q containing the *AT1* (angiotensin 1) receptor gene, although none of the polymorphisms in this gene were associated with diabetic nephropathy.

Family-based association analysis using the transmission disequilibrium test (**TDT**) can be used instead of linkage analysis. This involves analysis of the frequency of transmission of designated alleles from heterozygous parents to affected offspring. This method has been used for the first time in the genetics of nephropathy to examine the angiotensinogen gene. There was no evidence of preferential transmission of the *T* allele from parents to patients with nephropathy. In preliminary studies, the TDT method has, however, shown a positive association for the apolipoprotein E *ε2* allele and the endothelial nitric oxide synthase gene.[20]

The pathology of diabetic nephropathy

The characteristic intra-glomerular light microscopic changes of established diabetic nephropathy may be broadly divided into four categories.[1]

(1) The Diffuse Lesion. This common pattern represents an increase in the volume fraction of the mesangial region of the glomerulus in a relatively uniform distribution.

(2) The Nodular Lesion. The nodules are well-demarcated hard masses, eosinophilic and PAS-positive, irregular in size and distribution, located in the central regions of peripheral glomerular lobules. They are observed in more advanced glomerulosclerosis and after at least 14 years of diabetes. Several nodules may be present in each glomerulus and the remaining non-nodular mesangial regions frequently exhibit diffuse lesions.

(3) The Fibrinoid Cap. These lesions are highly eosinophilic, rounded, homogeneous structures, situated within the peripheral capillary wall. They are not common.

(4) The Capsular Drop. These exudative lesions, similar to the previous one, are also rarely observed, and may occur on the glomerular side of Bowman's capsule. They are appropriately named as they are frequently drop-shaped.

The tubules and interstitium show a variety of non-specific changes as seen in other causes of chronic renal disease. However arteriolar hyalinosis is characteristic of diabetic renal disease. This is due to extra-glomerular deposits of eosinophilic material which accumulates in the media or intima of afferent and efferent arterioles and is often the first pathological change of diabetic nephropathy detected using light microscopy. It is considered to be virtually pathognomonic. As glomerulopathy advances the expanded mesangium encroaches on the filtration surface ultimately leading to glomerular sclerosis.

Glomerular and extra-glomerular parameters seen on either light or electron microscopic sections can be quantitatively described using stereological methods. The peripheral glomerular basement membrane thickness, the volume of the glomerular mesangium expressed as a fraction of the glomerular volume are commonly quoted, as are estimates of filtration surface.

In non-diabetic subjects glomerular capillary basement membrane thickness ranges widely from 250 to 450 nm. It increases by about 30 per cent in the first five years of diabetes. The basement membrane thickness further increases with the transition from normo-albuminuria through micro-albuminuria to proteinuria. However, from cross-sectional studies it is clear that there is overlap between cases with normo-albuminuria and proteinuria.

Mesangial expansion is the most characteristic electron microscopic change seen in patients with all forms of diabetic nephropathy. The mesangium is composed of mesangial cells and associated matrix and in a large study of 150 type 1 diabetic patients with renal function ranging from normal to established proteinuria with reduced glomerular filtration rate, Steffes et al. demonstrated that mesangial expansion is characterized by mesangial matrix expansion, rather than cellular expansion.[21] In patients with micro-albuminuria mean mesangial volume is clearly increased; however, there is some overlap with non-diabetic controls and normo-albuminuric diabetic patients. As albuminuria increases so the relative volume of mesangium increases and the available filtration surface necessarily decreases, thereby reducing the glomerular filtration rate. Progressive mesangial expansion ultimately results in glomerular occlusion and sclerosis with further loss of glomerular filtration rate.[22]

The precise relationship between glomerular, tubular and interstitial structure and albuminuria is still not clear. Certainly the glomerular basement membrane is thickened and the mesangium expanded but these changes are unlikely to lead directly to an increased transglomerular passage of albumin. The most plausible structural causes would be the epithelial cell and the filtration slits. Recent prospective studies in the Pima Indians suggest that epithelial cell number is reduced in those who progress to albuminuria.

Monitoring renal function in diabetic nephropathy

Though albumin excretion rate is a reliable indicator of the risk for overt renal disease and appears to be related to the severity of renal damage, its day-to-day variability makes it relatively inaccurate for monitoring renal function over time. To evaluate the progression of renal disease and the impact of therapeutic intervention, a more precise method for the measurement of renal function is needed. Serum creatinine determination is the most commonly used, but has several disadvantages. The relationship between serum creatinine and glomerular filtration rate is asymptotic in nature, and normal concentrations of serum creatinine are still found even when as much as 50 per cent of renal function is already lost. In addition, protein

intake, lean body mass, metabolic disturbances and fluid losses can all influence serum creatinine levels. Endogenous creatinine clearance has similar shortcomings and, in renal insufficiency, overestimates renal function because of an increased tubular secretion of creatinine.

The renal clearance of inulin, using a primed continuous infusion technique, is the 'gold standard' for the determination of glomerular filtration rate, but is time consuming and relies on frequent urine sampling. These are some of the reasons that have led to the development of the plasma clearance of radioactive tracers. In Europe, the plasma disappearance of ^{51}Cr-ethylenediaminetetra-acetic acid (EDTA) after a single injection is one of the most widely used methods to evaluate glomerular filtration rate in diabetic patients and has proven reliable in several studies. Several blood samples over a period of at least four hours should be collected for a precise estimation of renal function and an allowance should be made for an extrarenal clearance of about 4 ml/min, particularly in patients with advanced renal failure (glomerular filtration rate below 20 ml/min). As an alternative to tracer methods (for example, ^{125}I-iothalamate, ^{125}I-diatrizoate, ^{99}Tc-diethylenetriaminepenta-acetic acid [DTPA]), methods based on non-ionic, radiocontrast media (for example, iohexol) have been proposed.

In diabetic patients with macroalbuminuria and overt nephropathy, glomerular filtration rate should be determined yearly to assess progression and the effect of any therapeutic intervention. Plotting glomerular filtration rate values over time is a useful method for predicting the likely date for initiation of renal replacement therapy.

Box 2 summarizes the investigations that should be routinely performed on all diabetic patients with abnormal albumin excretion rate. All patients should be carefully followed up on a regular basis.

Box 2 Investigations routinely performed on all patients with abnormal albumin excretion rate

- General physical examination and dietary assessment (every 3–6 months)
- Blood pressure (every 3–6 months)
- Visual acuity (at least yearly)
- Fundoscopy (at least yearly)
- 12 lead ECG/echocardiogram/exercise test
- Serum urea and creatinine (yearly)
- Fasting lipid profile (yearly)
- Assessment of peripheral vascular disease (yearly)
- Glycated haemoglobin (every 3 months)
- Albumin excretion rates (every 6 months)
- Urinanalysis (every 6 months)
- ^{51}Cr-EDTA glomerular filtration rate (yearly if albumin excretion rate is more than 300 mg/24 h)
- Renal ultrasound (initially)
- Serum complement levels (initially)
- Anti-nuclear factor (initially)

Treatment

Control of arterial hypertension

The positive relationship between levels of blood pressure and albumin excretion rates and rate of progression of renal failure has led to intensification in the treatment of hypertension in diabetic renal disease. Effective antihypertensive treatment significantly reduces the rate of decline of glomerular filtration rate, sometimes to less than one-fifth of pretreatment values. Such dramatic improvement in the rate of progression of renal disease could almost double the 'renal survival' of diabetic patients with nephropathy. Recent retrospective studies have suggested a marked decrease in cumulative mortality rate 10 years after onset of nephropathy from approximately 60 per cent to 18 per cent in type 1 diabetic patients with clinical albuminuria receiving antihypertensive treatment.

In the early studies, blood pressure was lowered using multiple drugs, including beta-blockers, diuretics and vasodilators. More recently, angiotensin-converting enzyme inhibitors have been used to obtain significant reduction of albuminuria and to retard the fall of glomerular filtration rate. A prospective study of 409 type 1 diabetic patients with overt nephropathy provided clear evidence that captopril preserves renal function in patients with type 1 diabetes better than placebo and, more importantly, reduces both the need for dialysis or transplantation and the mortality rate.[23] The renoprotective effect of angiotensin converting enzyme-inhibition appeared independent of its antihypertensive property. For patients with type 2 diabetes and overt nephropathy, antihypertensive treatment has been shown to be renoprotective although the role of angiotensin-converting enzyme inhibitors is not as clearly defined as in patients with type 1 diabetes. Angiotensin converting enzyme-inhibitors are more effective than other antihypertensive drugs (such as atenolol) in reducing albuminuria, but most classes of antihypertensive agents seem to have similar efficacy in affecting the rate of decline in glomerular filtration rate. In type 2 diabetic patients, the combination of a non-dihydropyridine calcium antagonist with an angiotensin converting enzyme-inhibitor seems to result in a greater reduction in urinary protein excretion and retardation of progression of nephropathy.[24] Most diabetic patients with diabetic nephropathy will require multiple drugs (of which a diuretic should always be part) to control blood pressure. The focus for treatment in this population must be on aggressive blood pressure reduction.

In patients with micro-albuminuria, independently of the baseline levels of blood pressure, angiotensin converting enzyme-inhibitors retard progression to clinical proteinuria and lower the rate of rise in albumin excretion rate.[25] A stabilizing effect of angiotensin converting enzyme-inhibition on albumin excretion rate and serum creatinine has also been reported in a 5-year controlled trial in normotensive type 2 diabetic patients who had micro-albuminuria.[26] The recent sub-analysis of the HOPE study in patients with type 2 diabetes and micro-albuminuria provides compelling evidence that angiotensin converting enzyme-inhibition with ramipril not only reduces the risk of overt nephropathy, but also lowered the risk of myocardial infarction, stroke and cardiovascular death by 25 per cent.[27] These results raise the possibility that at the stage of micro-albuminuria, the progression of renal damage in diabetic patients might be arrested. Recent guidelines advocate angiotensin converting enzyme-inhibition treatment of patients with micro-albuminuria regardless of blood pressure levels.

The optimal blood pressure levels necessary to prevent kidney damage is still a matter of debate. However, analysis of several small studies in type 1 diabetic patients suggest that the progressive fall of glomerular filtration rate might be halted by lowering mean arterial blood pressure to below 105 mmHg; the progression of micro-albuminuria should be stopped if mean arterial blood pressure is kept below 93 mmHg. The recent UKPDS study has demonstrated that intensive management of blood pressure aiming at values below 140/90 mmHg significantly reduced the risk of micro- and macro-vascular complications in hypertensive type 2 diabetic patients of recent onset, even before the appearance of micro-albuminuria.[28] Furthermore, the HOT study showed that the reduction of diastolic blood pressure from 90 to 80 mmHg in diabetic patients was able to induce a 50 per cent reduction in cardiovascular mortality.[29] The guidelines outlined in the sixth report of the Joint National Committee on Prevention, Detection, Evaluation and Treatment of High Blood Pressure recommended an aggressive programme of blood pressure reduction aiming for a target of less than 130/85 mmHg in all diabetic patients and a target of 125/75 mmHg in those patients with a proteinuria greater than 1 g per day.[30]

Dietary treatment

Restriction of dietary protein limits further damage both in animal models of renal disease and in human renal failure. In a five years self-controlled study of 19 diabetic patients with mean glomerular filtration rate at entry of 60 ml/min, Walker et al. demonstrated a reduction of the rate of decline of renal function from 0.61 to 0.14 ml/min/month when the protein intake was decreased to 0.67 from an initial intake of 1.13 g/kg body weight per day. There was also a significant decrease in albumin excretion rate. This effect, comparable to that obtained with intensive antihypertensive treatment, was independent of systemic blood pressure changes. The individual response to a low protein diet was, however, heterogeneous, with some patients showing no reduction in the speed of progression of renal failure.[31] The reason for this variability is not known; it was independent of dietary compliance, blood glucose control, blood pressure, and glomerular filtration rate at entry. A recent meta-analysis examining the effects of dietary protein restriction (0.5–0.85 g/kg body weight/day) in patients with diabetes, confirmed a beneficial effect on renal function and albuminuria but some caution should be applied.[32] Another trial in patients with various chronic non-diabetic renal diseases was unable to show clear benefit of 2.2 years of low-protein diet. Therefore, although it seems reasonable to introduce a low protein diet in the management of a diabetic patient with an advanced renal failure, the real value of this therapeutic manoeuvre in those patients with a renal function still in the normal range remains doubtful.

Control of hyperglycaemia

Diabetic nephropathy is to a considerable extent the result of the disturbed metabolism of the diabetic state. Patients who develop nephropathy have on average a record of poorer metabolic control than those who do not. Good metabolic control can postpone or possibly even halt progression to overt clinical nephropathy if applied at an early stage. A recent metanalysis found an association between metabolic control and urinary albumin excretion rate, and suggested that the rate of decline of glomerular filtration rate could be retarded by several years of improved glycaemic control. More recently, the DCCT has demonstrated that the rate of development of albuminuria may be significantly reduced by intensive therapy and good metabolic control.[9] The UKPS provided direct evidence for patients with recently diagnosed type 2 diabetes that a policy of intensive blood glucose control induced a 25 per cent reduction in overall microvascular complications with a 0.9 per cent separation in median glycosylated haemoglobin throughout the study.[10]

The role of intensified glycaemic control in patients with persistent micro-albuminuria or overt nephropathy remains controversial. Although several Scandinavian studies, based on small numbers of patients, have shown a reduced progression in patients with type 1 diabetes and micro-albuminuria with intensified insulin therapy, the DCCT and Micro-albuminuria Collaborative Study Group were unable to show a clear advantage of strict metabolic control on the progression of micro-albuminuria in type 1 diabetic patients.

No intervention trial of any significant size or duration is available for overt nephropathy, but recent observational data suggest that glycaemic control may have a role in the progression of the disease, particularly in patients in whom blood pressure is well controlled.[33]

Other treatments

Multifactorial intervention has recently been advocated and a prospective study from Denmark has shown that intensive stepwise control of risk factors (such as blood pressure, hyperglycaemia, hyperlipidaemia, smoking) specifically slows progression to nephropathy and progression of retinopathy in type 2 diabetic patients with micro-albuminuria.[34] However, further studies are needed to establish the effect of intensified multifactorial treatment, in particular, the possible role of lipid lowering therapy on progression of renal disease in diabetic patients.

Renal replacement therapy

An increasing number of diabetic patients enter renal replacement treatment (RRT) programmes throughout the world. Incidence and prevalence figures vary between countries and reflect different rates of diabetic nephropathy, availability of renal replacement facilities and treatment policies. The number of new patients with diabetes taken onto RRT programmes varies from 7 per cent in France to over 40 per cent in United States. Asian and Black patients have a higher rate of ESRF than their White counterparts. 16 per cent of new renal replacement patients in Europe have diabetic nephropathy (1991 data) whereas the figure for the USA is now (1999 data) at 41 per cent.

Renal transplantation should be the aim for all patients with diabetes in ESRF. Patient and graft survival and rehabilitation are all superior after transplantation when compared to dialysis. Clearly, this procedure is limited by the availability of grafts and the local policies for organ harvesting. In Europe approximately 60–70 per cent of diabetic patients are treated by haemodialysis, 15–20 per cent by peritoneal dialysis and about 20 per cent have a functioning graft (1991 data).

Foot problems due to a combination of peripheral neuropathy with peripheral vascular disease are a constant source of morbidity especially in patients who have received a renal transplant. Approximately 30 per cent of transplanted patients have had a major

amputation after 10 years. A careful watch must be kept on the feet in these patients with podiatry advice on foot care and footwear.

For all types of renal replacement therapy, actuarial survival in patients with diabetes is worse than in matched non-diabetic patients. Cardiovascular disease and infection are the principal causes of death with relative mortality being three to fourfold higher in diabetic patients under the age of 54 compared to non-diabetic patients on RRT. For the diabetic ESRF population aged 45–54, the death rate due to ischaemic heart disease is 20–50 times that of the general population. Coronary angiography in asymptomatic diabetic peer patients prior to renal transplantation should be performed routinely.

Simultaneous pancreas and kidney transplantation is more technically challenging than renal transplantation alone; it requires higher levels of immunosuppression, carries an increased rate of infection and cancer and has little or no proven benefits on the chronic complications of diabetes. A successful kidney/pancreas transplant significantly improves the quality of life of a long-standing type 1 diabetic patient. A fully functioning pancreas will enable the relaxation of dietary restrictions, allow the cessation of insulin injections and blood glucose monitoring and lift the fear of hypoglycaemia. Against this must be balanced the data on survival and the progression of other diabetic complications. A recent paper demonstrated that the simultaneous kidney and pancreas transplantation significantly decrease mortality in patients with type 1 diabetes mellitus and ESRF[35] and there is preliminary evidence that long-term (10 years) successful pancreas transplantation may lead to regression of renal lesions.[36]

References

1. Trevisan R, Walker JD, Viberti GC. Diabetic nephropathy. In: Rex Jamison, Robert Wilkinson, eds. *Nephrology*, 2nd edn. London: Chapman & Hall, 1997: 551–74.

2. Mogensen CE. Definition of diabetic renal disease in insulin-dependent diabetes mellitus based on renal function tests. In: Mogensen CE, ed. *The Kidney and Hypertension in Diabetes Mellitus*, 4th edn. Kluwer Academic Publishers, Boston, Dordrecht, London, 1998: 17–30.

3. Rudberg S, Persson B, Dalquist G. Increased glomerular filtration rate as a predictor of diabetic nephropathy: an 8 year prospective study. *Kidney International*, 1992; **41**: 822–8.

4. Yip JW, Jones SL, Wiseman M, Viberti CC. Glomerular hyperfiltration in the prediction of nephropathy in IDDM: a 10 year follow-up study. *Diabetes*, 1996; **45**: 1729–33.

5. Mogensen CE. Micro-albuminuria, blood pressure and diabetic renal disease: origin and development of ideas. *Diabetologia*, 1999; **42**: 263–85.

6. Remuzzi G, Bertani T. Pathophysiology of progressive nephropathies. *New England Journal of Medicine*, 1998; **339**: 1448–56.

7. Ritz E, Orth SR. Nephropathy in patients with type 2 diabetes mellitus. *New England Journal of Medicine*, 1999; **341**: 1127–33.

8. Dinneen S, Gerstein HC. The association of micro-albuminuria and mortality in non-insulin-dependent diabetes mellitus. A systematic overview of the literature. *Archives of Internal Medicine*, 1997; **157**: 1413–18.

9. The Diabetes Control and Complications Trial Research Group. The effect of intensive treatment on the development and progression of long-term complications in insulin-dependent diabetes mellitus. *New England Journal of Medicine*, 1993; **329**: 977–86.

10. UK Prospective Diabetes Study Group. Intensive blood-glucose control with sulphonylureas or insulin compared with conventional treatment and risk of complications in patients with type 2 diabetes (UKPDS 33). *Lancet*, 1998; **352**: 837–53.

11. Buccala R, Vlassara H. Advanced glycosylation end products in diabetic renal and vascular disease. *American Journal of Kidney Disease*, 1995; **26**: 875–88.

12. Koya D, King Gl. Protein kinase C activation and the development of diabetic complications. *Diabetes*, 1998; **47**: 859–66.

13. Zatz R, Meyer TW, Rennke HG, Brenner BM. Predominance of hemodynamic rather than metabolic factors in the pathogenesis of diabetic glomerulopathy. *Proceedings of the National Academy of Sciences of the United States of America*, 1985; **82**: 5963–7.

14. Quinn M, Angelico MC, Warram JH, Krolewski AS. Familial factors determine the development of diabetic nephropathy in patients with IDDM. *Diabetologia*, 1996; **39**: 940–5.

15. Trevisan R *et al.* Clustering of risk factors in hypertensive insulin-dependent diabetics with high sodium–lithium countertransport. *Kidney International*, 1992; **41**: 855–61.

16. Trevisan R, Fioretto P, Barbosa J, Mauer M. Insulin-dependent diabetic sibling pairs are concordant for sodium–hydrogen antiport activity. *Kidney International*, 1999; **55**: 2383–9.

17. Marre M *et al.* Contribution of genetic polymorphism in the renin-angiotensin system to the development of renal complications in insulin-dependent diabetes. *Journal of Clinical Investigation*, 1997; **99**: 1585–95.

18. Bowden DW *et al.* Linkage of genetic markers on human chromosomes 20 and 12 to NIDDM in Caucasian sib-pairs with a history of diabetic nephropathy. *Diabetes*, 1997; **46**: 882–6.

19. Fujusawa T *et al.* Meta-analysis of association of insertion/deletion polymorphism of angiotensin-I converting enzyme gene with diabetic nephropathy and retinopathy. *Diabetologia*, 1998; **41**: 47–53.

20. Chowdhury TA, Dyer PH, Kumar S, Barnett AH, Bain SC. Genetic determinants of diabetic nephropathy. *Clinical Science*, 1999; **96**: 221–30.

21. Steffes MW, Bilous RW, Sutherland DER, Mauer SM. Cell and matrix components of the glomerulus in type 1 diabetes. *Diabetes*, 1992; **41**: 679–84.

22. Mauer SM, Steffes MW, Ellis EN, Sutherland DER, Brown DM, Goetz FC. Structural-functional realtionships in diabetic nephropathy. *Journal of Clinical Investigation*, 1984; **74**: 1143–55.

23. Lewis EJ, Hunsicker LG, Bain RP, Rohde RD. The effect of angiotensin converting enzyme inhibition on diabetic nephropathy. *New England Journal of Medicine*, 1993; **329**: 1456–62.

24. Bakris GL, Wier MR, DeQuattro V, McMahon FG. Effects of an ACE-inhibitor/calcium antagonist combination on proteinuria in diabetic nephropathy. *Kidney International*, 1998; **54**: 1283–9.

25. The Micro-albuminuria Captopril Study Group. Captopril reduces the risk of nephropathy in IDDM patients with micro-albuminuria. *Diabetologia*, 1996; **39**: 587–93.

26. Ravid M, Savin H, Jutrin I, Bental T, Katz B, Lishner M. Long-term stabilizing effect of angiotensin-converting enzyme inhibition on plasma creatinine and on proteinuria in normotensive type II diabetic patients. *Annals of Internal Medicine*, 1993; **118**: 577–81.

27. Heart Outcomes Prevention Evaluation (HOPE) Study Investigators. Effects of ramipril on cardiovascular and microvascular outcomes in people with diabetes mellitus: results of the HOPE study and MICRO-HOPE substudy. *Lancet*, 2000; **355**: 253–9.

28. UK Prospective Diabetes Study Group. Tight blood pressure control and risk of macrovascular and microvascular complications in type 2 diabetes (UKPDS 38). *British Medical Journal*, 1998; **317**: 703–13.

29. Hansson L, Zanchetti A, Carruthers SG *et al.* For the HOT Study Group. Effects of intensive blood-pressure lowering and low-dose aspirin in patients with hypertension: principal results of the Hypertension Optimal Treatment (HOT) randomised trial. *Lancet*, 1998; **351**: 1755–62.

30. The Sixth Report of the Joint National Committee on Prevention, Detection, Evaluation, and Treatment of High Blood Pressure. *Archives of Internal Medicine*, 1997; **157**: 2413–46.

31. Walker JD *et al.* Restriction of dietary protein and progression of renal failure in diabetic nephropathy. *Lancet*, 1989; **2**: 1411–14.

32. Pedrini MT, Levey AS, Lau J, Chalmers TC, Wang PH. The effect of dietary protein restriction on the progression of diabetic and non-diabetic renal disease: a meta-analysis. *Annals of Internal Medicine*, 1996; **124**: 627–32.

33. Alaveras AE, Thomas SM, Sagriotis A, Viberti GC. Promoters of progression of diabetic nephropathy: the relative roles of blood glucose and blood pressure control. *Nephrology Dialysis Transplantation*, 1994; **12**(suppl. 2): 71–4.

34. Gaede P, Vedel P, Parving HH, Pdersen O. Intensified multifactorial intervention in patients with type 2 diabetes mellitus and micro-albuminuria: the steno type 2 randomised study. *Lancet*, 1999; **353**: 617–22.

35. Smets YF *et al.* Effects of simultaneous pancreas–kidney transplantation on mortality of patients with type 1 diabetes mellitus and end-stage renal failure. *Lancet*, 1999; **353**: 1915–19.

36. Fioretto P, Steffes MW, Sutherland DE, Goetz FC, Mauer SM. Reversal of lesion of diabetic nephropathy after pancreas transplantation. *New England Journal of Medicine*, 1998; **339**: 69–75.

6 Diabetic neuropathy

Solomon Tesfaye

Diabetic neuropathy is one of the most common complications of diabetes. Its clinical manifestations include; numbness in the feet which often results in ulceration and infection, neuropathic pain which can be severe and disabling, and autonomic neuropathy which can involve several systems. Clinic and population based studies have shown surprisingly similar prevalence rates for diabetic polyneuropathy, approximately 30 per cent of all diabetic people.[1,2] The prevalence of neuropathy is related to age, duration of diabetes and the quality of metabolic control.[1,2] Furthermore, neuropathy appears to be related to other microvascular complications of diabetes: by the time a diabetic patient has severe neuropathy, retinopathy and albuminuria are also usually present.[3] Evidence is emerging that increasing height and cardiovascular risk factors (cigarette smoking, hypertension, hyperlipidaemia) may also be related to increased prevalence of neuropathy.[1,2,4] The type of diabetes does not appear to influence the prevalence of neuropathy, with reported prevalence rates being similar in both type 1 and type 2 diabetes of similar duration.

Classification and clinical features of diabetic neuropathies

As there is considerable overlap in clinical features, clinical classification of the various syndromes of diabetic neuropathies is difficult. However attempts at classification stimulate thought as to the aetiology of the various syndromes and also assist in the planning of management strategy. Watkins and Edmonds[5] have recently suggested a classification for diabetic neuropathies that separate them into three groups (Box 1):

(1) Progressive neuropathies are associated with increasing duration of diabetes and with other diabetic complications. These are predominantly sensory, however autonomic involvement is also common. The onset is gradual and there is no recovery.

(2) Reversible neuropathies have rapid onset, often occurring at the presentation of diabetes itself. They are not related to diabetes duration or other diabetic complications. There is usually complete recovery.

(3) Pressure palsies occur more frequently in the diabetic state but are not specific to diabetes. There is no association with duration of diabetes or other complications.

Chronic sensory motor neuropathy (chronic distal symmetrical neuropathy)

This is the most common neuropathic syndrome, affecting over 80 per cent of all neuropathic patients. It is a diffuse symmetrical disorder, affecting principally the feet in a stocking distribution, involvement of the hands in a glove pattern being rare. The pattern of sensory loss is length-related, with sensory symptoms starting in the toes and then extending to involve the feet and legs. There is a similar progression proximally starting in the fingers when there is upper

Box 1 Classification of diabetic neuropathies. Watkins and Edmonds *(Reference 5)*

- ◆ Progressive neuropathies
  - ■ Chronic sensori-motor neuropathy
    - • Distal symmetrical
    - • Predominantly sensory
    - • Autonomic involvement
    - • Gradual onset
    - • Progressive with increasing duration of diabetes
    - • Related to glycaemic control
    - • Related to other microvascular complications
- ◆ Reversible neuropathies
  - ■ Mononeuropathies
    - • Proximal motor neuropathy (amyotrophy)
    - • Cranial nerve palsies (III, IV, VI)
    - • Truncal radiculopathies
  - ■ Acute painful neuropathies
    - • Associated with poor glycaemic control
    - • Associated with rapid glycaemic control
    - • Sudden onset
    - • Spontaneous recovery
    - • Not related to other microvascular complications
    - • Not related to duration of diabetes
- ◆ Pressure palsies
  - ■ For example, carpal tunnel syndrome

limb involvement, usually within the context of very severe neuropathy. Most patients with chronic sensory motor neuropathy will have an autonomic component which is often sub-clinical and detected only by formal testing. As the disease advances, it becomes a sensory motor neuropathy, although significant motor involvement is uncommon early in the course of the disease. The onset is gradual and progresses with increasing duration of diabetes. The incidence of chronic sensory motor neuropathy appears to be related to poor glycaemic control.

Symptoms

Some patients may not have any symptoms that makes them seek medical advice. These are precisely the patients that end up having foot ulceration, often complicated with infection, that may result in amputation. Careful routine clinical examination is therefore very important in identifying vulnerable subjects. When pain is a feature, a progressive build-up of unpleasant sensory symptoms is described: tingling ('pins and needles', paraesthesia); burning pain; shooting pains down the legs; lancinating pains; contact pain with day-time clothes or bedclothes (allodynia); sensation of heat or cold in the feet; persistent aching cramp-like sensations; occasional pain on walking, often described as 'walking barefoot on marbles', or 'walking barefoot on hot sand'. Patients also sometimes describe 'negative' symptoms such as numbness and dead feeling. Pain is a subjective experience which can have differing qualities in different patients and it is important that patients are allowed to describe their symptoms in their own words. The feet and legs are principally affected with these symptoms, similar symptoms being rare in the upper limbs. This has prompted a speculation that the standing position, with its effects on the peripheral vascular system, may have an aetiological role in the development of peripheral neuropathy. Others have suggested that the longer nerve fibres may be affected, resulting in distal neuro-pathy, an assertion which has had recent supporting epidemiological evidence, showing that neuropathy preferentially affects taller people.[1,6] This does suggest a distal axonopathy of the 'dying-back' type in which neurones with the longest axons are unable to support the more distal parts, possibly because of impairment of axonal transport of structural proteins.

Diabetic neuropathic pain is characteristically more severe at night, hence interfering with sleep.[7] Chronic loss of sleep and unremitting pain can lead to loss of employment and may result in significant limitation in exercise tolerance, social isolation and depression.[8] Severe pain may extend above the feet and can involve the whole leg, when there will also be upper limb involvement.

While autonomic dysfunction is common, symptoms of autonomic neuropathy are rare. Abnormal cardiovascular tests have been reported in 16–40 per cent of diabetic subjects.[9]

Clinical signs

The earliest and the most common presenting abnormality is a reduction or absence of vibration sense in the toes. With disease progression there is sensory loss in a 'stocking' and sometimes 'glove' distribution, involving all sensory modalities. Involvement of the small fibres causes a reduction in pinprick and temperature sensation in a 'stocking and glove' distribution. The ankle tendon reflex is usually reduced or absent and in severe disease the knee reflexes may also be absent. In advanced neuropathy there may be severe large

fibre disease, with impairment of proprioception. The patient may then have sensory ataxia associated with a positive Romberg's sign. Muscle power is usually normal, although mild weakness may be found in toe extensors, however there may be significant generalized muscular wasting, particularly in the small muscles of the hands and feet, with speedy progression. Wasting of the small muscles of the foot results in 'clawing', creating pressure points at the metatarsal heads, leading to callus formation and recurrent foot ulceration.

In patients with advanced neuropathy involvement of the upper limbs and the fine movements of the fingers are affected and the patient may complain of having difficulty in recognizing and handling small objects.

The feet should be carefully inspected, looking for foot ulceration and deformities. The skin is often dry and likely to crack as a result of autonomic neuropathy, pre-disposing to risk of foot ulceration and infection. When there is no peripheral vascular disease, the neuropathic foot is warm because of arterio-venous shunting.[10] The veins are distended and fail to collapse when the foot is elevated. The oxygen tension of blood in these veins is typically raised.[11,12] Autonomic neuropathy can also result in neuropathic leg oedema, which is resistant to treatment with diuretics and often interferes with the healing of diabetic foot ulcers. Rarely, patients with both somatic and autonomic neuropathy may develop Charcot's neuro-arthropathy (see Chapter 9, p. 107). Diabetes is now the leading cause of this condition. The Charcot foot has characteristic deformities which may be the result of repeated, apparently trivial, injuries which are not recognized by the patient because of impaired pain sensation. Blood flow to the foot is typically increased and peripheral vascular disease is usually absent.[12] In advanced Charcot joint there is destruction of joint surfaces and bones, resulting in gross anatomical deformities which make the foot vulnerable to ulceration.

Proximal motor neuropathy (amyotrophy, femoral neuropathy)

This syndrome of progressive asymmetrical proximal leg weakness and muscle atrophy usually affects diabetic patients over the age of 50.[13] An associated weight loss can sometimes be severe and raise the possibility of occult malignancy. On examination there is profound wasting of the quadriceps femoris with marked weakness in these muscle groups. Occasionally hip flexors and hip abductors can also be affected.[14] The patient may complain of difficulty in getting out of a low chair or climbing stairs. The patient also presents with severe pain deep in the thigh and often unremitting. Knee reflexes are depressed or absent. Sensory loss is unusual and if present indicates co-existent distal sensory neuropathy.

Other causes of quadriceps wasting such as nerve root and cauda aquina lesions and occult malignancy causing proximal myopathy should be carefully excluded. An X-ray of the lumbar sacral spine, an erythrocyte sedimentation rate (ESR), and an ultrasound of the abdomen may be required. Electrophysiological studies and magnetic resonance (MR) imaging of the lumbar spine may also be required.[14]

Coppak and Watkins reported that pain usually starts to settle after about three months and usually settles completely by one year, whereas the knee-jerk reflex is restored in 50 per cent of patients after two years.[13] Management is largely symptomatic and supportive. Patients should be reassured that the condition is likely to improve within a few months and is likely to resolve completely. Tight glycaemic control may be beneficial, although there is still controversy as to whether the use of insulin therapy influences the natural history of this syndrome.[13] Symptomatic treatment of the pain associated with this syndrome is often necessary with a tricyclic agent (for example, imipramine or amitriptyline 25–150 mg, taken before bed).

Cranial nerve palsy

The third cranial nerve palsy is by far the most common mononeuropathy (other than 'entrapment' neuropathies such as carpal tunnel syndrome). There is an acute presentation of pain in the orbit, or sometimes frontal headache.[15] On examination, there is ptosis and ophthalmoplegia often affecting the eye, the pupil usually being spared.[16] Complete recovery usually occurs within three months. The focal nature of the lesions on the third cranial nerve, and the clinical features with an acute onset and the time course taken for recovery, suggest a vascular aetiology.[15] Exclusion of any other cause for third cranial nerve palsy (aneurysm or tumour) by computerized tomographic (CT) or MR imaging is important. Sixth and seventh cranial nerve palsies have also been described in diabetic patients, but these are extremely rare.

Truncal radiculopathies

Diabetic truncal radiculopathies are characterized by an acute onset of pain in a dermatomal distribution over the lower thorax or the abdomen.[17] The pain is asymmetrical and can cause local bulging.[18] Associated patchy sensory loss is often a clue to the diagnosis. Exclusion of other causes of nerve root compression is important. Diagnosis can be difficult in those presenting with abdominal pain and some patients have undergone unnecessary investigations such as barium enema, colonoscopy and even laparotomy when the diagnosis could easily have been made by careful clinical history and examination. The patient can be reassured strongly as complete recovery is usual within a year, although occasionally symptoms can persist for a few years.

Acute painful neuropathies

These neuropathic syndromes are relatively uncommon and are characterized by a sudden onset of pain affecting the feet and legs in a symmetrical fashion. Two clinical syndromes have been identified – one occurring within the context of poor glycaemic control and the other within the context of rapid improvement in glycaemic control. Acute painful neuropathies are not related to the presence of other chronic diabetic complications.

Acute painful neuropathy of poor glycaemic control

This syndrome may occur in patients with poor glycaemic control. There is marked weight loss and Ellenburg coined the term 'neuropathic cachexia'. There is usually severe pain which is typically of burning quality and persistent, but some patients describe intermittent bouts of shooting pain as well. There may be a subjective feeling of the legs being swollen and there is usually contact pain (allodynia). The rapid onset, the severity and the nocturnal exacerbation of

symptoms often lead to depression. On clinical examination, there is little in the way of signs and sensory loss is often mild and sometimes absent. There are usually no motor signs although the ankle jerks are lost in a few. Nerve conduction tests are usually normal or mildly abnormal but temperature discrimination threshold is often reduced. There is complete resolution of symptoms within one year, and weight gain is usual with improvement in glycaemic control using exogenous insulin.

Acute painful neuropathy of rapid glycaemic control ('insulin neuritis')

This syndrome occurs within the setting of a rapid improvement of glycaemic control either with the start of insulin or hypoglycaemic oral agents.[19] There are burning pain, paraesthesia and allodynia, often with nocturnal exacerbation and depression may be a feature. There is no associated weight loss, sensory loss is mild or absent and there are no motor signs. Nerve conduction studies are normal but there is impaired exercise-induced increment in conduction velocity.[20] There is complete resolution of symptoms within one year.

Pressure (entrapment) neuropathies

Pressure (entrapment) neuropathies affecting the median and ulnar nerve are more common in the diabetic population than in the general population. Median nerve entrapment (carpal tunnel syndrome) causes pain and paraesthesiae in the hands, sometimes radiating to the forearm, particularly marked at night. Examination reveals a reduction of sensation in the median territory of the hand (lateral 3½ fingers) and wasting of muscle bulk in the thenar eminence. The diagnosis is confirmed by median nerve conduction studies and treatment involves surgical decompression of the carpal tunnel in the wrist. The response to surgery is usually good but occasionally painful symptoms may relapse.

Ulnar nerve entrapment at the ulnar groove in the elbow can also cause wasting of the dorsal interossia, particularly the first dorsal interossie. This is easily confirmed by ulnar electrophysiological studies that localize the lesion to the elbow. Other nerves that are vulnerable to entrapment are the lateral popliteal nerve which results in foot drop, the radial nerve which can result in wrist drop and the lateral cutaneous nerve of the thigh causing meralgia paraesthetica.

Pathogenesis of diabetic neuropathy

A number of peripheral nerve morphometric studies have demonstrated that distal symmetrical neuropathy is characterized by distal axonal loss, with a 'dying back' phenomenon. Myelinated fibre density is reduced.[21] The small and unmyelinated fibres that make up around 80 per cent of all nerve fibres are more difficult to assess. Teased fibre preparations also show focal areas of demyelination.[22] Nerve regenerative activity may also be seen with the emergence of 'regenerative clusters',[23] containing groups of myelinated and non-myelinated axon sprouts.

Despite considerable research, we still do not have a comprehensive explanation for the pathogenesis of diabetic neuropathy, although metabolic and vascular[24] hypotheses have been proposed (Box 2). There is now little doubt that chronic hyperglycaemia is implicated.

Box 2 Some of the proposed hypotheses of diabetic peripheral nerve damage

- Chronic hyperglycaemia
- Nerve microvascular dysfunction
- Polyol pathway hyperactivity
- Protein kinase C hyperactivity
- Non-enzymatic glycation
- Increased free radical formation
- Abnormalities of nerve growth factors

The EURODIAB IDDM Complications Study,[1] The Diabetes Control and Complications Trial (DCCT)[25] and more recently the United Kingdom Prospective Diabetes Study (UKPDS)[26] have demonstrated that poor glycaemic control is related to increased prevalence of neuropathy and other microvascular complications in diabetic patients and that, improved glycaemic control may prevent/reverse diabetic neuropathy. However, unravelling exactly how hyperglycaemia causes nerve damage has been a major stumbling block.

Polyol pathway hyperactivity

In 1966, Gabbay *et al.* postulated polyol pathway (Fig. 1) hyperactivity as a mechanism which could link hyperglycaemia to neuropathy.[27] Hyperglycaemia led to sorbitol accumulation in the peripheral nerve due to increased conversion from glucose, via the enzyme aldose reductase. This is supported by the demonstration of elevated sorbitol levels in diabetic nerves.[28,29] Elevated sorbitol levels are associated with depletion of myoinositol, which is important in phosphoinositide metabolism, and reduction in Na^+-K^+-ATPase which has an important role in the exchange of intra- and extra-cellular sodium and hence nerve membrane potential.[28,29] Aldose reductase inhibitors (ARIs) administered to either diabetic animals[30] or humans[31] result in an improvement in nerve conduction velocity. Some improvement in nerve fibre count has also been reported,[32] but there have been no unequivocal demonstration of amelioration of symptoms and clinical signs in humans. There is great controversy as to whether these agents should be used in routine clinical practice without definite proof of benefit and with the possibility of long-term side effects. A number of clinical trials are currently taking place with newer ARIs in early neuropathy (as in advanced neuropathy the nerve is highly disorganized and is unlikely to respond to treatment) and the results are eagerly awaited.

Non-enzymatic glycation

Non-enzymatic glycosylation of proteins is a feature of diabetes[33] and has been demonstrated in brain tubulin and peripheral nerve. This process may be an important initiating factor for nerve demyelination interfering with axonal transport. Advanced glycation end products (AGE) can also absorb ('quench') nitric oxide (NO), a potent vasodilator, and hence lead to impaired nerve blood flow.[34] Aminoguanidine, which inhibits AGE formation, has been shown to

Fig. 1 The polyol pathway.

improve nerve conduction deficits and blood flow in experimental diabetes,[35] although its role in human diabetic neuropathy is still undetermined.

Oxidative stress

In diabetes there is increased free radical generation partly as a result of non-enzymatic glycation and polyol pathway hyperactivity. The capacity to neutralize free radicals is also reduced, as polyol pathway hyperactivity leads to NADH depletion.[36] Thus, oxidative stress may impair nerve function by direct toxic effects or by reducing NO and nerve blood flow. Recent studies in rats with experimental diabetes have shown that free radical scavengers may improve nerve conduction velocity abnormalities[37] and these findings need to be proved in human diabetic neuropathy.

Neurotrophic factors

Neurotrophic factors are important in the growth and development of neurones. Amongst these are insulin-like growth factors-I and -II and the neurotrophin (NT) family. The NT family includes nerve growth factor (NGF), the levels of which are reduced in experimental diabetes.[38] NGF treatment corrects some aspects of sensory neuropathy related to small fibre dysfunction in diabetic rats. A recent clinical trial looking into the effect of parenteral NGF in human diabetic neuropathy was stopped because of lack of effect. The role of nerve growth factors in diabetic neuropathy needs to be explored further.

Protein kinase C activation

Diabetes leads to hyperactivity of vascular protein kinase C (PKC), in particular, the β-isoform,[39] via increased synthesis of diacylglycerol (DAG) from glucose. PKC activation is associated with abnormalities in vascular function. In rats with streptozotocin diabetes, retinal blood flow is decreased in parallel with an increase in retinal PKC activity. PKC inhibitor treatment corrected deficits in retinal perfusion and prevented the early glomerular hyperfiltration and increased urinary albumin excretion in diabetic rats and has recently been shown to correct nerve conduction velocity and perfusion deficits and to protect endothelial dependent relaxation.[40] There is currently a clinical trial of a PKC inhibitor in patients with mild to moderate neuropathy and the results are awaited.

Microvascular factors

There is now little doubt of the presence of severe microvascular disease at the stage of clinical diabetic neuropathy.[24,41] Several workers have demonstrated basal membrane thickening of endoneural capillaries, degeneration of pericytes, hyperplasia and swelling of endothelial cells and sometimes vessel closure. The degree of microvascular disease has been correlated with the severity of neuropathy.[42] *In vivo* studies in human subjects have demonstrated epineural arterio-venous shunting, diverting blood from the nutritive endoneural circulation, and impairing nerve blood flow.[43] The impairment of nerve blood flow causes a fall in endoneural oxygenation.[44]

In addition to direct measurement involving human peripheral nerve, other studies provide indirect evidence supporting a vascular aetiology for diabetic neuropathy. Strenuous exercise increases nerve blood flow and increases nerve conduction velocity by an average of 4 metres/sec in non-neuropathic diabetic patients. However, this increase is absent in neuropathic subjects, as the nerve microvasculature is severely diseased.[20] Moreover, there is a strong correlation between nerve conduction velocity and lower limb transcutaneous oxygenation measurements in diabetes; macrovascular disease appears to exacerbate neuropathy and surgical restoration of perfusion improves nerve conduction velocity.[45] A recent epidemiological study has also found a strong correlation between diabetic neuropathy and cardiovascular risk factors including body weight, hypertension, smoking and reduced high-density lipoprotein (HDL) cholesterol.[1]

In addition to human studies, impairment of blood flow has been found to be an early feature in rats with streptozotocin diabetes.[46] Several vasodilators have been found to enhance nerve blood flow and nerve function in diabetic animals.[34,47] In human diabetic neuropathy, angiotensin-converting enzyme inhibitors have been found to improve nerve function.[48,49] The presence of severe microvascular changes in subjects with acute painful neuropathy of rapid glycaemic control (insulin neuritis), hitherto thought to be purely metabolic in origin, provides an even more compelling evidence for the importance of microvascular factors in the pathogenesis of distal symmetric neuropathy.[19]

In summary, a number of metabolic derangements brought about by the diabetic state mentioned above have an impact on nerve perfusion, the vascular endothelium being a major target. Oxidative stress, activation of the PKC system and non-enzymatic glycation lead to reduced nerve NO. Occlusion of endoneural capillaries and the presence of haemorrhagic abnormalities associated with diabetes further exacerbate the impairment of nerve blood flow leading to nerve hypoxia and hence nerve structural and functional abnormalities (Fig. 2).

Autonomic neuropathy

Diabetes is a major cause of autonomic nervous system dysfunction affecting a number of systems (Box 3). Although abnormalities of autonomic function are very common in subjects with longstanding diabetes, clinically significant autonomic dysfunction is uncommon. Autonomic neuropathy has a gradual onset and is slowly progressive. The prevalence of diabetic autonomic neuropathy depends on the population studied and the number of tests of autonomic function employed. In the EURODIAB study, the prevalence of autonomic neuropathy, defined as the presence of two abnormal cardiovascular autonomic function tests, was 24 per cent. The neuropathy increased with age, duration of diabetes, glycaemic control and presence of cardiovascular risk factors (low HDL-cholesterol, hypertension and cigarette smoking).[50]

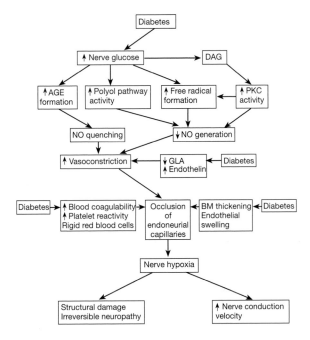

Fig. 2 A figure (adapted from Ward and Tesfaye. Pathogenesis of diabetic neuropathy. In: Pickup J, Williams G, eds. *Textbook of Diabetes*, 1997; **2**: 49.1–49.19) uniting biochemical and vascular factors in the pathogenesis of diabetic neuropathy. AGE: Advanced glycation end products; DAG: diacylglycerol; PKC: protein kinase C; BM: basement membrane; GLA: γ-linolenic acid; NO: nitric oxide.

Cardiovascular autonomic neuropathy

Cardiovascular autonomic neuropathy results in postural hypotension, change in peripheral blood flow and may be a cause of sudden death.

Postural hypotension

It is now generally accepted that a fall in systolic blood pressure of over 20 mmHg while standing is abnormal. Coincidental treatment with tricyclic antidepressants for neuropathic pain, or diuretic therapy may exacerbate postural hypotension, the chief symptom of which is dizziness on standing, although some patients may not have any symptoms. The symptoms can be disabling for some patients who may not be able to walk for more than a few minutes. In clinical practice, the severity of dizziness does not correlate with the postural drop in blood pressure. There is increased mortality in people with postural hypotension, although the reasons for this are not clear. The management of patients with postural hypotension poses major problems, and for some there may not be any satisfactory treatment. Current treatment includes improving glycaemic control, advising patients to get up from the sitting or lying position slowly, treatment with fludrocortisone (usual starting dose 0.1 mg which can be gradually increased to maximal daily dose of 0.5 mg) while carefully monitoring urea and electrolytes, and the use of support stockings. In severe cases, 'anti-gravity' or 'space suits' to compress the lower limbs, the α-1 adrenal receptor agonist, midodrine and octreotide may be used.

Box 3 Clinical manifestations of autonomic neuropathy

- ◆ Cardiovascular
  - ▪ Resting tachycardia
  - ▪ Heart rate abnormalities
  - ▪ Oedema
  - ▪ Postural hypotension
  - ▪ Arrhythmia
  - ▪ Sudden death
- ◆ Genitourinary
  - ▪ Erectile dysfunction
  - ▪ Retrograde ejaculation
  - ▪ Atonic bladder
  - ▪ Bladder infection
  - ▪ Abnormal renal sodium handling
- ◆ Gastrointestinal
  - ▪ Gastroparesis
  - ▪ Diarrhoea
  - ▪ Constipation
- ◆ Dermatological
  - ▪ Gustatory sweating
  - ▪ Dry skin
  - ▪ Sudomotor dysfunction
  - ▪ Arterio-venous shunting
- ◆ Neurological
  - ▪ Pupillary dysfunction
- ◆ Respiratory
  - ▪ Bronchoconstrictor dysfunction

Changes in peripheral blood flow

Autonomic neuropathy can cause arterio-venous shunting, with prominent veins in the neuropathic leg.[10] The venous oxygen tension,[11] skin blood flow,[51] and capillary pressure[52] are increased in the neuropathic leg due to sympathetic denervation. Thus in the absence of peripheral vascular disease the neuropathic foot is warm, and this may be one of the factors that causes the osteopenia associated with the development of Charcot neuro-arthropathy.

Cardiovascular autonomic function tests

Five cardiovascular autonomic function tests are now widely used for the assessment of autonomic function. These tests are non-invasive, and do not require sophisticated equipment (all that is required is an electrocardiogram machine, an aneroid pressure gauge attached to a mouthpiece, a hand grip dynamometer and sphygmomanometer). Table 1 shows reference values for cardiovascular autonomic function tests.[53]

Autonomic gastroparesis

Autonomic neuropathy can affect the upper gastrointestinal system by reducing oesophageal motility (causing dysphagia and heartburn), and gastroparesis (reduced gastric emptying causing bloating, early satiety, vomiting and swings in blood glucose).[54] The diagnosis of gastroparesis is often made on clinical grounds by the evaluation of symptoms and sometimes the presence of succussion splash, while barium swallow and follow through, or gastroscopy may reveal a large food residue in the stomach. Gastric motility and emptying studies can be performed in specialized units, and may help with diagnosis, but glycaemic control at the time of investigation is critical, as hyperglycaemia *per se* impairs gastric emptying.

Management of diabetic gastroparesis includes optimization of glycaemic control, the use of anti-emetics (metoclopramide and domperidone), the use of cholinergic agent which stimulates oesophageal motility (erythromycin enhances the activity of the gut peptide motilin) (Box 4). Severe gastroparesis causing recurrent vomiting is associated with dehydration, swings in blood glucose and weight loss and is an indication for hospital admission. The patient should be adequately hydrated with intravenous fluids and blood glucose should be stabilized by intravenous insulin. Anti-emetics are given intravenously and if the course is prolonged, total parenteral nutrition or feeding through a gastrostomy tube may be required. There is one recent report of surgical amelioration of symptomatic late gastroparesis[55] in carefully selected patients.

Autonomic diarrhoea

The patient may present with diarrhoea which tends to be worse at night, or alternatively some may present with constipation. Both the diarrhoea and constipation respond to conventional treatment (Box 4). Diarrhoea associated with bactrial overgrowth may respond to treatment with a broad spectrum antibiotic such as erythromycin, tetracycline, or ampicillin.

Abnormal sweating

Increased sweating usually affecting the face, and often brought about by eating (gustatory sweating) can be very embarrassing for the patients. Reduced sweating in the feet of affected patients can cause dry feet producing risk of fissuring and hence infection. Unfortunately, there is no satisfactory treatment for gustatory sweating, although the anti-cholinergic drug poldine may be useful in a minority of patients. Night sweating can also be problematic but must be differentiated from hypoglycaemia, menopausal flushing, chronic infection or malignancy.

Abnormalities of bladder function

Bladder dysfunction is a rare complication of autonomic neuropathy when there is sacral nerve involvement. The patient presents with hesitancy or increased frequency of micturition and, in serious cases, with urinary retention with overflow incontinence. Such a patient is prone to urinary tract infections. Ultrasound scanning of the urinary tract, cystometrography, and intravenous urography may be required for diagnosis. Treatment manoeuvres include mechanical methods of bladder emptying by applying supra-pubic pressure or intermittent

Table 1 Cardiovascular autonomic function test (Reference (53))

	Normal	**Borderline**	**Abnormal**
Heart rate tests			
Heart rate response to standing up (30 : 15 ratio)	$\geqslant 1.04$	1.01–1.03	$\leqslant 1.00$
Heart rate response to deep breathing (maximum minus minimum heart rate)	$\geqslant 15$ beats/min	11–14 beats/min	$\leqslant 10$ beats/min
Heart rate response to Valsalva manoeuvre (Valsalva ratio)	$\geqslant 1.21$	–	$\leqslant 1.20$
Blood pressure tests			
Blood pressure response to standing up (fall in systolic BP)	$\leqslant 10$ mmHg	11–29 mmHg	$\geqslant 30$ mmHg
Blood pressure response to sustained handgrip (increase in diastolic BP)	$\geqslant 16$ mmHg	11–15 mmHg	$\leqslant 10$ mmHg

Box 4 Treatment of diarrhoea and gastroparesis due to autonomic neuropathy

- ◆ Diarrhoea
  - ▪ Codeine phosphate 30 mg 3 times/day
  - ▪ Loperamide 2 mg 3 times/day
  - • Oxytetracycline 250 mg 4 times/day
  - • Erythromycin 250 mg 4 times/day
  } A one week course may suffice for bacterial overgrowth. Occasionally longer periods required at lower doses.

- ◆ Gastroparesis
  - ▪ Metoclopromide 10 mg 4 times/day
  - ▪ Domperidone 10–20 mg 3 times/day
  - ▪ Erythromycin 250 mg 3 times/day
  - ▪ Hospital admission required if severe for intravenous fluids and insulin

self-catheterization. Anticholinesterase drugs such as neostigmine or peridostigmine may be useful. Long-term indwelling catheterization may be required in some, but this predisposes the patient to urinary tract infections and long-term antibiotic prophylaxis may then be required.

Erectile dysfunction

Autonomic neuropathy also contributes to diabetic erectile dysfunction, as does vascular disease. Diabetic men are also not protected from the erectile dysfunction due to other illnesses; which includes poor glycaemic control, side-effects of other therapies (including anti-hypertensive medication) and as a result of psycho-sexual or social issues. Treatment with sildenafil may be used, if there are no contra-indications; or engorgement of the penile vasculature can be achieved mechanically using vacuum pumps or with vaso-active drugs such as papaverine (with or without phentolamine) or drosvaglandin E, which are given intracavernosally or via the urethra. Surgery may be required, where large vessel disease is a significant contributor.

Treatment

The two chief presentations of diabetic neuropathy are pain and numb foot, which predisposes the patient to foot ulceration. The problems associated with the numb foot are discussed in Chapter 9. The treatment scenario for painful neuropathy is less than satisfactory as currently available treatment approaches are highly symptomatic and often ineffective[7] (Box 5). Potential therapeutic agents that have the capacity to prevent or reverse the neuropathic process will emerge, as the pathological processes leading to diabetic nerve damage become clear.

A careful history and examination of the patient is essential in order to exclude other possible causes of leg pain such as peripheral vascular disease, prolapsed intervertebral discs, spinal canal stenosis and cauda aquina lesions. Unilateral leg pain should arouse a suspicion that the pain may be due to lumbar-sacral nerve root compression. These patients may well need to be investigated with a lumbar-sacral MR imaging. Other causes of peripheral neuropathy such as excessive alcohol intake and B_{12} deficiency should be excluded. The quality and severity should be assessed where pain is

Box 5 Management of painful diabetic neuropathy

- Exclusion of other causes of neuropathy
- Optimization of glycaemic control
- Psychological support for the patient
- Non pharmacological treatments: for example, bed cradle, opsite for contact pain
- Pharmacological treatments
  - Optimization of glycaemic control (if necessary with insulin in patients with type 2 diabetes)
  - Tricyclic antidepressants (imipramine or amitriptyline, 25–150 mg taken at night; SSRIs if tricyclics are not well tolerated)
  - Anticonvulsants (gabapentin 900–3600 mg/day in divided doses, carbamazepine 200–800 mg/day)
  - Tramadol (50–400 mg/day)
  - Capsaicin cream (0.075%)
  - IV lignocaine (0.5 mg/kg given over 30 min)
  - Electric spinal cord stimulation if no response or if there are unacceptable side effects to pharmacotherapy

the predominant symptom. Neuropathic pain can be disabling in some patients and an empathic approach is essential. Patients should be allowed to express their symptoms freely without too many interruptions. Psychological support of the patient with painful neuropathy is an important aspect of the overall management.

Symptomatic treatment

Glycaemic control

There is now little doubt that good blood sugar control is the only treatment that prevents/delays the onset of diabetic neuropathy.[25] In addition, painful neuropathic symptoms are also improved by tight metabolic control, if necessary with the use of insulin in type 2 diabetes.[56] The first step in the management of painful neuropathy is a concerted effort aimed at improving glycaemic control.

Tricyclic compounds

Tricyclic compounds are now regarded as the first line treatment for painful diabetic neuropathy.[7] A number of double blind clinical trials have confirmed their effectiveness beyond any doubt. These drugs have unwanted side-effects such as drowsiness, anti-cholinergic side-effects such as dry mouth and dizziness due to postural hypotension in those that have co-incidental autonomic neuropathy. Patients should be started on imipramine or amitriptyline at a low dose (25–50 mg taken before bed), the dose gradually titrated if necessary up to 150 mg per day. The mechanism of action of tricyclic compounds in improving neuropathic pain is not known, but their effect does not appear to be through their antidepressant property, as they are effective even in those with a depressed mood.[7]

Anticonvulsants

Anticonvulsants, including carbamazepine,[7] phenytoin[7] and more recently gabapentin[57] have also been found effective in the relief of moderate to severe neuropathic pain. Unfortunately, treatment with anticonvulsants is often complicated with troublesome side-effects such as sedation, dizziness and ataxia. Treatment should be started at a relatively low dose and gradually increased to maintenance dose of these drugs, while carefully monitoring potential side-effects (Box 5).

Topical capsaicin

Topical capsaicin (0.075 per cent) applied sparingly 3–4 times per day to the affected area has been found to relieve neuropathic pain. Topical capsaicin works by depleting substance 'P' from nerve terminals, and there may be worsening of neuropathic symptoms for the first 2–4 weeks of application.[58]

Intravenous lignocaine and oral mexiletine

Intravenous lignocaine at a dose of 5 mg/kg body-weight administered over 30 min with a cardiac monitor *in situ*, has also been found to be effective in relieving neuropathic pain for up to two weeks.[59] This form of treatment is useful in subjects that are having severe pain which is not responding to the above agents, although it does necessitate bringing the patient into hospital for a few hours. Oral mexiletine, which has similar structure to lignocaine, may have a beneficial effect at reducing neuropathic pain, given at the dose of 10 mg/kg body-weight.[7]

α-lipoic acid

Infusion of the antioxidant α-lipoic acid at a dose of 600 mg intravenously per day over a three week period (5–5–4 day), has also been found to be useful in reducing neuropathic pain.[60]

Management of disabling painful neuropathy not responding to pharmacological treatment

Neuropathic pain can be extremely severe, interfering significantly with a patient's daily activities and sleep. Some patients may not be helped by conventional pharmacological treatments. Such patients pose a major challenge as they are severely distressed and sometimes wheelchair bound. A recent study has demonstrated that such patients may respond to electrical spinal cord stimulation, which relieves both background and peak neuropathic pain.[8] This form of treatment is particularly advantageous, as the patient does not have to take any of the other pain relieving medications, with all their side effects. A recent follow-up of patients fitted with electrical spinal cord stimulators found that stimulators continued to be effective five years after implantation. Transcutaneous electrical nerve stimulation (TENS) may also be beneficial for the relief of localized neuropathic pain in one limb.[61]

Potential therapeutic agents

Based on the proposed hypotheses of nerve damage in diabetes, detailed above, a number of pharmacological agents have been studied, primarily in diabetic animals, to see if they could prevent/reverse conduction deficits associated with diabetes.

Aldose reductase inhibitors (ARIs)

In the polyol pathway, glucose is converted to sorbital, which is in turn converted to fructose (Fig. 1). The key enzyme in this pathway is aldose reductase. Over the past 20 years several studies have linked increased activity of this pathway with the various complications of diabetes, including neuropathy (see above). However, although ARIs appear to be effective in preventing/reversing nerve conduction deficits associated with neuropathy in animal models, the results are less convincing in human diabetic neuropathy. As a result no ARI has been licensed for the treatment of neuropathy in the Western world. Several, large multicentre trials are now taking place, with newer and more potent ARIs and hopefully these will provide more information about the potential value of ARIs for the treatment of clinical diabetic neuropathies.

Vaso-active agents

Studies in rats with streptozotocin diabetes have recently shown that several vaso-active agents that have the capacity to improve nerve blood flow, also have a beneficial effect in preventing/reversing peripheral nerve dysfunction. Among vaso-active agents that have the capacity to improve nerve blood flow are angiotensin-converting enzyme-inhibitors, angiotensin-II receptor blockers, calcium channel antagonists, prostanoid analogues, gamma linolenic acid, and antioxidants.[24,34] In human diabetic neuropathy, the angiotensin-converting enzyme inhibitor lisinopril,[48] and more recently trandolapril[49] have been shown to improve nerve function. Currently, clinical trials are taking place to assess the effectiveness of PKC-β inhibitors in improving several parameters of nerve function in subjects with early to moderate diabetic neuropathy.

Inhibitors of advanced glycation end products (AGE)

AGE have been implicated in the pathogenesis of chronic complications of diabetes. Aminoguanidine which inhibits AGE formation has been found to improve nerve function and blood flow in diabetic animals.[62] However, the role of aminoguanidine remains to be proven in human diabetic neuropathy.

Spinal cord involvement in diabetic neuropathy

Recently magnetic resonance imaging was used to measure spinal cord cross sectional area in diabetic subjects with and without peripheral neuropathy and in healthy controls.[63] A significant reduction in cord cross sectional area was found in people with diabetic peripheral neuropathy compared to normal control subjects.[63] This would indicate that at this stage of clinical diabetic neuropathy an extensive, and perhaps even irreversible, damage has occurred. Indeed, with this result in mind, perhaps it is not surprising that the variety of therapeutic options so far attempted in human diabetic neuropathy has not been successful. This does underpin the need to detect neuropathy early. The mechanism of spinal cord involvement is unclear. One possibility may be that damage to the peripheral nerves causes secondary spinal cord 'shrinkage' due to degeneration or atrophy. It is also possible that the primary insult may be to the central nervous system, with the well documented peripheral changes occurring as secondary phenomena. However, the published post-mortem findings of microvascular disease within the spinal cord, similar to that seen to the peripheral nerve, would suggest that the same pathogenic

mechanisms may be involved in both areas, and that the processes are concomitant. Further work is required to investigate if spinal cord involvement is an early feature in the neuropathic process.

References

1. **Tesfaye S** et al. The prevalence of diabetic neuropathy and its relation to glycaemic control and potential risk factors: the EURODIAB IDDM Complications Study. *Diabetologia*, 1996; **39**: 1377–84.

2. **Maser RE, Steenkiste AR, Dorman JS** et al. Epidemiological correlates of diabetic neuropathy. Report from Pittsburgh Epidemiology of Diabetes Complications Study. *Diabetes*, 1989; **38**: 1456–61.

3. **Pirart J.** Diabetes mellitus and its degenerative complications: a prospective study of 4000 patients observed. *Diabetes Care*, 1978; **1**: 168–88, 252–63.

4. **Shaw AE, Zimmet PZ.** The epidemiology of diabetic neuropathy. *Diabetes Reviews*, 1999; **7**: 245–52.

5. **Watkins PJ, Edmonds ME.** Clinical features of diabetic neuropathy. In: Pickup J, Williams G, eds. *Textbook of Diabetes*. Oxford: Blackwell Science, 1997; **2**: 50.1–50.20.

6. **Sosenko JM, Gadia MT, Fournier AM, O'Connell MT, Aguiar MC, Skyler JS.** Body stature as a risk factor for diabetic sensory neuropathy. *American Journal of Medicine*, 1986; **80**: 1031–4.

7. **Tesfaye S, Price D.** Therapeutic approaches in diabetic neuropathy and neuropathic pain. In: Boulton AJM, ed. *Diabetic Neuropathy*. Carnforth: Marius Press, 1997; **1**: 159–81.

8. **Tesfaye S, Watt J, Benbow SJ, Pang KA, Miles J, MacFarlane IA.** Electrical spinal cord stimulation for painful diabetic peripheral neuropathy. *Lancet*, 1996; **348**: 1696–701.

9. **Zeigler D** et al. Prevalence and clinical correlates of cardiovascular autonomic and peripheral diabetic neuropathy in patients attending diabetes centres. The Diacan Multicentre Study Group. *Diabetes and Metabolism*, 1993; **19**: 143–51.

10. **Ward JD, Simms JM, Knight G, Boulton AJM, Sandler DA.** Venous distension in the diabetic neuropathic foot (physical sign of arterio-venous shunting). *Journal of Royal Society of Medicine*, 1983; **76**: 1011–14.

11. **Boulton AJM, Scarpello JHB, Ward JD.** Venous oxygenation in the diabetic neuropathic foot: evidence of arterio-venous shunting? *Diabetologia*, 1982; **22**: 6–8.

12. **Shaw JE, Boulton AJM.** Charcot neuropathy. *The Foot*, 1995; **5**: 65–70.

13. **Coppack SW, Watkins PJ.** The natural history of femoral neuropathy *Quarterly Journal of Medicine*, 1991; **79**: 307–13.

14. **Subramony SH, Willbourn AJ.** Diabetic proximal neuropathy. Clinical and electromyographic studies. *Journal of Neurological Science*, 1982; **53**: 293–304.

15. **Asbury AK, Aldredge H, Hershberg R, Fisher CM.** Oculomotor palsy in diabetes mellitus: a clinicopathological study. *Brain*, 1970; **93**: 555–7.

16. **Goldstein JE, Cogan DG.** Diabetic ophthalmoplegia with special reference to the pupil. *Archives of Ophthalmology*, 1960; **64**: 592–600.

17. **Ellenberg M.** Diabetic truncal mononeuropathy – a new clinical syndrome. *Diabetes Care*, 1978; **1**: 10–13.

18. **Boulton AJM, Angus E, Ayyar DR, Weiss R.** Diabetic thoracic polyradiculopathy presenting as abdominal swelling. *British Medical Journal*, 1984; **289**: 798–9.

19. **Tesfaye S, Malik R, Harris N** et al. Arterio-venous shunting and proliferating new vessels in acute painful neuropathy of rapid glycaemic control (insulin neuritis). *Diabetologia*, 996; **39**: 329–35.

20. **Tesfaye S, Harris N, Wilson RM, Ward JD.** Exercise induced conduction velocity increment: a marker of impaired nerve blood flow in diabetic neuropathy. *Diabetologia*, 1992; **35**: 155–9.

21. **Llewelyn JG, Gilbey SG, Thomas BA, King RH, Muddle JR, Watkins BJ.** Sural nerve morphometry in diabetic autonomic and painful sensory neuropathy: a clinico-pathological study. *Brain*, 1991; **144**: 867–92.

22. Thomas PK, Lascelles RG. Schwann cell abnormalities in diabetic neuropathy. *Lancet*, 1965; **i**: 1355–7.

23. Britland ST, Young RJ, Sharma AK, Clark BF. Association of painful and painless diabetic polyneuropathy with different patterns of nerve fibre degeneration and regeneration. *Diabetes*, 1990; **39**: 898–908.

24. Cameron NE, Eaton SEM, Cotter MA, Tesfaye S. Vascular factors and metabolic interactions in the pathogenesis of diabetic neuropathy. *Diabetologia*, 2001; **44**: 1973–88.

25. The Diabetes Control and Complications Trial Research Group. The effect of intensive diabetes therapy on the development and progression of neuropathy. *Annals of Internal Medicine*, 1995; **122**: 561–8.

26. UK Prospective Diabetes Study (UKPDS) Group. Intensive blood-glucose control with conventional treatment and risk of complications in patients with type 2 diabetes. *Lancet*, 1998; **352**: 837–53.

27. Gabbay KH, Merola LO, Field RA. Sorbitol pathway: presence in nerve and cord with substrate accumulation in diabetes. *Science*, 1966; **151**: 209–10.

28. Greene DA, Lattimer SA, Simar AAF. Sorbitol, phosphoinositides and sodium-potassium ATPase in pathogenesis of diabetic complications. *New England Journal of Medicine*, 1987; **316**: 599–606.

29. Tomlinson DR. Polyols and myoinositol in diabetic neuropathy – of mice and men. *Mayo Clinical Proceedings*, 1989; **64**: 1030.

30. Tomlinson DR, Moriarty RJ, Mayer H. Prevention and reversal of defective axonal transport and motor nerve conduction velocity in rats with experimental diabetes by treatment with aldose reductase inhibitor sorbinil. *Diabetes*, 1984; **33**: 470–6.

31. Judzewitsch RG *et al*. Aldose reductase inhibition improves nerve conduction velocity in diabetic patients. *New England Journal of Medicine*, 1983; **308**: 119–25.

32. Sima AAF *et al*. Regeneration and repair of myelinated fibres in sural nerve biopsy specimens from patients with diabetic neuropathy treated with sorbinil. *New England Journal of Medicine*, 1988; **319**: 548–55.

33. Brownlee M, Cerami A, Vlassara H. Advanced glycosylation end products in tissue and the biochemical basis of diabetic complications. *New England Journal of Medicine*, 1988; **318**: 1315–21.

34. Cameron NE, Cotter MA. The relationship of vascular changes to metabolic factors in diabetic mellitus and their role in the development of peripheral nerve complications. *Diabetes/Metabolism Reviews*, 1994; **10**: 189–224.

35. Cameron NE, Cotter MA, Dines K, Love A. Effects of aminoguanidine on peripheral nerve function and polyol pathway metabolites in streptozotocin-diabetic rats. *Diabetologia*, 1992; **35**: 946–50.

36. Gingliano D, Ceriello A, Paolisso G. Oxidative stress and diabetic vascular complications. *Diabetes Care*, 1996; **19**: 257–67.

37. Cameron NE *et al*. Anti-oxidant and pro-oxidant effects on nerve conduction velocity, endoneural blood flow, and oxygen tension in non-diabetic and streptozotocin-diabetic rats. *Diabetologia*, 1994; **37**: 449–59.

38. Helleweg R, Hartung H-D. Endogenous levels of nerve growth factor (NGF) are altered in experimental diabetes mellitus: a possible role for NGF in the pathogenesis of diabetic neuropathy. *Journal of Neuroscience Research*, 1990; **26**: 258–67.

39. Koya D, King GL. Protein kinase C activation and the development of diabetic complications. *Diabetes*, 1998; **47**: 859–66.

40. Cameron NE, Cotter MA, Jack AM, Basso MD, Hohman TC. Protein kinase C effects on nerve function, perfusion, Na$^+$, K$^+$-ATPase activity and glutathione content in diabetic rats. *Diabetologia*, 1999; **42**: 1120–30.

41. Malik RA *et al*. Endoneural localization of microvascular damage in human diabetic neuropathy. *Diabetologia*, 1993; **36**: 454–9.

42. Malik RA *et al*. Microangiography in human diabetic neuropathy: relationship between capillary abnormalities and the severity of neuropathy. *Diabetologia*, 1989; **32**: 92–102.

43. Tesfaye S *et al*. Impaired blood flow and arterio-venous shunting in human diabetic neuropathy: a novel technique of nerve photography and fluorescein angiography. *Diabetologia*, 1993; **36**: 1266–74.

44. Newrick PG, Wilson AJ, Jakubowski J, Boulton AJM, Ward JD. Sural nerve oxygen tension in diabetes. *British Medical Journal*, 1986; **293**: 1053–4.

45. Young MJ, Veves A, Smith JV, Walker MG, Boulton AJM. Restoring lower limb blood flow improves conduction velocity in diabetic patients. *Diabetologia*, 1995; **38**: 1051–4.

46. Cameron NE, Cotter MA, Low PA. Nerve blood flow in early experimental diabetes in rats: relation to conduction deficits. *American Journal of Physiology*, 1991; **261**: E1–8.

47. Stevens MJ, Feldman EL, Thomas T, Greene DA. Pathogenesis of diabetic neuropathy. In: Veves A, ed. *Management of Diabetic Neuropathy*. Totowa-New Jersey: Humana Press, 1998: 13–48.

48. Reja A, Tesfaye S, Harris N, Ward JD. Improvement in nerve conduction and quantitative sensory tests after treatment with lisinopril. *Diabetic Medicine*, 1995; **12**: 307–9.

49. Malik RA *et al*. Effects of angiotensin converting enzymes (ACE) inhibitor transdolepril on human diabetic neuropathy: a randomised, double-blind, controlled trial. *Lancet*, 1998; **352**: 1978–81.

50. Kempler P, Tesfaye S, Chaturvedi N, Stevens LK, Ward JD, Fuller JH. Autonomic neuropathy and the cardiovascular risk. *Diabetologia*, 1998; **41**(suppl. 1): A51.

51. Watkins PJ *et al*. Severe sensory-autonomic neuropathy and endocrinopathy in insulin-dependent diabetes. *Quarterly Journal of Medicine*, 1995; **88**: 795–804.

52. Edmonds ME, Archer AG, Watkins PJ. Ephedrine: a new treatment for diabetic neuropathic oedema. *Lancet*, 1983; **i**: 548–51.

53. Ewing DJ, Clarke BF. Diagnosis and management of diabetic autonomic neuropathy. *British Medical Journal*, 1982; **285**: 916–18.

54. Horowitz M, Fraser R. Disordered gastric motor function in diabetes mellitus. *Diabetologia*, 1994; **37**: 543–51.

55. Ejjaskjaer NT *et al*. Novel surgical treatment and gastric pathology in diabetic gastroparesis. *Diabetic Medicine*, 1999; **16**: 488–95.

56. Boulton AJM, Drury J, Clarke B, Ward JD. Continuous subcutaneous insulin infusion in the management of painful diabetic neuropathy. *Diabetes Care*, 1982; **5**: 386–90.

57. Backonja M *et al*. Gabapentin for the symptomatic treatment of painful neuropathy in patients with diabetes mellitus: a randomised controlled trial. *Journal of the American Medical Association*, 1998; **280**: 1831–6.

58. Capsaicin Study Group. The effect of treatment with capsaicin on daily activities of patients with painful diabetic neuropathy. *Diabetes Care*, 1992; **15**: 159–65.

59. Kastrup J *et al*. Treatment of chronic painful neuropathy with intravenous lidocaine infusion. *British Medical Journal*, 1986; **292**: 173.

60. Zeigler D *et al*. Treatment of symptomatic diabetic peripheral neuropathy with the antioxidant α-lipoic acid. A 3-week multi-centred randomised, contolled trial. *Diabetologia*, 1995; **38**: 1425–33.

61. Tesfaye S. Painful diabetic neuropathy: aetiology and non-pharmacological treatment. In: Veves A, ed. *Management of Diabetic Neuropathy*. Totowa-New Jersey: Humana Press, 1998: 49–60.

62. Kilhara M *et al*. Aminoguanidine effects on nerve blood flow, vascular permeability, electrophysiology, and oxygen free radicals. *Proceedings of the National Academy of Sciences of the United States of America*, 1991; **88**: 6107–11.

63. Eaton SE *et al*. Spinal-cord involvement in diabetic peripheral neuropathy. *Lancet*, 2001; **358**: 35–6.

7 Pregnancy and diabetes

David R. Hadden

Introduction

Pregnancy in a diabetic mother carries a greater risk to both mother and the offspring than pregnancy in the general obstetric population. Perinatal mortality (fetal death between 24 weeks gestation and one week after delivery) is about four per cent overall for diabetic pregnancy (accounting for all such pregnancies at a regional level), compared to less than one per cent for the overall obstetric population. Somewhat better figures may be reported from centres of excellence but even there the increased risk persists. There is a two to four times increased risk of giving birth to a child with a congenital malformation. Risks to the mother include exacerbation of pre-existing diabetic microvascular and macrovascular complications, risks associated with pregnancy-induced hypertension and iatrogenic risks associated with more intensive blood glucose control.[1,2]

These adverse risks must be seen in the context of the very considerable improvement in the outcome of pregnancy in a diabetic mother over the past fifty years, which relate to aspects of obstetric surveillance as well as to better management of maternal hyperglycaemia.[3] It is now possible for the prospective diabetic mother to take a positive approach to achieving a normal pregnancy outcome, and it is important that her medical advisers avoid unnecessary interference with all of the normal physiological aspects of pregnancy and childbirth.

In European women, the frequency of diabetic pregnancy is relatively low, about 1 in 300 of all pregnancies but this depends on the local prevalence of both type 1 and type 2 diabetes in women of childbearing age. There are marked ethnic and national differences, including the ten-fold greater incidence of type 1 diabetes in women aged 15–40 years in northern European countries compared to southern Greece, and the younger age of onset observed in type 2 diabetes in Oriental, Middle Eastern, Hispanic American, African and Caribbean women which may allow a prevalence of diabetes as high as one in ten pregnancies in some communities.

The obstetric risks are modified between type 1 diabetes, where the hyperglycaemia usually precedes the pregnancy, and type 2 diabetes, which may present for the first time in late pregnancy. These diabetes classifications are often linked to classical obstetrical risk factors, including age, parity, weight, hypertension, smoking and drug abuse. Previous miscarriage, multiple pregnancy, nutritional deficiency, late booking and poor family planning are further obstetric risk factors. Fetal outcome is also affected by purely diabetic risks including the duration of pre-existing diabetes or the time of onset of hyperglycaemia in the pregnancy, the severity of hyperglycaemia or the occurrence of ketoacidosis, maternal insulin-induced hypoglycaemia and diabetes related hypertension, retinopathy, neuropathy or macrovascular disease. Educational aspects, especially the concept of pre-pregnancy counselling and regular antenatal clinic attendance are important modifiers of most of these risk factors.[4]

There are specific risks to the baby of the diabetic mother, including both intrauterine growth retardation (small for dates) and fetal overgrowth (macrosomia). The associated risks of prematurity and of operative delivery, and the risk of hypoglycaemia in the newborn, are short term but require expert neonatal supervision. Longer term risks to the developing child relate to intrauterine imprinting of islet cell development and insulin insensitivity and may be associated with childhood and adult obesity and the vicious cycle of type 2 diabetes in the next generation.

Nevertheless, the outcome of pregnancy in the diabetic women is generally successful, due to the combined attentions of a team which usually involves the diabetes physician and nurse specialist, obstetrician, midwife and neonatologist, each with a special interest in diabetic pregnancy; the family doctor and the often meticulous and enthusiastic cooperation of the diabetic mother herself. It is the aim of this team to achieve as normal as possible maternal blood glucose levels both before and during pregnancy, so that the normal physiological adaptations of maternal metabolism in pregnancy will occur and a normal baby be born by normal delivery at the expected full term gestation[5] (Fig. 1).

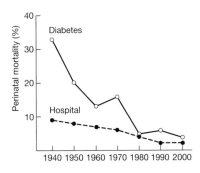

Fig. 1 Perinatal mortality in diabetic pregnancy at the Royal Maternity Hospital, Belfast over 60 years; compared with the overall hospital outcome.

Definitions

The internationally agreed definitions of type 1 and type 2 diabetes mellitus apply in principle during pregnancy. However, the specific metabolic adaptations of pregnancy, which affect both the fasting and the postprandial blood glucose, suggest that non-pregnancy derived criteria for diagnosis of diabetes in pregnancy may not be sufficiently exact. Several approaches to this problem exist, causing confusion. The term gestational diabetes is applied to hyperglycaemia first recognized in pregnancy and is usually defined as any degree of glucose intolerance detected by an oral glucose tolerance test (OGTT). Gestational diabetes may in due course be shown to represent the onset of type 1 or type 2 diabetes which persist after delivery, or it may resolve after delivery for an indefinite time. The published guidelines from the United Kingdom, Europe and USA reflect these real, but relatively minor, differences in diagnostic criteria (see Table 1).[6–9]

The two different diagnostic schemes for diagnosing gestational diabetes use venous plasma glucose levels from either the 75 g or the 100 g OGTT and will continue to be used until an internationally agreed study on the 75 g OGTT in pregnancy, the Hyperglycaemia and Adverse Pregnancy Outcome study (HAPO) reports on the pregnancy outcome for mothers with lesser degrees of hyperglycaemia in sixteen centres worldwide. There is already evidence that fetal macrosomia is related to maternal blood glucose as a continuum and also that intervention with insulin therapy in later pregnancy will prevent the fetal overgrowth. It is probable but not yet proven that more intensive blood glucose control for milder degrees of maternal hyperglycaemia will also be beneficial to the future health of the baby.

Raised maternal blood pressure in a diabetic pregnancy also requires definition. Pregnancy induced hypertension may be due to pre-eclampsia or gestational hypertension (according to the presence or absence of proteinuria respectively) and these may have different pathophysiological mechanisms. The usual obstetrical definition of hypertension is systolic blood pressure above 140 mmHg or diastolic blood pressure above 90 mmHg on two or more measurements more than six hours apart. As pregnancy induced hypertension is the leading cause of maternal death in late pregnancy, and is associated with several risk factors for gestational diabetes, it is important that blood pressure and proteinuria status are observed before and during diabetic pregnancy.

The obstetrical indicator used to assess outcome is perinatal mortality (fetal death between 24 weeks gestation and one week after delivery) but this is becoming less effective in judging outcome as overall experience improves and expert neonatal care prolongs life for very premature babies. As the spontaneous abortion rate is also increased for diabetic pregnancy, the concept of total fetal loss due to all causes of pregnancy failure may become useful, including fertilization and implantation problems, early spontaneous abortion and late unexplained stillbirths, with extention of the post-delivery time for neonatal death to one month.

It is difficult to classify congenital malformations further than by the generally accepted definition of a major malformation recognized by ultrasound scan or at birth by clinical examination. Minor skin blemishes or congenital problems not recognized until later life are not at present recorded. Macrosomia is better defined as large for dates using locally derived birthweight criteria but specific indicators of fetal adiposity may become available.

Screening for hyperglycaemia in pregnancy

Because of the variable prevalence of hyperglycaemia in pregnancy and the different definitions of gestational diabetes, a number of different methods of screening mothers in early or later pregnancy have developed. There is still no international agreement and in particular there has been confusion between the use of testing glucose tolerance in pregnancies with clinical risk factors (family history of diabetes, previous pregnancy, hyperglycaemia or a large for date baby) with a random blood glucose measurement, or the use of a screening 50 g oral glucose load with a one hour plasma glucose

Table 1 Definitions of gestational diabetes

	Fasting	1 h	2 h	3 h
World Health Organisation: revised criteria (1999)				
75 g OGTT: venous plasma glucose in mmol/l				
Gestational diabetes (includes both)				
Gestational 'IGT'	>7.0	–	and 7.8–11.1	–
AND				
Gestational 'Diabetes'	<7.0	–	and/or >11.1	–
American Diabetes Association				
100 g OGTT: venous plasma glucose in mg/dl (two or more results abnormal)				
Gestational Diabetes	105	190	165	145
	(5.8 mmol/l	10.6	9.2	8.1)
4th ADA International Workshop on Gestational Diabetes (1998) in mg/dl				
100 g glucose tolerance test (Carpenter and Coustan criteria)				
Gestational Diabetes	95	180	155	140
	(5.3 mmol/l	10.0	8.6	7.8)
75 g Oral glucose tolerance test (1998) (two or more results abnormal)				
Gestational Diabetes	95	180	155	–
	(5.3 mmol/l	10.0	8.6)	

OGTT: Oral glucose tolerance test; IGT: Impaired glucose tolerance.

Box 1 Screening for gestational diabetes

- Urine should be tested for glycosuria (and proteinuria) at every antenatal visit.

- Timed random laboratory venous plasma glucose whenever glycosuria detected, and routinely at first booking visit and at 28 weeks gestation.

- Proceed to 75 g oral glucose tolerance test if blood glucose greater than 6.0 mmol fasting or more than two hours after food, or greater than 7.0 mmol/l within two hours of food.

measurement in all pregnancies. In the United Kingdom there is now general agreement on the protocol shown in Box 1.[6]

The main concept is that routine measurement of urine glucose, although very non-specific and frequently positive due to the lowered renal threshold of pregnancy, will identify the otherwise unrecognized diabetic mother presenting for the first time in pregnancy, and this suspicion at any time during the pregnancy must then be confirmed by blood glucose measurement. An untimed postprandial plasma glucose at first booking and again at about 28 weeks will further serve to confirm the absence of diabetes at two important points – early in pregnancy for unrecognized type 1, and in the third trimester for type 2 gestational diabetes associated with the increasing insulin resistance of late pregnancy respectively.

The diagnosis of gestational diabetes will require a 75 g oral glucose tolerance test, however pregnancies are screened, using fasting and two hour values. More precise definitions of milder degrees of hyperglycaemia in pregnancy using the 75 g test will be developed, based on outcome measures of fetal macrosomia rather than on statistical analysis of blood glucose distribution in normal populations. These values will be important if intervention by dietary alteration or insulin therapy is envisaged. At present insulin treatment is advised for all mothers with gestational diabetes whose venous plasma glucose remains above 6.0 mmol/l fasting, or 8.0 mmol/l two hours after 75 g glucose. It may be that even lower criteria will be shown to reduce the prevalence of fetal macrosomia.

All diabetic women contemplating pregnancy should be reviewed prior to conception, including assessment of glycaemic control, blood pressure, urine microalbumin (with further renal function testing if necessary) and examination of the retina through appropriately dilated pupils. During pregnancy, further measurement of blood pressure and proteinuria will be routine. Weight gain in pregnancy is important at the upper and lower extremes but may not be necessary to document in otherwise normal women. Newer protocols for assessment of fetal development including ultrasound assessment of fetal fat deposition may lead to better detection of pathological macrosomia in late gestation, as well as confirming congenital fetal abnormality at an early date.

Pathophysiology

Pregnancy in the normal female involves both biochemical and immunological adaptation during the nine-month gestation. Metabolic changes will optimize conditions for fetal growth and immunological tolerance will minimize any cellular or humoral incompatibility between fetus and mother. The added energy demand requires an increased maternal food intake, use of endogenous energy stores and more efficient energy conservation.

The increase in food intake which is desirable is modest, perhaps only 200 kcal per day in the third trimester, allowing an average weight gain of 11–16 kg for a woman of normal body mass index. A 6 g increment of dietary protein to the daily recommendation for women of childbearing age, in a diet prescription still relatively low in fat (but not less than 30 per cent of total energy) is reasonable. For overweight women with gestational diabetes, dietary restriction to 1200–1800 kcal per day to discourage weight gain after 28 weeks has been shown to improve maternal blood glucose, but the lower caloric intake produces measurable ketonuria.

One of the first metabolic effects of normal pregnancy is a fall in fasting plasma glucose, related to increased renal clearance and decreased gluconeogenesis. In a type 1 diabetic mother this may cause unexpected hypoglycaemia and the insulin dose for those who have achieved tight control pre-pregnancy may have to be temporarily reduced or more widely distributed with more frequent meals.

Subsequently, a marked decrease in insulin sensitivity (increased insulin resistance) parallels the growth of the feto-placental unit, reversing abruptly following delivery. By full term insulin mediated glucose uptake into maternal skeletal muscle will have fallen by approximately 40 per cent. The normal response to this diminished insulin sensitivity is an increase in insulin secretion and in healthy pregnancy there is a 10–15 per cent increase in postprandial blood insulin levels. The physiological changes in carbohydrate, fat and protein metabolism that usually occur during transition from feeding to fasting are exaggerated in pregnancy, with more rapid swings between the anabolic state of feeding and the catabolic state of fasting. These changes are largely due to placental hormones, notably human placental lactogen, increasing lipolysis for maternal energy while sparing carbohydrate nutrients for the fetus (Fig. 2).

Women who lack the necessary pancreatic β-cell reserve, either absolutely as in type 1 diabetes or relatively as in type 2 diabetes, will have abnormal adaptation of carbohydrate, protein and fat metabolism. Uncorrected, these can adversely affect maternal well-being and fetal development. The insulin dose to maintain normoglycaemia and prevent maternal ketosis may increase up to three-fold in the course of pregnancy in type 1 diabetes and women with type 2 diabetes will usually require insulin treatment in pregnancy, often at high dose because of their obesity and physical inactivity. The

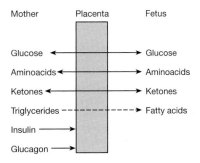

Fig. 2 Diagram showing the concentration dependent transport of glucose, aminoacids and ketones across the placenta, and the relation of maternal triglyceride to fetal fatty acids following hydrolysis in the placenta. Insulin and glucagon do not cross the placenta.

physiological acceleration of fat catabolism means that maternal ketoacidosis is a greater risk and can be precipitated by nausea and anorexia in early pregnancy, or by urinary tract infection. The use of β-sympathomimetic drugs to inhibit pre-term labour, and of high dose steroids to improve fetal lung maturity, will need careful monitoring of the blood glucose and adjustment of the insulin dose.

Similar changes in intermediary metabolism occur in gestational diabetes, with elevation of serum glucose, non-esterified fatty acids (NEFA), triglycerides and amino acids. These can be returned to normal by insulin therapy. These women are at increased risk of progression to established type 2 diabetes, especially if there is a family history, or a relatively poor insulin response to oral glucose, or following a subsequent pregnancy. About five per cent will develop type 1 diabetes, and these may show islet cell antibodies or glutamic acid decarboxylase antibodies during pregnancy.

Changes in circulating nutrient levels in the mother will influence nutrient concentrations in the fetal circulation (Fig. 2). The metabolic changes of diabetic pregnancy can be returned towards normal if the maternal blood glucose is tightly controlled, and an understanding of the underlying pathophysiological mechanisms is important to all physicians who look after these women.[10,11]

Management

Diabetes onset prior to pregnancy

Introduction

Also known to obstetricians as 'pregestational diabetes', these mothers may have type 1 or type 2 diabetes. In northern Europeans type 1 diabetes predominates. The essential basis of treatment is good metabolic control, beginning before conception. Intensive management of blood glucose will require more frequent capillary blood glucose measurements made by the patient, more aggressive insulin therapy, stricter food and exercise schedules and more frequent contact with the diabetes team.

Preconception counselling

All sexually active, fertile diabetic women should use effective contraception unless they are in good control and aim to conceive. Diabetes related fetal congenital abnormalities are initiated very early in pregnancy and may be prevented by tight blood glucose control. It is therefore essential that all diabetic women of childbearing age are aware of the risks of birth defects and miscarriages related to high blood glucose at this time. Any method of contraception is acceptable, but it should be used effectively.[12]

The main points of preconception counselling include discussion of the risk of pregnancy to the mother herself, the risk of fetal abnormalities, the implications of a tight blood glucose regimen and the ultimate risk of diabetes developing in the offspring. If necessary a preconception review should include a specialist ophthalmological examination, with laser photocoagulation if indicated prior to the institution of tight blood glucose control. Serum creatinine and urinary microalbumin should be measured and assessment made of possible coronary artery disease, autonomic neuropathy or gastroparesis. A 24 h urine protein and creatinine clearance will be needed if there is evidence of incipient diabetic nephropathy, with a specialist renal consultation. A review of drug therapy for hypertension, hyperlipidaemia and epilepsy is necessary, and as far as possible all drugs discontinued. For persistent

hypertension methyldopa has proven to be effective and safe, with nifedipine and labetolol considered acceptable second line agents if methyldopa alone cannot produce adequate control as pregnancy progresses (women whose hypertension is severe pre-pregnancy should be advised that they are at very high risk of complications and that the medical advice would be to avoid pregnancy). Thiazide diuretics and β-blockers should be stopped, because of concerns about possible teratogenicity. Angiotensin-converting enzyme inhibitors should also be stopped because of the possibility of fetal and neonatal renal failure. This effect occurs in later pregnancy and there is no cause for concern in a woman presenting early in pregnancy, having been on angiotensin-converting enzyme inhibitors at conception. Lipid lowering drugs should be stopped, with appropriate dietary advice. Persistent epileptic seizures require careful neurological assessment and advice, as some form of therapy will probably be needed and these drugs have their own teratological potential. The distinction between epileptic and hypoglycaemic seizures is thus of major importance and can be difficult.

Preconception management

The risk of fetal abnormalities is largely related to maternal blood glucose control in the first weeks of gestation, although glucose may not be the sole teratogen. There is evidence that most diabetic women who give birth to an abnormal infant had mean capillary blood glucose levels greater than 10 mmol/l (mean of a fasting and three post-meal measurements daily) in early pregnancy. In the randomized, prospective Diabetes Control and Complications Trial, eight out of nine pregnancies which resulted in a fetal congenital malformation occurred in women who had not been assigned to intensive insulin therapy.[3] The mean maternal HbA$_{1c}$ close to conception was 8.1 per cent (standard deviation +1.7 per cent) for the conventionally treated and 7.4 per cent (standard deviation +1.3 per cent) for the intensively treated mothers ($p = 0.0001$), with a non-diabetic range of up to 6.1 per cent. It must be recognized that some diabetic women will not be able to achieve perfect blood glucose or HbA$_{1c}$ levels and there is evidence that completely normal values are not necessary to minimize the risks of miscarriage or congenital abnormalities. Generally accepted targets would be capillary blood glucose levels of 3.5–5.0 mmol/l before meals and 4.5–7.0 mmol/l one hour after meals, with HbA$_{1c}$ 6.0 per cent (upper limit of non-diabetic normal range 5.3 per cent). The increased risk of maternal hypoglycaemia (which is exacerbated in early pregnancy) must be explained to the potential mother and her family as a consequence of tight blood glucose control (see Chapter 1). The lowered threshold for adrenaline release for the classical symptoms of a hypoglycaemic reaction will allow the neuroglycopaenic symptoms of confusion and loss of consciousness to occur without warning, and instruction on early self treatment, with rapidly absorbed glucose tablets is important. Family members should be instructed in the use of subcutaneous glucagon (1 mg injection) and encouraged to use this if necessary. These problems are much less likely to occur in type 2 diabetic patients due to their greater insulin resistance.

The insulin regimen used will be determined by the diabetes physician. Although twice daily short and intermediate insulin mixtures can achieve the levels of tight control desired in some patients, this is at a significant risk of hypoglycaemia due to the relatively larger doses of the intermediate insulins and the need for very regular meal times and life style compared to more intensified insulin regimens. For this reason, the basal/bolus regimen using a long acting insulin as a basal injection at bedtime (or twice daily, on rising and at bedtime), with short acting bolus injections before each meal has been widely used, with appropriate pen injectors. This regimen is similar in principle to the effect of a basal rate constant infusion pump with premeal bolus infusions, but is much simpler in general use. A prepregnancy consultation to initiate intensive therapy is always desirable: if pregnancy occurs without adequate planning it is still worthwhile making the change to multiple daily injections.

Pre-pregnancy and in the first trimester, the total dose of insulin may not be greatly different from in the non-pregnant state and it can be equally distributed between the four injections of a pre-meal and pre-bed insulin injection regimen: in later pregnancy, careful patient self monitoring of blood glucose and dose increases will be needed. A 24-h telephone consultation service will be appreciated by the patient, but the staff who give advice must be aware of the aims of the tight control regimen and the associated problems. Oral hypoglycaemic agents should not be used in pregnancy, so type 2 diabetic women, controlled on tablets, should be converted to insulin use pre-conception and enough time allowed for stable glycaemic control to be achieved. At the same time as intensive blood glucose control is initiated, a dietetic consultation, with discussion of pregnancy nutritional needs, is necessary. A supplement of folic acid 400 mg daily is standard advice for all diabetic pregnancies, to minimize risk of central nervous system abnormalities. Any medications taken to treat other conditions, including hypertension and hyperlipidaemia, should be adjusted as discussed above. Furthermore, every effort should be made to stop the mother smoking. These concepts should be discussed widely at all times when pregnancy education takes place.

First trimester management

Accurate dating of the pregnancy is an obstetric imperative, and is best achieved by ultrasound examination at 8–10 weeks. The insulin dependent diabetic mother will already have established contact with her diabetes team by this time and the possibility of fetal growth delay related to poor metabolic control should have already been considered. From early pregnancy onwards, there is benefit in regular maternal diabetes attendance, usually every two weeks for discussion of blood glucose self monitoring results and advice on increasing the insulin dose. Diabetic attendance is more beneficial than obstetric at this stage.

Second and third trimester management

After 12–16 weeks gestation, the increasing degree of maternal insulin resistance necessitates an increased insulin dose to maintain normal blood glucose control. There is a shift in emphasis from generally good blood glucose levels to very tight control, related to evidence that the risk of fetal macrosomia is closely related to maternal postprandial blood glucose control. To achieve this very tight control the target capillary blood glucose should be 4.0–5.0 mmol/l fasting, and 4.5–7.0 mmol/l postprandially. Self monitoring before meals may not be sufficient to achieve such tight control and one hour post meal testing becomes useful. Occasional checking for nocturnal hypoglycaemia may be necessary, especially if the mother appears to be losing her ability to sense acute hypoglycaemia. A doubling of insulin dose is often necessary during the period 14–30 weeks, with frequent adjustment and consultation. After about 36 weeks a steady state occurs and a small reduction in dose may be necessary.

Severe diabetic ketoacidosis is a serious problem to fetal health and even viability, and diabetic mothers should be able to monitor urinary ketones in case of intercurrent urine infection or other illnesses, knowing how to obtain urgent advice if needed. Mild ketonuria with normal or low blood glucose usually represents inadequate food intake related to the physiological acceleration of carbohydrate metabolism, or 'starvation ketosis': it is probably of little if any significance, although the question of subsequent impaired motor and intellectual development of the child has been raised. To avoid this possibility an increased caloric intake of about 150 kcal/d has been suggested in the second trimester, and a routine bedtime snack.

Obstetric supervision by a specialized midwife and obstetrician should be more frequent than for uncomplicated pregnancy. Ultrasound examination every four weeks will allow detection of intrauterine growth retardation or evolving macrosomia and hydramnios. The risk of late unexplained fetal death may be less when glucose control is good but remains an occasional unexpected disaster. Various biophysical tests of fetal viability have been proposed, from maternal 'kick counting' to contraction stress tests, with the possibility of early delivery in mind. Pregnancy induced hypertension may require hospital admission and close supervision. More complex investigations, including amniocentesis for detection of fetal abnormality, or measurement of amniotic fluid insulin to confirm fetal hyperinsulinism, or cordocentesis to confirm fetal hypoxia are presently research oriented rather than routine procedures.

Diabetes with onset or first recognition in pregnancy (gestational diabetes)

Introduction

The prevalence of gestational diabetes defined either by the World Health Organization criteria or by the American Diabetes Association criteria (Table 1) varies between populations.[13] The main determinant is the age of onset and frequency of type 2 diabetes in a given ethnic group of females in a particular environment. Obesity, exercise, parity and maternal age are also important. The highest prevalence may be up to 20 per cent of pregnancies, as in some Native American groups and Pacific Islanders, where major lifestyle changes have occurred over several generations. In London the prevalence varies from four per cent in Asian immigrant mothers, followed by those from Chinese, African and Caribbean backgrounds, to less than 0.5 per cent in Caucasian mothers. These prevalences are likely to change with changing nutritional habits. Ultimately it is the level of blood glucose in the mother which has an effect on the developing fetus and this is likely to be a continuous variable. The HAPO study will set a new baseline in this controversial area.

Prepregnancy counselling for women at risk of gestational diabetes

In women who have a high risk of gestational diabetes, a prepregnancy educational programme on nutrition and lifestyle will reduce the number who require active treatment.[12] Previous gestational diabetes is very likely to recur, and often becomes permanent. Programmes for prevention of type 2 diabetes may include prophylactic oral hypoglycaemic therapy, which should be reconsidered if pregnancy occurs. Low dose oral contraception has a minimal effect on the risk of developing type 2 diabetes and any effective form of pregnancy planning is acceptable.[14] Careful management of hypertension and hyperlipidaemia in these women, with appropriate prepregnancy consultation for those with established retinopathy and nephropathy is also necessary. Nutritional advice and folic acid supplementation and specific drug precautions otherwise follow standard obstetrical practice, as for type 1 diabetes.

First trimester management

Gestational diabetes does not usually develop until later in the pregnancy. Hyperglycaemia developing for the first time in early pregnancy is probably type 1 diabetes and insulin should be started at once to prevent the unexpected development of ketoacidosis. Often short/intermediate acting insulin mixtures taken twice daily will provide excellent blood glucose control in these women but the dose will increase as pregnancy proceeds. Self blood glucose monitoring and the targets for blood glucose control are as for pre-existing type 1 diabetes.

Second and third trimester management

Diet instruction is essential and a degree of energy restriction, with advice on exercise and dietary fibre content is usually helpful. A safe level of energy restriction has been shown to be 30 kcal/kg (about 1800 kcal per day) and 25 kcal/kg may be advised for more obese mothers. This level of energy restriction did not result in small for dates babies, even though maternal weight gain after 28 weeks was less than 2 kg.

Self monitoring of capillary blood glucose is a useful skill for these mothers to acquire. At a minimum a fasting and post meal plasma glucose should be measured weekly as the pregnancy progresses. HbA$_{1c}$ values are less immediately helpful because of the six-week time lag in the glycosylation process and the more rapid rise of plasma glucose in later pregnancy, but a measurement in late pregnancy is necessary to identify overall control.

Oral hypoglycaemic therapy is not generally advised on pharmaceutical grounds, although it is probable that a high glucose itself rather than any of the drugs presently used for type 2 diabetes has the more potent adverse effect on pregnancy outcome. A few studies have suggested that oral hypoglycaemic agents can safely be used in carefully designated type 2 diabetic pregnancy, but there is no consensus view. Standard practice is to advise insulin therapy for persistent maternal hyperglycaemia in order to prevent fetal complications, especially those related to the compensatory fetal hyperinsulinaemia and ensuing macrosomia. There is good evidence that such therapy is successful and safe. A twice daily mixture of short/medium acting insulin should be advised if the laboratory venous plasma glucose or accurate capillary blood glucose remains above 6.0 mmol/l fasting or 8.0 mmol/l at any time postprandially and some authorities recommend the use of intensified insulin treatment regimes as for type 1 diabetes for these women too.[15] It is not necessary to wait for the result of a formal 75 g OGTT to start insulin therapy in a woman with diagnostic hyperglycaemia but the OGTT may be the determining factor if a screening programme is in use. The starting dose of insulin can safely be 1.0 U/kg/day, so that for a 60 kg woman the dose will be 30 U of insulin before breakfast and before the evening meal. This insulin regimen may be initiated as a day patient in a diabetes centre, as hospital admission is often difficult for these mothers, but the process must be rapid in keeping with the advancing pregnancy.

Pregnancy with diabetic nephropathy or severe proliferative retinopathy

The former high perinatal mortality of up to 30 per cent in women with established nephropathy, and the risk of acceleration of the maternal renal disease during and after pregnancy led to specific advice that these women should avoid pregnancy. There are still hazards, especially of accelerated hypertension, clinically indistinguishable from severe pre-eclampsia. Total proteinuria will increase considerably in these mothers. Proliferative retinopathy will also be adversely affected by the worsening hypertension. Overall, a woman with established diabetic nephropathy still remains at high risk in pregnancy, and counselling must emphasize the progressive nature of the renal disease as well as the poorer fetal outcome. Hypertension control may be difficult and the intensification of treatment essential to control maternal hypertension can increase the risk of a small for dates baby. Renal transplantation may be an option prior to considering a pregnancy as successful outcomes following transplantation have been recorded.[16]

There are also real risks of exacerbation of proliferative retinopathy and every effort to recognize and treat this prior to considering pregnancy must be made. If effective and extensive panretinal photocoagulation has been achieved, pregnancy is relatively safe from the retinal point of view. In contrast a patient who has established proliferative retinopathy with a long history of poor blood glucose control, especially if associated with renal impairment and hypertension, is at a real risk of visual deterioration, with retinal or intraocular haemorrhage. Careful examination of the retina is necessary before and during the pregnancy and expert ophthalmological advice should be obtained if necessary. For women with normal retinae at the start of pregnancy, especially if diabetic control has not been drastically altered, once each trimester is probably sufficient but for women with pre-existing retinopathy, more frequent monitoring may be required, especially if overall glycaemic control has been significantly improved over a short space of time.

When counselling a woman with advanced diabetic complications about pregnancy the risk not just to herself but also to the baby must be discussed, as intrauterine growth retardation may occur in pregnancy in women with advanced microvascular disease. The potential parents must both be aware of the risks to mother and baby and make their decision whether to proceed or not with the best risk assessment information possible.

Labour and delivery

Relatively little is known of the best way to monitor fetal well being in a diabetic pregnancy. The main concerns are of late unexplained intrauterine death and problems with excessive or deficient fetal growth and liquor volume. At present regular two weekly ultrasound scans allow the best measurements, and are better than simple clinical assessment. Neither umbilical artery blood flow nor routine cardiotocography seem to be predictive and maternal 'kick-counts' are generally too imprecise. Excellent blood glucose control is a positive benefit, and if this has not been achieved in later gestation and especially if other obstetric complications such as pre-eclampsia occur, careful consideration to early delivery by the safest route must be given, bearing in mind the possible risks of fetal prematurity.

There is evidence that an uncomplicated diabetic pregnancy can safely be allowed to continue to term, provided that there has been tight blood glucose control, that there is no evidence of fetal macrosomia or polyhydramnios, that fetoplacental function is judged to be normal and there are no obstetric complications such as severe pre-eclampsia, placenta praevia or intrauterine growth retardation. The well controlled diabetic mother should be reassured that normal delivery at the normal time is the overall aim.

Nevertheless a proportion of diabetic pregnancies will require delivery by caesarean section for obstetric reasons. The risk of shoulder dystocia due to fetal macrosomia and the fear of late fetal death will always influence the obstetrician in making the decision. Induction of labour is now a reasonably standard procedure, and intrapartum fetal monitoring by cardiotocography or other means should be available. The clinical experience of the obstetrician is still very important, which is a major reason for a degree of centralization of these high risk pregnancies.

Management of diabetes in labour is straightforward, provided it is recognized that the normal woman eats very little during this time and that the insulin dose is appropriately reduced. It is important for fetal well-being to maintain the maternal blood glucose 3–5 mmol/l during labour and delivery. One recent report suggests that it is adequate to keep the blood glucose under 8 mmol/l.[17] Accurate capillary blood glucose monitoring at hourly intervals is helpful. For spontaneous labour a five per cent glucose infusion with six units of short-acting insulin per 500 ml can be used to maintain blood glucose control, with adjustment of the rate of infusion as necessary. For induced labour, where other intravenous infusions are in progress, care must be taken not to over-hydrate. The usual doses of insulin are taken the day before, omitting the evening intermediate or long-acting insulin, and on the morning of delivery the five per cent dextrose infusion with short-acting insulin started. A light breakfast may be possible. A suggested insulin regimen is shown in Table 2.

For elective caesarean section, the previous evening intermediate or long-acting insulin should also be omitted. In the labour ward the same five per cent dextrose infusion with six units short-acting insulin is used. The protocol shown in the table has proved safe but individual decisions should be made by the labour ward staff on the amount of insulin required to maintain the maternal blood glucose in the range 3–5 mmol/l. An unthinking adherence to a so called 'sliding scale' is unwise. The pre-delivery dose of insulin may have been increased two or three times above the woman's non-pregnant dose, and care must be taken to adjust the labour ward protocol appropriately. The insulin requirement may fall to pre-pregnancy levels immediately after placental delivery. On the first day after delivery, the intravenous glucose and insulin infusion can continue until normal light meals are taken. At this time the insulin dose can revert towards the pre-pregnancy regimen, initially at about half the final pregnancy dose, to maintain maternal blood glucose at a rather higher range of 6–8 mmol/l before meals.

Breastfeeding is important and requires dietetic advice to increase the mother's energy intake – breast feeding is a high energy activity and the mother's insulin dose usually needs to be decreased. The baby may be slow to feed, and care must be taken to ensure that the mother has her own food before breastfeeding to avoid the risk of maternal hypoglycaemia.

Neonatal complications

The major complications to the newborn baby of a diabetic mother include neonatal hypoglycaemia, macrosomia and the risk of congenital abnormalities. Other complications which have been recorded are the respiratory distress syndrome, hypocalcaemia and polycythaemia.

Neonatal hypoglycaemia, the direct result of neonatal hyperinsulinism secondary to fetal hyperglycaemia, is particularly problematic because of the difficulty in defining a normal range for the physiological transient fall in neonatal blood glucose and uncertainty as to whether either transient self-limiting hypoglycaemia or persistent hypoglycaemia following normal feeding is associated with neurological damage.[18] The prevalence of neonatal hypoglycaemia, using definitions ranging from less than 1.1 mmol/l to less than 2.2 mmol/l at various times between 2–24 h, with or without early feeding, varies from 8–61 per cent in published series. More definite studies of insulin/glucose relationships, and measures of alternative brain fuels such as NEFA, lactate and ketones are needed to relate to neurological outcomes. It is probable that the early neonatal blood glucose, within two hours of birth, can fall transiently to 1.5 mmol/l physiologically and that this initial fall may be greater in the infant of a hyperglycaemic diabetic mother. After 24 h there will be no difference between the normal and the diabetic pregnancy, even if neonatal hyperinsulinaemia persists for several days. There is no evidence to link this transient fall in blood glucose with any permanent neurological damage, nor is there agreement that early feeding or glucose infusions are in any way beneficial. An important point to remember is that blood glucose measurements by heelprick using test strips and meters are less accurate at very low values, so that only laboratory values are reliable. Normal practice is to concentrate on the at risk baby (where the mother was hyperglycaemic) and consider supplementary formula feeds if the blood glucose remains less than 2.0 mmol/l in the first

Table 2 Labour ward guide lines for glucose/insulin infusion

Maternal capillary blood glucose (mmol/l)	Infusion 5% dextrose (ml)	Short-acting insulin added to infusion (U)	Approximate time per infusion (h)	Supplementary subcutaneous short acting insulin every 6 h
<2.0	500 ml	0	2 h	0
2.0–3.9	500 ml	0	6 h	0
4.0–7.9	500 ml	6 U	6 h	0
8.0–11.9	500 ml	6 U	6 h	6 U
12.0–15.9	500 ml	6 U	6 h	10 U
>16.0	contact diabetes staff			

24 h. If the baby has a seizure or reduced level of consciousness, intravenous glucose (10 per cent glucose 3 ml/kg/h, or 5 mg/kg/min) should be established. Normal feeds should be continued and the intravenous glucose gradually reduced. It is important not to compromise successful breast feeding by overzealous glucose supplementation, and overfrequent blood glucose monitoring should be discouraged. Experienced neonatal advice should be at hand to facilitate these decisions.

Macrosomia in the infant of a poorly controlled diabetic mother is largely due to excess fat deposition, but there is also increased protein anabolism. The excess fat is rapidly lost and by six months these babies are indistinguishable from normal. Measures of skinfold thickness in the newborn will confirm the adiposity present prior to delivery. Labour and delivery may be prolonged for a macrosomic baby, with risks of premature onset of labour, perinatal asphyxia and birth trauma (notably shoulder dystocia), but these risks must be weighed against those of anaesthesia in the mother and respiratory morbidity in the infant following caesarean delivery.

Some infants of diabetic mothers are small for dates due to intrauterine growth retardation, usually due to placental insufficiency related to pre-eclampsia, or to maternal antenatal blood glucose concentrations which have been too low. There is a suggestion that early fetal growth retardation also occurs due to maternal hyperglycaemia in early pregnancy. These small-for-dates babies may present more problems and require expert neonatal attention in a special care unit.

The respiratory distress syndrome played a major part in the higher mortality of infants of diabetic mothers when poorly controlled mothers were delivered prematurely by caesarean section. This situation is now much less common due to the improved metabolic control related to self monitoring of blood glucose. Delivery as close to term as possible will minimize the risk, and antenatal steroid treatment to the mother will enhance fetal lung maturity, although the diabetes team and the mother should be warned on the day of therapy so that the insulin dose can be temporarily increased if appropriate. Admission for glucose monitoring and supplemental intravenous insulin infusion therapy is used in some units to cover the steroid administration.

Hypocalcaemia (less than 2.0 mmol/l in full term infants) can occur in about 15 per cent of infants of well controlled diabetic mothers, and more often when control is poor. It is usually self limiting and very rarely causes any clinical signs. Routine monitoring of neonatal calcium is not necessary in otherwise healthy infants. Polycythaemia and hyperbilirubinaemia are likewise occasionally found, but do not generally require routine assessment or special treatment.

Congenital fetal abnormalities are two to four times more common in diabetic pregnancy, although the reported incidence varies between centres and time periods.[19] There is strong embryological evidence that most of these abnormalities are determined in the teratologically susceptible time period up to the seventh gestational week. The exact nature of the teratogenic insult is not known, although there is good evidence that glucose itself is the main problem. Experimental studies of hyperglycaemic rat pregnancy suggest that the mechanism may be an embryonic excess of free oxygen radicals, with accumulation of sorbitol and depletion of myoinositol and arachidonic acid, all secondary to maternal hyperglycaemia.

Cardiac abnormalities are the most common, with an incidence of one in 100 diabetic pregnancies, about four times greater than in nondiabetic pregnancies. Some of these abnormalities can be recognized by ultrasound at 18 weeks or after. There are also reversible cardiac problems such as cardiomyopathy and asymmetric septal hypertrophy equally related to maternal hyperglycaemia. Renal problems from total agenesis to renal cysts and ureteric maldevelopment, and neural tube defects and anencephaly are also more common. Many other congenital abnormalities have been reported, of varying degrees of severity. The varying degrees of the caudal regression syndrome, from total maldevelopment of the lower limbs (sirenomelia) to relatively minor problems of sacral dysplasia and bladder dysfunction are thought to be specifically diabetes related but are relatively uncommon.

Management of the pregnancy where a congenital malformation is detected by ultrasound requires sensitive counselling, and if appropriate delivery in a specialized unit with expert neonatal and surgical support. Prevention of these congenital abnormalities is a major goal of pre-pregnancy counselling and of better blood glucose control of all women at risk of pregnancy. Folic acid supplementation, and probably other free radical scavengers such as vitamin C, which should be available in a well balanced diet with fresh fruit and vegetables, are important aspects of preparation for pregnancy.

Contraception

The importance of reliable family planning in allowing careful control of blood glucose prepregnancy and at conception means that considerable value must be placed on a simple, reliable, easily available and acceptable method. The progesterone-only pill is a medically attractive option but needs careful compliance with its 24 h regimen for administration if it is going to be effective. Progestogen depot injections may be particularly effective and acceptable for younger women, although they should be warned about some initially irregular bleeding followed by amenorrhoea. After more than five years' use, there may be an increased risk of osteoporosis and oestradiol levels should be monitored after this duration. At present, the most effective and acceptable option is probably the low dose combined oral contraceptive pill. Although there are some theoretical problems, the 30 μg oestrogen formulation with a standard progestogen has proved itself in diabetic practice. The risks of dyslipidaemia, hyperglycaemia and coagulopathies have been extensively studied, and a number of reassuring reports are available. Measurement of blood pressure, lipids and HbA_{1c} on an annual review, should be standard practice for all diabetic people. The usual absolute contraindications, such as migraine, apply in diabetes. The use of gestogen and desogestrel, as the progestogens in combined oral contraception, with concerns about the increased risk of venous thromboembolism, including pulmonary emboli, is best restricted to patients with additional risk factors for cardiovascular disease, such as relevant family history or hyperlipidaemia and the potential risks must be discussed carefully with the patients.

Other contraceptive techniques are also acceptable. Intrauterine devices used carefully do not produce increased salpingitis in diabetic women. The new small devices that also deliver a progestogen may be particularly suitable, although the woman should be warned about the possibility of erratic bleeding in the first few months, often followed by oligomenorrhoea or even amenorrhoea. Many couples will wish to use barrier methods. Particular thought must be given to the possibility of teenage pregnancy, and the diabetes team is often in a special position in this respect. A simple leaflet which can be easily and openly discussed with all diabetic women of childbearing age is an essential part of day-to-day diabetes consultation.

Some parents will wish to discuss the risk of their babies developing diabetes. This requires sensitive handling – for type 1 diabetes the risk is quoted at 2–3 per cent if the mother is diabetic, 4–6 per cent if the father is diabetic and 5–10 per cent if a sibling is diabetic.

Outcome

The target for women with diabetes is that their pregnancy outcome should be at least as good as that for non-diabetic women. Although in some centres of excellence for both diabetes and obstetric care this target seems within reach, audit of larger unselected United Kingdom populations show that for type 1 diabetes infants still have a ten-fold greater risk of a congenital malformation and a five-fold greater risk of stillbirth than in the general obstetric population.[20] For gestational diabetes the risks of congenital malformation and stillbirth are very much less, but the long-term risks to the infant of having been macrosomic at birth and to the mother of developing permanent type 2 diabetes are being established for different ethnic groups. It is probable that these risks can be reduced by measures to reduce maternal blood glucose in pregnancy.

Although the outcomes of pregnancy for the diabetic woman have improved very much since the discovery of insulin there is a realization that diabetes services before and during pregnancy require a more integrated approach to the specific problem of optimizing blood glucose control, with implementation of existing guidelines and maximizing of maternal empowerment. From a broader viewpoint the maternal intrauterine environment – whether overnutrition or undernutrition, expressed as glycaemia or as other factors – will affect fetal development and particularly fetal insulin secretion.[21,22] Maternal glucose control may have an important influence on susceptibility to diabetes, hypertension and cardiovascular disease in the next generation.[23] Measures to modify the abnormal intrauterine environment would be expected to be beneficial in the longer term, but evidence to prove this in a practical manner, and to assess the actual risks and benefits to an individual mother and child will require very long-term observation.

References

1. **Hadden DR.** Diabetes in pregnancy: past, present and future. In: Dornhorst A, Hadden DR, eds. *Diabetes and Pregnancy. An International Approach to Diagnosis and Management.* Chichester: Wiley, 1996: 3–21.

2. **Buchanan TA, Coustan DR.** Diabetes mellitus. In: Burrow GD, Ferris TF, eds. *Medical Complications During Pregnancy.* 4th edn. Philadelphia: WB Saunders, 1995: 29–61.

3. **The Diabetes Control and Complications Trial Research Group.** Pregnancy outcomes in the Diabetes Control and Complications Trial. *American Journal of Obstetrics and Gynaecology,* 1996; **174:** 1343–53.

4. **Casson IF** *et al.* Outcomes of pregnancy in insulin dependant diabetic women: results of a five year population cohort study. *British Medical Journal,* 1997; **315:** 275–8.

5. **Hadden DR.** The management of diabetes in pregnancy. *Postgraduate Medical Journal,* 1996; **72:** 525–31.

6. **Jardine Brown C** *et al.* Report of the pregnancy and neonatal care group. *Diabetic Medicine,* 1996; **13:** 543–53.

7. **European Diabetes Policy Group 1998.** *A Desktop Guide to Type 1: (Insulin-Dependent) Diabetes Mellitus.* International Diabetes Federation (Europe). Brussels, 1998; 29–30.

8. **European Diabetes Policy Group 1999.** *A Desktop Guide to Type 2 (Non-Insulin-dependent) Diabetes Mellitus.* International Diabetes Federation (Europe). Brussels, 1999; 30–1.

9. **Metzger BE, Coustan DR** and the organizing committee. Summary and recommendations of the fourth international workshop conference on gestational diabetes mellitus. *Diabetes Care,* 1998; **21:** B161–7.

10. **Pedersen J.** *The Pregnant Diabetic and her Newborn: Problems and Management.* Baltimore: Williams and Wilkins, 1977: 211–20.

11. **Freinkel N.** Of pregnancy and progeny. *Diabetes,* 1980; **27:** 1023–35.

12. **Steele JM, Johnstone FD, Smith AF, Duncan LJP.** Five years experience of a pre-pregnancy clinic for insulin dependent diabetes. *British Medical Journal,* 1982; **285:** 3555–6.

13. **Hadden DR.** Geographic, ethnic and racial variations in the incidence of gestational diabetes mellitus. *Diabetes,* 1985; **34**(suppl.): 8–12.

14. **Kjos SL** *et al.* Effect of low dose oral contraceptives on carbohydrate and lipid metabolism in women with recent gestational diabetes: results of a controlled randomized prospective study. *American Journal of Obstetrics and Gynecology,* 1990; **163:** 1822–7.

15. **Jovanovic L.** American Diabetes Association's Fourth International Workshop-Conference on Gestational Diabetes Mellitus: summary and discussion. Therapeutic interventions. *Diabetes Care,* 1998 August; **21** (suppl. 2): B131–7.

16. **Kitzmiller JL, Combs AC.** Diabetic nephropathy. In: Reece EA, Coustan DR, eds. *Diabetes Mellitus in Pregnancy.* 2nd edn. Edinburgh: Churchill Livingstone, 1995: 315–44.

17. **Carron Brown S, Kyne-Grzebalski D, Mwangi B, Taylor R.** Effect of management policy upon 120 type 1 diabetic pregnancies: policy decisions in practice. *Diabetic Medicine,* 1999; **16:** 573–8.

18. **Cornblath M, Schwartz R, Aynsley-Green A, Lloyd JK.** Hypoglycaemia in infancy: the need for a rational definition. A Ciba Foundation discussion meeting. *Paediatrics,* 1990; **85:** 834–7.

19. **Mills JL** *et al.* Lack of relation of increased malformation rates in infants of diabetic mothers to glycemic control during organogenesis. *New England Journal of Medicine,* 1988; **319:** 1617–23.

20. **Hadden DR, Alexander A, McCance DR, Traub AL.** Obstetric and diabetic care for pregnancy in diabetic women: ten year outcome analysis, 1985–1995. *Diabetic Medicine,* 2001; **18:** 546–53.

21. **Hales CN, Barker DJP.** Type 2 (non insulin dependent) diabetes mellitus: the thrifty phenotype hypothesis. *Diabetologia,* 1992; **35:** 595–601.

22. **Hattersley AT, Tooke JE.** The fetal insulin hypothesis: an alternative explanation of the association of low birthweight with diabetes and vascular disease. *Lancet,* 1999; **353:** 1789–92.

23. **Pettit DJ, Knowler WL.** Diabetes and obesity in the Pima Indians: a cross generational vicious cycle. *Journal of Obesity and Weight Regulation,* 1988; **7:** 61–75.

8 Macrovascular disease and diabetes

Arshia Panahloo and John S. Yudkin

Introduction

Macrovascular disease is an important complication of diabetes and its prevention and management must form an integral part of the patient's care plan. Macrovascular disease is at least two to three times more prevalent in diabetic than non-diabetic patients.[1] In type 2 diabetes up to 75 per cent of all deaths are attributed to macrovascular disease, yet the significance of this is often neglected. The treatment of diabetic patients is often centered on the treatment of hyperglycaemia and relatively little attention is paid to other risk factors for macrovascular disease.

With improvements in glycaemic control there has been a reduction in the microvascular complications of diabetes. Unfortunately this has not been so firmly established in relation to macrovascular disease.[2] Atheroma is more frequent, more severe and more rapidly progressive in diabetes. Coronary heart disease, followed by stroke, are the commonest causes of death in type 2 diabetes. Results from recent large trials, the DCCT (Diabetes Control and Complications Trial)[3] and UKPDS (United Kingdom Prospective Diabetes Study),[4] provide concrete evidence that good glycaemic control prevents the onset and progression of diabetic microvascular disease. In consequence, the approaches to prevention of macrovascular disease take on an even greater significance. Recent data suggest that glycaemic exposure has relatively little part to play in this process. In this chapter we discuss the risk factors for macrovascular disease in diabetes, the clinical manifestations of macrovascular disease and strategies for risk factor reduction.

Risk factors for macrovascular disease

After adjusting for known risk factors for macrovascular disease, such as hypertension, dyslipidaemia and smoking, the presence of the diabetic state itself confers most of the excess coronary heart disease risk in diabetes. Furthermore, after taking into account the increased prevalence of hypertension in diabetes, diabetes itself is the major factor predisposing to stroke. In patients with diabetes conventional risk factors such as hyperlipidaemia, hypertension and smoking have a synergistic effect and should be treated aggressively. After adjustment for age, gender, smoking, hypertension, low-density lipoprotein (LDL) and high-density lipoprotein (HDL) cholesterol, diabetic subjects without prior coronary heart disease have a similar risk of cardiovascular events to non-diabetic subjects with previous coronary heart disease.[5]

Smoking is a major risk factor for coronary heart disease in diabetic subjects. Figure 1 shows the effect of risk factors and intervention on life expectancy in a 45 year old diabetic man. As shown smoking results in the largest reduction in life expectancy, while smoking cessation is more effective than treatment with antihypertensives, statins or aspirin. Diabetic patients should not only be encouraged to stop smoking, but all relevant approaches, including prescription of nicotine patches, should be employed to help patients with smoking cessation.

The following risk factors for macrovascular disease will be discussed: glycaemic control; hyperlipidaemia; hypertension; microalbuminuria; insulin; proinsulin-like molecules; and coagulation and fibrinolysis.

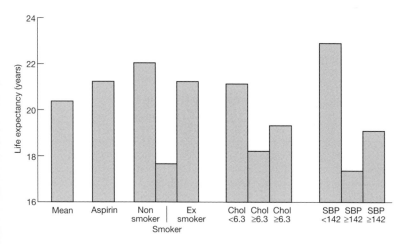

Fig. 1 Effects of risk factors and interventions on life expectancy in a 45 year old diabetic man.

Glycaemic control and macrovascular disease

The fact that the increased risk of coronary heart disease in diabetes is not fully explained by conventional risk factors has prompted speculation that hyperglycaemia itself is responsible for the enhanced cardiovascular risk. The relationship between hyperglycaemia and the development of coronary heart disease remains controversial.[7,8]

Several studies have shown an association between glycated haemoglobin and mortality from coronary heart disease, this association being stronger in younger (type 1) patients than older (type 2) patients. Epidemiological data have not resolved the causal association between glycaemia and coronary heart disease. Hyperglycaemia may have a direct effect on endothelial cell function leading to atherosclerotic change. The accumulation of advanced glycosylation end product (AGE) proteins over time has been implicated in atherosclerosis. AGEs induce excess cross-linking of collagen and other extracellular matrix proteins in the vascular wall. AGE products stimulate the release of cytokines that induce cell proliferation. Hyperglycaemia also results in glycosylation of LDL and HDL altering their function: LDL becomes more prone to oxidation and the transport of cholesterol by HDL is impaired, both factors promoting atherosclerosis.

DCCT has convincingly shown a relationship between glycaemic control and microvascular complications in patients with type 1 diabetes.[3] The study however was not designed to show a reduction in coronary heart disease – the subjects studied were young, and events were few. However, intensive therapy reduced the development of hypercholesterolaemia by 34 per cent in the combined cohort. When all major cardiovascular and peripheral vascular events were combined, intensive therapy reduced the risk of macrovascular disease by 41 per cent, but this did not reach statistical significance.

UKPDS[4] was designed in the mid 1970s. Its aim was to find out whether intensive management of blood glucose produced better long-term outcomes than conventional therapy in people newly diagnosed with type 2 diabetes. The hypothesis was that lowering blood glucose to the normal range would reduce diabetic complications and macrovascular events. A second question was whether any hypoglycaemic agent had particular advantages. A hypertension study was superimposed on the glucose control study and will be discussed below. The benefits of the intensive policy were mainly due to improved microvascular outcomes, with a borderline support for decrease in macrovascular events, as in the DCCT (16 per cent risk reduction for fatal and non-fatal myocardial infarction, $p = 0.052$). Macrovascular events outnumbered microvascular events in the study, and should have provided reasonable power for the detection of any difference. The 10-year follow-up period may have been too short to find changes in atheroma. There were no differences in cardiovascular outcomes between individual therapies.

A link between postprandial hyperglycaemia and coronary heart disease was first suggested in the 1950s. Prospective epidemiological studies provide further evidence for a link between impaired glucose tolerance (which means post-glucose load hyperglycaemia) and coronary heart disease.[8] Postprandial or post-glucose load hyperglycaemia may however, simply be a marker of increasing insulin resistance and hyperinsulinaemia which is associated with coronary heart disease.

Hyperlipidaemia

Lipid abnormalities in diabetes

Lipid and lipoprotein abnormalities occur more frequently in type 2 diabetic patients than in type 1 patients. In well-controlled type-1 diabetes, serum lipids are similar to those of non-diabetic subjects, although HDL levels may be higher. With poor glycaemic control, there is a rise in concentration of triglyceride-rich lipoproteins, chylomicrons and very low-density lipoprotein (VLDL). The abnormalities are corrected with improved insulin therapy. The major determinants of hyperlipidaemia in type 1 diabetes are poor glycaemic control, age, obesity and the presence of nephropathy.[9] Indeed, in type 1 diabetes, lipoprotein abnormalities begin to develop at the stage of microalbuminuria (see Chapter 5).

The dyslipidaemia of type 2 diabetes is, however, more closely related to insulin resistance. The characteristic dyslipidaemia consists of hypertriglyceridaemia, with low levels of HDL cholesterol. Levels of total and LDL cholesterol are usually normal. The distribution of LDL particles is however abnormal, with a prevalence of small dense LDL particles, which are strongly related to vascular risk, probably because of their predisposition to oxidation.

The relationship between lipids and macrovascular disease in diabetes

In the Multiple Risk Factor Intervention Trial Research Group (MRFIT) study, during the 12-year follow-up period, the absolute risk of cardiovascular death was increased three-fold in diabetic men after adjustment for age, race, income, serum cholesterol, systolic blood pressure, and cigarette smoking.[1] Cardiovascular death rates increased with increasing cholesterol in both non-diabetic and diabetic men. The absolute increase in risk per unit rise in serum cholesterol was steeper in subjects with diabetes, even though the proportionate risk increase was less. LDL cholesterol concentrations are a risk factor for macrovascular disease in both type 1 and type 2 diabetes. Furthermore, HDL cholesterol concentrations are inversely related to vascular disease, particularly in type 2 diabetes. In type 1 diabetes, some studies have found lower HDL cholesterol and apoprotein A1 concentrations specifically in those with coronary heart disease.[10] Serum triglyceride levels have been associated with clinical vascular disease in diabetic subjects in both cross-sectional and prospective studies. In the Paris prospective study, baseline triglyceride levels were related to subsequent coronary heart disease death after allowing for total cholesterol, systolic blood pressure, obesity and smoking.[11] Similar associations have been found in both type 1 and type 2 diabetes.[10] This may be explained by the relationship between triglyceride and LDL cholesterol, as triglyceride levels are proportional to small dense LDL and to the fall in HDL cholesterol.

Management of lipid disorders in diabetes

Total serum cholesterol, total triglyceride and HDL cholesterol concentrations should be measured annually on a fasting sample. Weight reduction and exercise are the most important lifestyle changes in patients with type 2 diabetes, leading not only to improvement in glycaemic control but also to improved insulin sensitivity, lipid profiles and blood pressure. Only when these measures have failed should drug treatment for dyslipidaemia be initiated.

The treatment of lipid abnormalities in diabetic patients should be considered as secondary prevention, regarding the diabetes as a major 'primary event'. The threshold for treating hyperlipidaemia should be lower than in the general population. In diabetes, premenopausal women lose their relative protection against cardiovascular disease, thus coronary risk should be assessed in diabetic premenopausal women as in men. While identifying patients who would benefit most from lipid-lowering therapy can be performed using a variety of risk stratification approaches,[12] the threshold for intervention remains controversial. At present, the standing medical advisory committee in the UK has recommended a coronary risk of over 3 per cent per year as the threshold for starting therapy with a statin. Recent primary and secondary prevention trials of cholesterol lowering with 3-hydroxy-3-methylglutaryl-CoA reductase inhibitors in non-diabetic populations have shown reductions in mortality and morbidity from coronary heart disease without adverse effects.[13,14] The Scandinavian Simvastatin Survival Study (4S)[13] included just over 200 diabetic patients and lipid-lowering therapy with simvastatin produced a greater reduction in coronary events in the diabetic than in non-diabetic subjects (55 per cent versus 32 per cent). However in the Cholesterol and Recurrent Events (CARE) study,[15] there were similar reductions in coronary events in a rather larger number of diabetic subjects as in the non-diabetic subjects (27 per cent versus 25 per cent). There are no trial data on which to base recommendations for the treatment of hypertriglyceridaemia and low HDL cholesterol.

The joint British recommendations on prevention of coronary heart disease in clinical practice, suggest a target of total cholesterol of less than 5.0 mmol/l and LDL cholesterol of less than 3.0 mmol/l, in subjects with coronary heart disease or atherosclerotic disease.[16] At present, the statin group of drugs are recommended for coronary risk prevention. Fibrates lower serum triglyceride levels, but, while awaiting the results of large intervention studies, no clinical trial data exist showing prevention of coronary events. The combination of a statin and fibrate can be useful in some situations, but liver transaminases and creatine kinase (CK) should be monitored. It is important to stress that all modifiable risk factors to reduce coronary heart disease should be targeted. Risk stratification charts for diabetes are further discussed below.

Hormone replacement therapy (HRT) and lipids

Oestrogen therapy in postmenopausal women lowers serum LDL cholesterol and raises serum HDL cholesterol levels. HRT should be used with caution in patients with hypertension and hypertriglyceridaemia, as HRT may aggravate these. Although there have been no studies of HRT in diabetic patients, these agents are believed – largely through epidemiological rather than clinical trial evidence to have a favourable impact on cardiovascular risk. HRT might be used more widely in patients with diabetes as their theoretical cardiovascular protective effect outweighs their side-effects. However, a randomized controlled trial showed no benefit for HRT, with early increase in thromboembolic events in the actively treated group, so the other indications for HRT should be used in women with diabetes.[17]

Hypertension

Prevalence of hypertension in diabetes and relationship to cardiac risk

Hypertension is an important cardiovascular risk factor in diabetic patients and is twice as common as in the non-diabetic population.

In type 1 diabetes hypertension is closely associated with diabetic nephropathy and begins to develop at the early stage of microalbuminuria. Susceptibility to both hypertension and nephropathy may be genetic, manifested by increased sodium–lithium counter-transport activity in red cells. This is discussed further in Chapter 5.

The prevalence of hypertension in type 2 diabetes is also higher than in the general population especially in younger patients.[18] At the age of 45, forty per cent of patients with type 2 diabetes have hypertension, the proportion increasing to sixty per cent by the age of 75.[18] Not only does hypertension add to the excess cardiovascular risk of type 2 diabetes but it is also a risk factor for the development of microalbuminuria and retinopathy. Lowering blood pressure decreases albuminuria in both type 1 and type 2 diabetes and slows the rate of decline in renal function in type 1 diabetes (Chapter 5).

Treatment of hypertension in diabetes

Hypertension remains underrecognized and undertreated in patients with diabetes. Yet hypertension in diabetes aggravates both micro- and macrovascular disease and should be treated aggressively at thresholds below those used for the non-diabetic population. Patients with microalbuminuria benefit from treatment with angiotensin-converting enzyme inhibitors while still normotensive.

The hypertension in diabetes study was a randomized controlled trial encapsulated as a Latin square design within the UKPDS. It examined whether tight blood pressure control prevented macrovascular and microvascular complications of diabetes.[19] Mean blood pressure during follow-up was significantly reduced in the group assigned tight blood pressure control (144/82), compared to the less tight control group (154/87). In the group with tight control there was a 24 per cent reduction in all diabetes related end-points, 32 per cent reduction in deaths due to diabetes (two thirds of which were the consequence of cardiovascular events) (Fig. 2), 37 per cent in microvascular end points (Fig. 3a) and 44 per cent in strokes (Fig. 3b). The group assigned to tight blood pressure control had

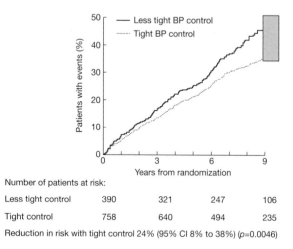

Number of patients at risk:

Less tight control	390	321	247	106
Tight control	758	640	494	235

Reduction in risk with tight control 24% (95% CI 8% to 38%) (p=0.0046)

Fig. 2 Kaplan–Meier plots of proportions of patients with any clinical end point, fatal or non-fatal, related to diabetes. (Adapted from *British Medical Journal*, 1998; **317**: 703–13.)

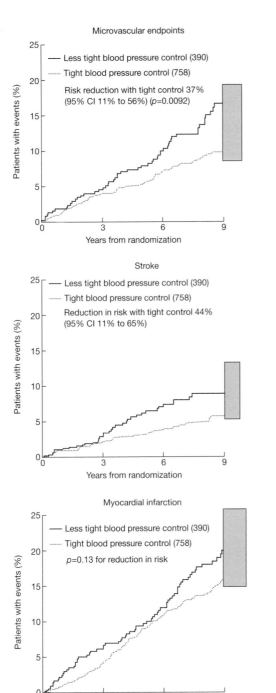

Fig. 3 (a)–(c) Kaplan–Meier plots of proportions of patients who developed microvascular end points (mostly retinal photocoagulation), fatal or non-fatal myocardial infarction or sudden death, and fatal or non-fatal strokes. (Adapted from *British Medical Journal*, 1998; **317**: 703–13.)

a non-significant reduction of 21 per cent in myocardial infarction (Fig. 3c). However when all macrovascular disease was combined, including myocardial infarction, sudden death, stroke and peripheral vascular disease, the group assigned tight blood pressure control had a 34 per cent reduction in risk compared with the group assigned to less tight control. However, the efficacy of antihypertensive therapy in diabetic patients is gained only at the expense of substantial polypharmacy. Twenty nine per cent of the tight control group required three or more hypotensive agents to achieve their target blood pressure.

The UKPDS also examined the efficacy of different antihypertensive therapies in reducing macrovascular and microvascular complications in type 2 diabetes.[20] Subjects were randomized to treatment with a β-blocker (atenolol) or angiotensin-converting enzyme inhibitor (captopril). They were both equally effective in reducing blood pressure, with a similar proportion of patients (27 per cent and 31 per cent) requiring three or more antihypertensive agents. Captopril and atenolol were equally effective in reducing the risk of macrovascular end points (Fig. 4). Interestingly, there were no advantages apparent with angiotensin-converting enzyme inhibitor therapy in terms of any of the other major end points, and, although none of the differences was significant, for 18 of the 23 individual or composite end points the point estimate of advantage favoured atenolol. The study was not fully powered to address this issue conclusively. However β-blockade resulted in more weight gain, and these patients needed greater increases in hypoglycaemic therapy than those allocated to captopril. The results of this trial have had a major impact on the management of hypertensive patients with diabetes.

From the practical point of view the therapeutic target for blood pressure in all patients with diabetes must be substantially less than 150/85 mmHg, and the data from the Hypertension Optimal Treatment (HOT) study[21] supports the UKPDS in suggesting that a target of 140/80 mmHg is appropriate. In the presence of microalbuminuria or proteinuria even lower thresholds may be logical, perhaps with a target of less than 120/70 mmHg with proteinuria greater than 1 g/24 h.[22]

There is little evidence that, compared to the importance of the degree of control, it makes much difference in regard to the clinical outcomes whether the agent used is an angiotensin-converting enzyme inhibitor, a β-blocker, a calcium-channel blocker or a thiazide diuretic – the agent of first choice in the systolic hypertension in the elderly program.[23] Certain calcium-channel blockers have been implicated in an increased coronary heart disease risk in diabetic subjects, but the results of the HOT trial[21] and the Systolic Hypertension in Europe (SYST-EUR)[23,24] trial suggest that this is not so.

Angiotensin-converting enzyme inhibitors may be useful as first line agents in subjects with microalbuminuria or proteinuria; they are efficacious, do not have deleterious metabolic side-effects and have a renoprotective effect. They can be used in combination with other agents such as selective β-blockers, thiazide diuretics, α-blockers and calcium-channel blockers. Deleterious metabolic side effects do not occur or are rare when thiazides are used in low doses (for example, bendrofluazide 1.25–2.5 mg daily) and these drugs combine well with angiotensin-converting enzyme inhibitors. Renal function should be monitored during angiotensin-converting enzyme inhibitor therapy as they may cause hyperkalaemia and renal impairment.

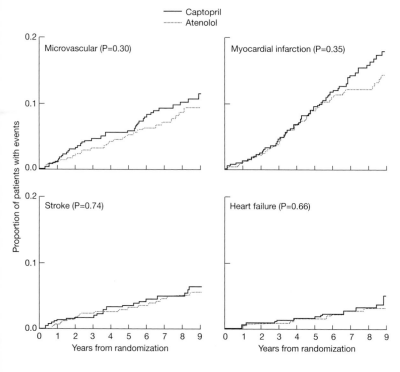

Fig. 4 Kaplan–Meier plots of proportions of patients who developed microvascular end points (mostly retinal photocoagulation), fatal or non-fatal myocardial infarction (including sudden death), and fatal or non-fatal strokes and heart failure. (Adapted from *British Medical Journal*, 1998; **317**: 713–20.)

Microalbuminuria

Microalbuminuria and proteinuria in the context of diabetic nephropathy are discussed in Chapter 5. Microalbuminuria and proteinuria are markers of cardiovascular risk in subjects with both type 1 and type 2 diabetes. Adverse changes in several cardiovascular risk factors have been found in microalbuminuric diabetic subjects, including hypertension, raised levels of triglyceride, lipoprotein(a), fibrinogen and plasminogen activator inhibitor-1 (PAI-1), but these factors alone do not seem to explain the excess risk, with microalbuminuria in consequence being an independent risk factor for cardiovascular disease. It has been postulated that microalbuminuria is a marker for the endothelial injury that initiates the atherothrombotic process.[25]

All cardiovascular risk factors should be targeted aggressively in diabetic subjects with microalbuminuria and proteinuria. Patients should be advised to stop smoking and should be treated with low-dose aspirin.

Insulin

Subjects with type 2 diabetes have raised levels of circulating insulin, although these concentrations decline later in the natural history of the condition. Subjects with type 1 diabetes also have peripheral hyperinsulinaemia compared to normal subjects, in whom insulin secreted physiologically into the portal vein is cleared by the liver.

There is some evidence that raised plasma insulin itself may be a risk factor for cardiovascular disease, although this remains controversial.[26] Insulin may be directly involved in atherogenesis.[27] In animal studies, high insulin concentrations have been shown to stimulate cholesterol synthesis in smooth muscle cells and in macrophages in the arterial wall. It also stimulates proliferation and migration of smooth muscle cells and enhances the binding of LDL to smooth muscle cells and macrophages. These changes result in the thickening of the arterial wall and are influenced by hypertension and other haemodynamic factors to which insulin may contribute. There is however no evidence of a deleterious effect of insulin on the arterial wall in humans.

It has been postulated that hyperinsulinaemia may contribute to hypertension by stimulating the sympathetic nervous system, promoting renal sodium retention and inducing vascular smooth muscle cell hypertrophy. However, patients treated with insulin or those with high insulin concentrations as a result of insulinoma do not have elevated blood pressure levels, suggesting that the relationship between hyperinsulinaemia and hypertension is the consequence of other mechanisms. The fact that the insulin treated type 2 diabetic patients in the UKPDS showed no excess cardiovascular morbidity or mortality has ended much of the theorizing about the potentially adverse effects of insulin.[4]

Raised insulin levels and insulin resistance are associated with inhibition of fibrinolysis, mainly through an effect on PAI-1. PAI-1 levels are elevated in subjects with type 2 diabetes, and insulin is thought to have a direct effect in stimulating PAI-1 release from endothelial cells and hepatocytes. PAI-1 as a cardiovascular risk factor will be discussed further below.

Proinsulin-like molecules

In diabetic subjects approximately 30 per cent of insulin measured in an insulin radioimmunoassay consists of proinsulin-like molecules, which are intact and des 31,32 proinsulin.[28] As with insulin, concentrations of proinsulin-like molecules correlate with cardiovascular risk factors. Clinical trials of human proinsulin were discontinued due to an increase in cardiovascular events. The mechanisms whereby proinsulin-like molecules may confer increased cardiovascular risk are not apparent. In type 2 diabetes insulin treatment reduces levels of proinsulin-like molecules. In a cross-over study a reduction in levels of proinsulin correlated with a reduction in PAI-1 activity. This may suggest that proinsulin augments PAI-1 expression independently of insulin. Both intact and des 31,32 proinsulin have been shown to stimulate PAI-1 expression *in vitro*.[29]

Coagulation and fibrinolysis

Figure 5 shows a simplified scheme of the coagulation and fibrinolytic pathways. Diabetes is associated with several defects in the pathway, predisposing to procoagulant changes in the blood. These defects are marked on Fig. 5. An atherosclerotic plaque alone is not sufficient for the development of coronary heart disease, there being a need for superimposed inflammation, plaque rupture and thrombosis. The procoagulant changes in diabetes contribute to plaque thrombosis precipitating acute myocardial infarction (AMI).

PAI-1 is a major regulator of fibrinolysis. Levels are raised in subjects with type 2 diabetes and probably contribute to their poor outcome following thrombolytic therapy. PAI-1 is produced by endothelial cells and hepatocytes, and plasma levels show a strong correlation with serum insulin-like molecules and triglyceride levels. PAI-1 levels are elevated post AMI, and diabetic subjects admitted with AMI have higher PAI-1 levels than non-diabetic subjects, this being associated with reduced efficacy of thrombolytic therapy, higher rise in cardiac enzymes (indicating impaired reperfusion), and an increased risk of early and delayed reinfarction. The molecular basis of variations in PAI-1 levels will be further discussed in Chapter 3.2.

Clinical manifestations of macrovascular disease
Presentation of macrovascular disease

The presentation of cardiovascular disease in diabetes is similar to that in non-diabetic subjects, with angina, myocardial infarction and heart failure being the most prominent. Classical symptoms occur, although angina and myocardial infarction can be painless, possibly due to an autonomic neuropathy. Ischaemic events may present atypically, with sweating, malaise, dyspnoea and syncope, often confused with hypoglycaemia. Silent ischaemia apparent on Holter monitoring or ECG is more common in diabetes and has a worse prognosis.[30]

Both immediate and long-term mortality from myocardial infarction are increased in diabetic subjects. Myocardial infarction runs a more complicated course in diabetes, with an increased risk of cardiogenic shock and congestive heart failure. This increased risk persists despite a similar infarct size to that of non-diabetic subjects. Despite overall improvements in outcome of AMI, the excess risk of the diabetic patient persists into the thrombolytic era.

The clinical presentation of stroke is similar to that in non-diabetic subjects, although the mortality and disability following stroke is increased in diabetes. Arterial disease in the leg presents with typical intermittent claudication. Peripheral vascular disease in the context of the diabetic foot is discussed further in Chapter 9.

The management of acute myocardial infarction[31]
Thrombolytic therapy

Thrombolytic therapy in diabetic patients is proportionately of similar advantage as in patients without diabetes. The higher absolute

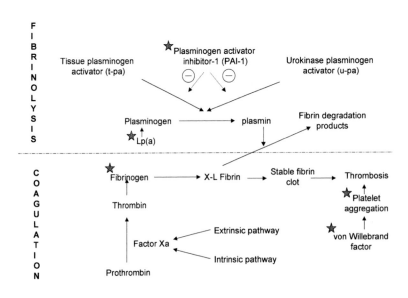

Fig. 5 The coagulation and fibrinolytic pathway. The defects that favor coagulation and impair fibrinolysis are marked with a star.

risk translates into greater absolute benefit than for non-diabetic patients in terms of lives saved per treatment given. Proliferative retinopathy is no longer considered a contraindication to thrombolytic therapy. A review of the literature has found only one case of retinal haemorrhage in a diabetic patient given thrombolysis, and this resolved in three weeks. The Global Utilization of Streptokinase and tissue plasminogen activator for Occluded Coronary Arteries Study included 6011 patients with diabetes who were given thrombolysis. There was only one case noted of an ocular complication – a periorbital haematoma. As it can be calculated from meta-analysis that administering thrombolytic therapy to 1000 diabetic patients would result in 37 fewer deaths at 35 days, treating these 6000 patients with thrombolysis would have resulted in over 200 fewer deaths to set against this one periorbital haematoma.

There is no evidence regarding the advantages of one thrombolytic therapy over another. As mentioned above, angiographic and enzyme release studies suggest that the diabetic coronary thrombus is more resistant to thrombolytic therapy, perhaps due to the higher concentrations of PAI-1. This would suggest, in theory at least, that subjects with diabetes might benefit from higher doses of thrombolytic agents. This has not been tested in clinical practice.

Aspirin[32]

Debate on the use of aspirin in subjects with diabetes continues. In the Second International Study of Infarct Survival study, the 35-day mortality in all subjects was reduced to a similar degree by either streptokinase or 165 mg of aspirin started on admission. However the subgroup analysis of diabetic patients found a significant interaction, implying that they did not benefit from aspirin. But caution was expressed in interpreting results from multiple subgroups. Other diabetic subgroups in major thrombolytic studies and investigations of aspirin show similar benefits to those in non-diabetic subjects (Fig. 6). Some studies, based on platelet thromboxane levels after different doses of aspirin, suggest that diabetic patients might need higher doses of aspirin (300 mg rather than the more usual 75–150 mg) than patients without diabetes. This has not been evaluated clinically.

Strong evidence therefore exists for treating with aspirin any diabetic patient with a history of myocardial infarction, angina, thrombotic stroke or transient ischaemic attacks, provided that there are no contraindications. It would also be valid to consider aspirin treatment for any diabetic patient without known macrovascular disease considered to be of high cardiovascular risk.

Glycaemic control (insulin–glucose infusion)

Thrombolytic therapy and aspirin have improved the prognosis of patients presenting with AMI, however, diabetic patients continue to do badly, with greater morbidity and mortality. Around 20–25 per cent of patients admitted to coronary care units will be found to be hyperglycaemic, although in many instances this is stress hyperglycaemia rather than newly diagnosed diabetes. The findings of the DIGAMI (Diabetes Mellitus, Insulin Glucose Infusion in Acute Myocardial Infarction) study[33] have shown a major advantage of improved glycaemic control during and after myocardial infarction and suggest that known diabetic and hyperglycaemic patients post AMI should be managed with insulin rather than with continuing oral hypoglycaemic agents. In this study 620 patients with known or newly diagnosed diabetes, and plasma glucose concentrations exceeding 11 mmol/l on admission with AMI, were randomized to receive either an intensified intravenous insulin regimen or hypoglycaemic therapy at the discretion of the physician. The intensified regimen comprised the use of insulin and glucose infusions in hospital, followed by multiple insulin injections for at least three months. There was a significant improvement in glycaemic control at 24 h and at discharge. Although there was no significant difference in in-hospital deaths, the 12 month mortality was reduced by 30 per cent in the infusion group. At a mean follow-up of 3.4 years mortality in the infusion group was reduced by 28 per cent.

The most striking benefit of intravenous insulin treatment was seen in the large sub-group (44 per cent of the study population) who were not taking insulin on admission, and with a low cardiovascular risk profile. Questions however, remain unanswered, whether the benefit resulted from insulin infusion during the acute event, from improved glycaemic control following discharge, or from a pharmacological benefit of withdrawing oral hypoglycaemic agents.

The controversial UGDP study in the 1970s suggested a higher cardiovascular mortality in type 2 diabetic patients treated with oral hypoglycaemic agents and one interpretation was to attribute the excess cardiac events to the sulphonylureas. Sulphonylureas act by inhibiting the K_{ATP} channel, which is present not only in the pancreas but also in the heart and vascular smooth muscle. Blockade of these channels has been shown to prevent cardiac preconditioning and reduce reactive hyperaemia under experimental conditions. In theory, this could lead to a worse outcome after AMI. The UKPDS study has however not shown any adverse cardiovascular events of sulphonylureas.

A meta-analysis of nine randomized trials using glucose-insulin-potassium (GIK) infusions in the treatment of AMI, predominantly in patients without diabetes, showed a significant reduction in in-patient mortality in patients treated with GIK compared to placebo.[34] Five of these studies excluded subjects with type 1 diabetes, and two excluded all subjects with diabetes. One postulated mechanism for the beneficial action of GIK infusions may be the use of exogenous glucose as fuel rather than non-esterified fatty acids, thus preventing ischaemic myocardial injury. Thus it is possible that patients in the DIGAMI Study had diabetes was irrelevant to their benefiting from insulin.

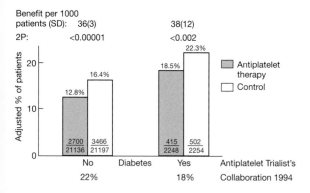

Fig. 6 The benefits of aspirin on cardiovascular events in non-diabetic and diabetic subjects. (Adapted from *Diabetic Medicine*, 1998; **15**: 275–81.)

Despite the important results, the DIGAMI study had major limitations – such as in providing a mechanism of benefit, in terms of the relative advantages of early versus late insulin treatment, and the need for twice-daily versus multiple injection therapy in these patients. The results of the DIGAMI 2 Study are awaited to answer many of the questions regarding mechanisms of action. Debate continues as to whether long-term insulin therapy should be continued post AMI. Significant survival benefit from the whole DIGAMI population were not seen until 12 months, perhaps as a consequence of questions of study power, but possibly suggesting that long-term insulin therapy played an important role. We advocate that all diabetic patients post AMI should be treated long-term with insulin, in twice- or multiple daily injection regimens. Local policies should be developed to implement a DIGAMI-like protocol.

Secondary prevention post AMI

In addition to the long-term use of aspirin and insulin, β-blockers and angiotensin-converting enzyme inhibitors should be considered in diabetic patients post AMI.

β-blockers

Early introduction of cardioselective β-blockade in diabetic subjects is associated with substantial reduction in overall mortality, sudden death and non-fatal reinfarction.[35] Meta-analyses suggest a reduction in mortality of 35 per cent.[36] There is now compelling evidence that β-blockers reduce reinfarction and sudden death in diabetic patients at least as effectively, and probably to a greater extent than in non-diabetic patients. β-blockers do not affect the intensity or number of hypoglycaemic attacks and should not be withheld from diabetic patients. Deterioration in glycaemic control or blunted counterregulatory responses to hypoglycaemia are seldom clinically important problems, especially with the cardioselective β-blockers. Critical limb ischaemia is an absolute contraindication. Heart failure is no longer considered a contraindication, since trials with cavedilol have shown improved morbidity and mortality in mild to moderate heart failure. In summary, all diabetic patients should receive intravenous β-blockers acutely followed by oral therapy post AMI, unless there is an absolute contraindication.[36]

Angiotensin-converting enzyme inhibitors

Angiotensin-converting enzyme inhibitors have protective properties both when started early during the acute phase of AMI or months post AMI in patients with diabetes.[37] As mentioned previously, several mechanisms may contribute to the increased in-hospital mortality in diabetic patients; more extensive atherosclerosis, clinical or sub-clinical diabetic cardiomyopathy with systolic or diastolic dysfunction, alterations in the fibrinolytic system, impaired reperfusion and reocclusion after fibrinolysis, diabetic neuropathy with sympathetic/parasympathetic imbalance, and endothelial dysfunction. Angiotensin-converting enzyme inhibitors have the potential to interfere with most of these mechanisms either directly through the renin–angiotensin and bradykinin systems or indirectly through their haemodynamic effects. Several recent trials have shown significant benefit of long-term angiotensin-converting enzyme inhibitor therapy with a risk reduction in mortality of 19 per cent to 27 per cent over 2.5 to 4 years of follow-up.[37] The Trandolapril Cardiac

Evaluation (TRACE) study showed that angiotensin-converting enzyme inhibitor treatment post AMI in patients with left ventricular dysfunction increased life expectancy, the effect being greater in subjects with diabetes, almost doubling life expectancy.[38] In summary, diabetic patients with left ventricular dysfunction post AMI should routinely be treated with angiotensin-converting enzyme inhibitors both in the acute and long-term setting.

Coronary surgery in diabetic subjects

Coronary artery disease in diabetic subjects is often considered to be diffuse, severe and unsuited to surgery.[39] Angiographic and necropsy evidence on this matter is inconclusive but coronary artery disease may progress more rapidly in the presence of diabetes. Angiographic appearances of advanced disease may therefore be a result of delay in investigation. Although surgery may be more complicated by infection, symptom relief by coronary artery bypass surgery, including internal mammary grafting, is comparable to that achieved among non-diabetic patients, although long-term survival is less good. A reduced long-term survival does not in itself justify withholding surgery from diabetic patients. Diabetic patients with angina experience good results from angioplasty. The St. Vincent task force for diabetes cardiovascular disease sub-group called for more active consideration for revascularization procedures for diabetic patients by cardiologists and cardiac surgeons.[39]

Risk factor reduction

The concept of numbers needed to treat (NNT) has been popularized by the proponents of evidence based medicine. If an intervention reduces the risk of an event by, say, 25 per cent in all groups of subjects treated, the intervention will be 10 times more effective, in terms of events prevented per treatment given, if applied to a population with a 40 per cent risk of the event as compared to one with a 4 per cent risk. This means that, both in terms of cost-benefit and risk-benefit, it would be more advantageous to treat more subjects at high risk than at low risk – even if that high level of risk is not a consequence of the risk factor which is being treated. In terms of how this relates to patients with diabetes, the quantitation of level of risk merely allows calculation of something which has been done qualitatively by clinicians for years – in that levels of cholesterol or blood pressure which might remain untreated in patients without coronary heart disease or nephropathy would be considered as warranting therapy in a patient with such a complication.

A number of approaches have been devised to allow easy quantitation of overall levels of risk. Some of these, such as the Sheffield cholesterol tables, derive threshold concentrations of total cholesterol which would predict certain risks of coronary heart disease events or death (for example, 1.5 per cent, 3 per cent, 4.5 per cent per annum) in men and women of different ages and with or without other risk factors. Others, such as the Dundee risk disk, allow quantitation of relative or absolute levels of coronary heart disease risk respectively for individuals based on categoric and continuous variables.

The task force of the European Society for Cardiology, European Atherosclerosis Society and European Society of Hypertension ('European task force') has produced a Risk Table for coronary heart disease incidence in the form of colour charts based on Framingham coefficients. These permit estimation of 10 year risk of coronary heart disease for men and women, smokers and non-smokers, of different ages and at different levels of blood pressure and cholesterol. Persuaded by the advantages of colour charts which simultaneously integrate several risk factors, the approach has been expanded to provide Risk Charts for diabetic, as well as non-diabetic, subjects.[12] Furthermore, because the presence of microalbuminuria in diabetic subjects acts as an important predictor for cardiovascular disease, a recent meta-analysis has been employed to calculate additional risk in the presence of microalbuminuria, permitting the derivation of a Risk Chart for microalbuminuric diabetic subjects.[12] The colour charts are reproduced as Figs 7–9.

The influence of a risk factor is not usually fully reversible. In order to estimate the benefit of risk factor reduction, one needs to apply the findings of intervention trials, or their meta-analyses. If the risk of a coronary heart disease event can be reduced by 25 per cent by a lifestyle or therapeutic intervention, treating a person with a predicted 10 year risk of 40 per cent will reduce this to 30 per cent. Thus treating 100 such people for 10 years will cut the number of events from 40 to 30. These figures translate as numbers needed to treat – 10 people for 10 years to prevent one event, or 100 person-years of treatment per event prevented. The colour codes are translated into numbers needed to treat in Fig. 10. The figure of 25 per cent risk reduction is an approximation as to the benefits of cholesterol lowering with an 3-hydroxy-3 methylglutaryl-CoA reductase

inhibitor, and of aspirin treatment, on vascular events. Overviews of the benefits of blood pressure lowering on coronary heart disease incidence from the UKPDS, the Hypertension Optimal Treatment and the Systolic Hypertension in the Elderly Program Studies have estimated a reduction of between 20 per cent and 30 per cent, but treating hypertension has a much more dramatic impact on reducing the incidence of stroke, such that a net figure of 25 per cent of total events prevented may be an underestimate.

Table 1 combines the estimates from a variety of intervention studies in patients with diabetes to calculate numbers needed to treat to prevent a coronary heart disease event and to prevent death. As previously emphasized, cigarette smoking is not only the risk factor which has the greatest impact on both coronary heart disease risk and on total mortality, it is also the one which shows the greatest reversibility. Because of the impact of smoking cessation on a variety of other conditions, life expectancy is affected to a much greater extent than would be expected by the influence on coronary heart disease alone (Fig. 1).

These Risk Charts provide an easily accessible, but of preliminary necessity, approach to estimating levels of coronary heart disease risk in non-diabetic and diabetic subjects. It is proposed that they might be used to make decisions on thresholds for intervention for cholesterol and blood pressure lowering and for aspirin treatment. We also propose that their accessibility may make them useful for patient education.

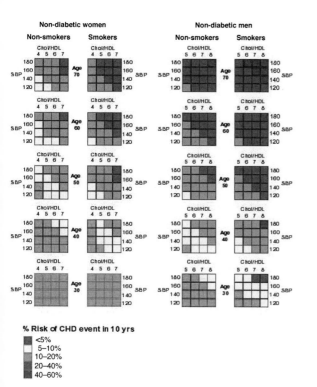

Fig. 7 Ten-year risk of coronary heart disease events in non-diabetic men and women. (Adapted from *Diabetic Medicine*, 1999; **16**: 219–27.)

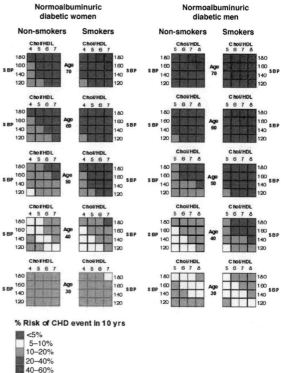

Fig. 8 Ten-year risk of coronary heart disease events in diabetic men and women with normal albumin excretion. (Adapted from *Diabetic Medicine*, 1999; **16**: 219–27.)

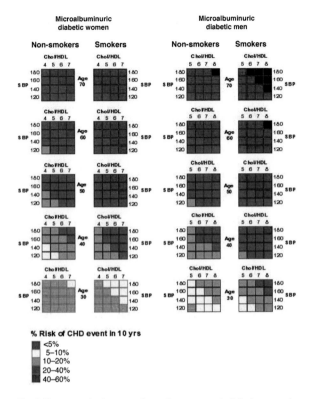

Fig. 9 Ten-year risk of coronary heart disease events in diabetic men and women with microalbuminuria. (Adapted from *Diabetic Medicine*, 1999; **16**: 219–27.) (See Plate 39.)

Background risk per 10 years	Effect of treatment on events per 100 subject per 10 years	Reduction in events per 100 subject per 10 years	Numbers needed to treat for 10 years to prevent one event
80%	⟹60%	20	5
70%	⟹53%	17.5	6
60%	⟹45%	15	6.7
50%	⟹38%	12.5	8
40%	⟹30%	10	10
30%	⟹23%	7.5	13.3
20%	⟹15%	5	20
15%	⟹11%	3.75	26.7
10%	⟹ 8%	2.5	40
7.5%	⟹ 6%	1.87	53.3
5%	⟹ 4%	1.25	80
2.5%	⟹ 2%	0.53	160

Fig. 10 Number needed to treat for ten years to prevent one event. (Adapted from *Diabetic Medicine*, 1999; **16**: 219–27.)

Table 1 Numbers needed to treat for 10 years to prevent 1 chd event if background risk is 30%

Glucose lowering	20.8
Blood pressure	15.9
Cholesterol lowering	29.8
Aspirin	15.2
Stopping smoking	17.4

Conclusion

In conclusion macrovascular disease is an important complication of diabetes and attention to risk factor reduction should play an important and integral part of diabetes care.

Acknowledgement

We would like to thank Sara Stanner for kindly producing the risk stratification charts.

References

1. Stamler J, Vaccaro O, Neaton JD, Wentworth D. Multiple Risk factor Intervention Trial Research Group. Diabetes, other risk factors, and 12 year cardiovascular mortality for men screened in the Multiple Risk Factor Intervention Trial. *Diabetes Care*, 1993; **16**: 434–44.

2. Chaturvedi N, Jarrett J, Shipley MJ, Fuller JH. Socioeconomic gradient in morbidity and mortality in people with diabetes: cohort study findings from the Whitehall study and the WHO multinational study of vascular disease in diabetes. *British Medical Journal*, 1998; **316**: 100–5.

3. The Diabetes Control and Complications Trial Group. The effect of treatment of diabetes on the development and progression of long-term complications. *New England Journal of Medicine*, 1993; **329**: 977–86.

4. UK Prospective Diabetes Study (UKPDS) Group. Intensive blood-glucose control with sulphonylureas or insulin compared with conventional treatment and risk of complications in patients with type 2 diabetes (UKPDS 33). *Lancet*, 1998; **352**: 837–53.

5. Haffner SM, Lehto S, Ronnemaa T, Pyörälä K, Laakso M. Mortality from coronary heart disease in subjects with type 2 diabetes and in nondiabetic subjects with and without prior myocardial infarction. *New England Journal of Medicine*, 1988; **339**: 229–34.

6. Yudkin JS, Blauth C, Drury P *et al*. Prevention and management of cardiovascular disease in patients with diabetes mellitus: an evidence base. *Diabetic Medicine*, 1996; **13**: S101–21.

7. Barrett-Connor E. Does hyperglycemia really cause coronary heart disease? *Diabetes Care*, 1997; **20**: 1620–3.

8. Haffner SM. The importance of hyperglycaemia in the non-fasting state to the development of cardiovascular disease. *Endocrine Reviews*, 1998; **19**(5): 583–92.

9. Haaber AB, Kofoed-Enevoldsen A, Jensen T. The prevalence of hypercholesterolaemia and its relationship with albuminuria in insulin-dependent diabetic patients; an epidemiological study. *Diabetic Medicine*, 1992; **9**: 557–61.

10. Laakso M, Pyörälä K, Sarlund H, Voutilainen E. Lipid and lipoprotein abnormalities associated with coronary heart disease in patients with insulin dependent diabetes mellitus. *Arteriosclerosis*, 1986; **6**: 679–84.

11. Fontbonne A, Eschwège E, Cambien F *et al*. Hypertriglyceridaemia as a risk factor for coronary heart disease mortality in subjects with impaired glucose tolerance or diabetes. *Diabetologia*, 1989; **32**: 300–4.

12. Yudkin JS, Chaturvedi N. Developing risk stratification charts for diabetic and nondiabetic subjects. *Diabetic Medicine*, 1999; **16**: 219–27.

13. Pyörälä K, Pedersen TR, Kjekshus J, Feargeman O, Olsson AG, Thorgiersson G. Cholesterol lowering with simvastatin improves prognosis of diabetic patients with coronary heart disease. A subgroup analysis of the Scandinavian Simvastatin Survival Study (4S). *Diabetes Care*, 1997; **20**: 614–20.

14. Shephard J, Cobbe SM, Ford I. West of Scotland Coronary Prevention Study Group Prevention of coronary heart disease with pravastatin in men with hypercholesterolemia. *New England Journal of Medicine*, 1995; **333**: 1301–7.

15. Sacks FM *et al*. The effect of pravastatin on coronary events after myocardial infarction in patients with average cholesterol levels. *New England Journal of Medicine*, 1996; **335**: 1001–9.

16. Joint British recommendations for the prevention of coronary heart disease in clinical practice. British Cardiac Society, British Hyperlipidaemia Association, British Hypertension Society, endorsed by the British Diabetic Association. *Heart*, 1998; **80**: S2.

17. Hulley S *et al*. Randomized trial of estrogen plus progestin for secondary prevention of coronary heart disease in postmenopausal women. Heart and Estrogen/progestin Replacement Study (HERS) Research Group *Journal of the American Medical Association*, 1998; **280**: 605–13.

18. Hypertension in Diabetes Study Group. HDS 1: prevalence of hypertension in newly presenting type 2 diabetic patients and the association with risk factors for cardio-vascular and diabetic complications. *Journal of Hypertension*, 1993; **11**: 309–17.

19. UK Prospective Diabetes Study Group. Tight blood pressure control and risk of macrovascular and microvascular complications in type 2 diabetes: UKPDS 38. *British Medical Journal*, 1998; **317**: 703–13.

20. UK Prospective Diabetes Study Group. Efficacy of atenolol and captopril in reducing risk of macrovascular and microvascular complications in type 2 diabetes: UKPDS 39. *British Medical Journal*, 1998; **317**: 713–20.

21. Hansson L *et al*. Effects of intensive blood pressure lowering and low-dose aspirin in patients with hypertension: principal results of the Hypertension Optimal Treatment (HOT) randomised trial. *Lancet*, 1998; **351**: 1755–62.

22. Lazarus JM *et al*. Modification of Diet in Renal Disease Study Group. Achievement and safety of a low blood pressure goal in chronic renal disease. *Hypertension*, 1997; **29**: 641–50.

23. Curb JD *et al*. Effect of diuretic-based antihypertensive treatment on cardiovascular disease risk in older diabetic patients with isolated systolic hypertension. *Journal of the American Medical Association*, 1996; **276**: 1886–92.

24. Staessen JA *et al*. Randomised double-blind comparison of placebo and active treatment for older patients with isolated systolic hypertension. The Systolic Hypertension in Europe (Syst-Eur) Trial Investigators. *Lancet*, 1997; **350**: 757–64.

25. Deckert T, Feldt-Rasmussen B, Borch-Johnsen K, Jensen T, Kofoed-Enevoldsen A. Albuminuria reflects widespread vascular damage: the Steno hypothesis. *Diabetologia*, 1989; **32**: 219–26.

26. Jarrett RJ. Why is insulin not a risk factor for coronary heart disease? *Diabetologia*, 1994; **37**: 945–7.

27. Stout RW. Insulin and atheroma. 20 year perspective. *Diabetes Care*, 1990; **13**: 631–54.

28. Yudkin JS. Circulating proinsulin-like molecules. *Journal of Diabetes Complications*, 1993; **7**: 113–23.

29. Panahloo A, Yudkin JS. Diminished fibrinolysis in diabetes mellitus and its implication for diabetic vascular disease. *Coronary Artery Disease*, 1996; **7**: 724–31.

30. Schneidt-Nave C, Barrett-Connor E, Wingard DL. Resting electrocardiographic abnormalities suggestive of asymptomatic ischemic heart disease associated with non insulin dependent diabetes mellitus in a defined population. *Circulation*, 1990; **81**: 899–906.

31. Yudkin JS. Managing the diabetic patient with acute myocardial infarction. *Diabetic Medicine*, 1998; **15**: 276–81.

32. Yudkin JS. Which diabetic patients should be taking aspirin? *British Medical Journal*, 1995; **311**: 641–2.

33. Malmberg K. DIGAMI (Diabetes Mellitus, Insulin Glucose Infusion in Acute Myocardial Infarction) Study Group. Prospective randomised study of intensive insulin treatment on long term survival after acute myocardial infarction in patients with diabetes. *British Medical Journal*, 1997; **314**: 1512–5.

34. Fath-Ordoubadi F, Beatt KJ. Glucose-insulin-potassium therapy for treatment of acute myocardial infarction. An overview of randomised placebo-controlled trials. *Circulation*, 1997; **96**: 1152–6.

35. Kjekshus J, Gilpin E, Cali G. Diabetic patients and beta-blockers after acute myocardial infarction. *European Heart Journal*, 1990; **11**: 43–50.

36. McDonald TM, Butler R, Newton RW, Morris AD. Which drugs benefit diabetic patients for secondary prevention of myocardial infarction? DARTS/MEMO collaboration. *Diabetic Medicine*, 1998; **15**: 282–9.

37. Zuanetti G, Latini R, Maggioni AP, Franzosi MG, Santoro L, Tognoni G. GISSI-3 investigators. Effect of the ACE inhibitor lisinopril on mortality in diabetic patients with acute myocardial infarction. *Circulation*, 1997; **96**: 4239–45.

38. Torp-Pedersen C, Køber L. TRACE Study Group. Effect of ACE inhibitor trandolapril on life expectancy of patients with reduced left-ventricular function after acute myocardial infarction. *Lancet*, 1999; **354**: 9–12.

9 The diabetic foot

Michael Edmonds and V.M. Foster

Introduction

These are exciting times for the diabetic foot. Major advances in the last decade have led to improved outcomes in ulcer management and reduced numbers of amputations.[1] Increased interest in the diabetic foot has resulted in systematic reviews,[2–4] guidelines[5] and consensus development.[6,7] These reports have stressed the importance of early recognition of the 'at risk' foot, the prompt institution of preventive measures, and the provision of rapid and intensive treatment of foot infection in multidisciplinary foot clinics. Such measures can reduce the number of amputations in diabetic patients.

This chapter outlines a simple classification of the diabetic foot into the neuropathic and neuroischaemic foot. It then describes a simple staging system of the natural history of the diabetic foot and a treatment plan for each stage.[8] Successful management of the diabetic foot needs the expertise of a multidisciplinary team which should include physician, podiatrist, nurse, orthotist, radiologist and surgeon working closely together, within the focus of a diabetic foot clinic.

Classification

An important prelude to proper management of the diabetic foot is the correct diagnosis of its two main syndromes; the neuropathic foot, in which neuropathy predominates but the major arterial supply to the foot is intact, and the neuroischaemic foot, where both neuropathy and ischaemia resulting from a reduced arterial supply, contribute to the clinical presentation.[9]

The significance of structural abnormalities of the skin microcirculation is not fully understood, although there are numerous functional abnormalities which may be important. These include increased blood flow, widespread vascular dilatation, increased vascular permeability, impaired vascular activity and limitation of hyperaemia.[10]

Infection is rarely a sole factor but often complicates neuropathy and ischaemia and is responsible for considerable tissue necrosis in the diabetic patient. Effective neutrophil microbial action depends on the generation of several oxygen-derived free radicals. These toxic species, which include the superoxide anion, are formed during the respiratory burst activated after chemotaxis and phagocytosis. In diabetes, especially if poorly controlled, deficiencies in neutrophil chemotaxis, phagocytosis, superoxide production, respiratory burst activity and intracellular killing have all been described.[11]

The neuropathic foot

This is a warm, well-perfused foot with sensory deficit and autonomic dysfunction leading to arteriovenous shunting and distended dorsal veins. Peripheral auto-sympathectomy damages the neurogenic control mechanisms which regulate capillary and arteriovenous shunt flow and loss of pre-capillary vasoconstriction.[10] The pulses are palpable. Sweating is diminished and the skin may be dry and prone to fissuring. Motor neuropathy resulting in paralysis of the small muscles may contribute to structural deformities such as a high arch and claw toes. This leads to prominence of the metatarsal heads (Fig. 1). It has two main complications, the neuropathic ulcer and the neuropathic (Charcot) foot.

The neuroischaemic foot

This is a cool, pulseless foot with poor perfusion. It also has neuropathy. Ischaemia results from atherosclerosis of the leg vessels. This is often bilateral, multisegmental and distal, involving arteries below the knee. Intermittent claudication and rest pain may be absent because of coexisting neuropathy and the distal distribution of the arterial disease. Ulcers in the neuroischaemic foot develop on the margins of the foot, at sites made vulnerable by underlying ischaemia to moderate but continuous pressure, often from poorly fitting shoes (Fig. 2).

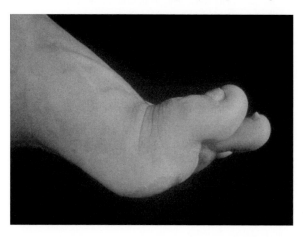

Fig. 1 Neuropathic foot showing dilated dorsal veins secondary to autonomic neuropathy and high medical longitudinal arch leading to prominent metatarsal heads secondary to motor neuropathy.

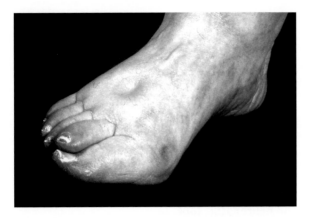

Fig. 2 Neuroischaemic foot with pitting oedema secondary to cardiac failure. There is also hallux valgus and erythema from pressure of tight shoe on medial aspect of the first metatarso-phalangeal joint.

The natural history of the diabetic foot

The natural history of the diabetic foot can be divided into six stages:[8]

(1) The foot is normal and not at risk. The patient does not have the risk factors that render him vulnerable to foot ulcers (neuropathy, ischaemia, deformity, callus and oedema).

(2) High risk foot. The patient has developed one or more of the risk factors for ulceration of the foot.

(3) Foot with ulcer. Ulceration is on the plantar surface in the neuropathic foot (Fig. 1) and on the margin in the neuroischaemic foot (Fig. 2).

(4) Foot with cellulitis. The ulcer has developed infection with the presence of cellulitis, which can complicate both the neuropathic and the neuroischaemic foot.

(5) Foot with necrosis. In the neuropathic foot, infection is usually the cause of necrosis. In the neuroischaemic foot, infection is still the most common reason, although severe ischaemia can lead to necrosis directly.

(6) The foot cannot be saved and will need a major amputation.

Every diabetic patient can be placed into one of these stages and then managed appropriately. In stages 1 and 2, the emphasis is on prevention of ulceration. In stage 3 the presentation and management of foot ulceration is critical. Finally, in stages 4 and 5, the complications of foot ulceration, notably, cellulitis and necrosis must be managed.

The management of the diabetic foot

At each stage, it is necessary to take control to prevent progression. Management will be considered under the following headings:

- wound control
- microbiological control
- mechanical control
- vascular control
- metabolic control
- educational control.

Metabolic control is important at every stage. Tight control of blood glucose, blood pressure and blood cholesterol and triglycerides should be achieved to preserve neurological and cardiovascular function. Advice should be given to stop smoking. In stages 4 and 5, metabolic decompensation may occur in the presence of infection, and intensive management of the diabetic state is often required.[8]

Stage 1 – normal foot

Presentation

By definition, the foot does not have the risk factors for foot ulcers, namely, neuropathy, ischaemia, deformity, callus, and swelling. The diagnosis of stage 1 is made by screening patients and excluding these factors.

Neuropathy

A simple technique for detecting patients with loss of protective pain sensation is to use a nylon monofilament, which, when applied perpendicular to the foot, buckles at a given force of 10 g. The filament should be pressed against several sites including the plantar aspect of the first toe, the first, third and metatarsal heads, the plantar surface of the heel and the dorsum of the foot. The filament should not be applied over callus until that has been removed. If the patient cannot feel the filament at any of these sites, then significant neuropathy is present with loss of protective pain sensation. Prospective studies have shown that the inability to perceive the 10 g monofilament at the toes or the dorsum of the foot predicts future development of an ulcer.[12]

Ischaemia

The most important manoeuvre to detect ischaemia is the palpation of the foot pulses, namely the dorsalis pedis pulse and the posterior tibial pulse. If either of these foot pulses can be felt then it is highly unlikely that there is significant ischaemia. A small hand held Doppler probe can be used to confirm the presence of pulses and to quantitate the vascular supply. Used together with a sphygmomanometer, the brachial systolic pressure and ankle systolic pressure can be measured. The pressure index, which is the ratio of ankle systolic pressure to brachial systolic pressure, can be calculated. In normal subjects, the pressure index is usually more than one, but in the presence of ischaemia it is below one. Thus, absence of pulses and a pressure index of less than one confirms ischaemia. Conversely, the presence of pulses and a pressure index over one rules out ischaemia and further vascular investigations are not necessary.

Many diabetic patients have medial arterial calcification, giving an artificially elevated systolic pressure, even in the presence of ischaemia. It is thus difficult to assess the diabetic foot when the pulses are not palpable, but the pressure index is more than one. It is then necessary to use other methods to assess flow in the arteries of the foot, such as examining the pattern of the Doppler arterial waveform or measuring transcutaneous oxygen tension or toe systolic pressures.[13]

Deformity

Deformity often leads to bony prominences, which are associated with high mechanical pressures on the overlying skin. This leads to ulceration, particularly in the absence of protective pain sensation and when shoes are unsuitable. Common deformities that should be noted include claw toes, pes cavus, hallux valgus, hallux rigidus, hammer toe, and nail deformities and Charcot foot (see below).

Callus

This is a thickened area of epidermis which develops at sites of high pressure and friction. It should not be allowed to become excessive as this can be a forerunner of ulceration in the presence of neuropathy.

Oedema

Oedema is a major factor predisposing to ulceration, reducing skin oxygenation and often exacerbating a tight fit inside poorly fitting shoes.

Management

This stage by definition does not have any evidence of skin breakdown or ischaemia. However, mechanical and educational control are important to prevent the development of ulceration.

Mechanical control

Mechanical control is based upon wearing sensible footwear. Shoes should have broad rounded or square toes, adequate toe depth, low heels to avoid excessive toe pressure on the forefoot and lace up, velcro or buckle straps to prevent movement within the shoe.[14]

Educational control

Advice on basic foot care including nail cutting techniques, the treatment of minor injuries and the purchase of shoes should be given. Educational programmes involving behavioural contracts and organizational intervention for health care providers have shown a significant reduction in foot ulceration at one year follow up.[15]

Stage 2 – the high risk foot

Presentation

The foot has developed one or more of the risk factors for ulceration. It is important to detect these by a regular screening examination. Referral of these patients at risk to a multidisciplinary programme of care has been shown to reduce amputations.[16]

The Charcot foot is a particularly devastating deformity which needs prompt diagnosis and treatment and is described at the end of this section.

Management

Mechanical, vascular and educational control are important.

Mechanical control

Deformity must be accommodated and callus, dry skin, fissures and oedema must be treated.

Deformities

Deformities in the neuropathic foot render the plantar surface vulnerable to ulcers, best prevented by using special insoles, whereas

in the neuroischaemic foot the foot margins need protection and appropriately wide shoes should therefore be advised.

Footwear can be divided into three broad types: sensible shoes (from high street shops) for patients with minimal sensory loss; ready made stock (off the shelf) shoes for neuroischaemic feet that are not greatly deformed but that need protection along the foot margins and customized or bespoke (made to measure) shoes containing cradled, cushioned insoles, necessary to redistribute the high pressures on the plantar surface of the markedly neuropathic foot.

Callus

Patients should never trim their own callus or use callus removers. Callus should be removed regularly by sharp debridement.

Dry skin and fissures

Dry skin should be treated with an emollient such as E45 cream or calmurid cream.

Oedema

Oedema may complicate both the neuropathic and the neuroischaemic foot. Its main cause will be impaired cardiac and renal function, which should be treated. Oedema may rarely be secondary to neuropathy, and will respond to ephedrine (initial dose 10 mg thrice daily and increasing up to 30–60 mg tds).

Vascular control

Patients with absent foot pulses should have their pressure indices measured to confirm ischaemia and to provide a baseline, so that subsequent deterioration can be detected. If the patient has rest pain, disabling claudication, or the pressure index is below 0.5, then severe ischaemia is present and the patient should be referred for a vascular opinion. All diabetic patients with evidence of peripheral vascular disease may benefit from anti-platelet agents: 75 mg aspirin daily, or clopidrogel 75 mg daily.

Educational control

Patients who have lost protective pain sensation need advice on how to protect their feet from mechanical, thermal and chemical trauma. They should establish a habit of regular inspection of the feet so that problems can be detected quickly and they seek help early.

Charcot foot

The term Charcot foot refers to bone and joint destruction that occurs in the neuropathic foot.[17] It can be divided into three phases:

(1) acute onset

(2) bony destruction/deformity

(3) stabilization

Acute onset

The foot presents with unilateral erythema, warmth and oedema (Fig. 3). There may be a history of minor trauma. About 30 per cent of patients complain of pain or discomfort. X-ray may be normal. However, a technetium-99m diphosphonate bone scan will detect early evidence of bony destruction. Early diagnosis is essential. Cellulitis, gout and deep vein thrombosis may masquerade as a Charcot foot. Initially the foot is immobilized in a non-weight

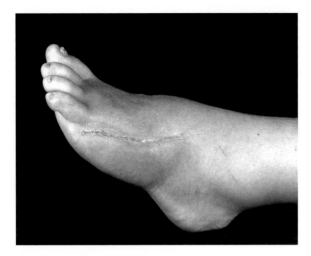

Fig. 3 Charcot foot – acute stage, showing redness and swelling. The Charcot deformity was precipitated by amputation of the fifth toe.

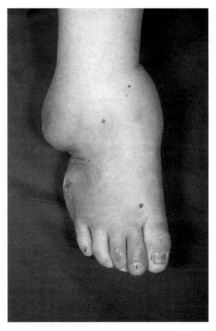

Fig. 4 Charcot foot – chronic stage with ankle and subtalar subluxation.

bearing cast to prevent deformity. After one month, a total contact cast is applied and the patient may mobilize for brief periods. However, the patient is given crutches and encouraged to keep walking to a minimum. An alternative is the Aircast (see below), but a cradled moulded insole should protect the sole. Such treatment if given early should help to prevent the second phase, that of bony destruction and deformity. Bisphosphonates are under trial in the treatment of the Charcot foot.[18]

Bony destruction

Clinical signs are swelling, warmth and deformities, including the rocker bottom deformity and medial convexity of the foot (Fig. 4). X-ray reveals fragmentation, fracture, new bone formation, subluxation and dislocation. The aim of treatment is immobilization until there is no longer evidence on X-ray of continuing bone destruction and the foot temperature is within 2 °C of the contralateral foot. Deformity in a Charcot foot can predispose to ulceration, which may become infected and lead to osteomyelitis. This may be difficult to distinguish from neuropathic bone and joint changes, as on X-ray, bone scan or magnetic resonance imaging (MRI), appearances may be similar. However, if the ulcer can be probed to bone, osteomyelitis is the more likely diagnosis.

Stabilization

The foot is no longer warm and red. There may still be oedema but the difference in skin temperature between the feet is less than 2 °C. X-ray shows fracture healing, sclerosis, and bone remodelling. The patient can now progress from a total contact or Aircast to an orthotic walker, fitted with cradled moulded insoles. However, too rapid mobilization can be disastrous, resulting in further bone destruction. Extremely careful rehabilitation should be the rule. Finally, the patient may progress to bespoke footwear with moulded insoles.

The rocker bottom Charcot foot with plantar bony prominence is a site of very high pressure. Regular reduction of callus can prevent ulceration. If ulceration does occur, an exostectomy may be needed. The

most serious complication of a Charcot foot is instability of the hind foot and ankle joint. This can lead to a flail ankle on which it is impossible to walk. Reconstructive surgery and arthrodesis, with a long term ankle foot orthosis, has resulted in better outcome and limb salvage.[19]

Stage 3 – the ulcerated foot

Presentation

It is essential to differentiate between ulceration in the neuropathic foot and that in the neuroischaemic foot.

Neuropathic ulcer

Neuropathic ulcers result from mechanical, thermal or chemical injuries that are unperceived by the patient because of loss of pain sensation. The classical position is under the metatarsal heads, but they are more frequently found on the plantar aspects of the toes. Direct mechanical injuries may result from treading on sharp objects, but the most frequent cause of ulceration is the repetitive mechanical forces of gait, which result in callosity formation, inflammatory autolysis and subkeratotic haematomas. Tissue necrosis occurs below the plaque of callus resulting in a small cavity filled with serous fluid which eventually breaks through to the surface with ulcer formation.

Neuroischaemic ulcer

Ulceration in the neuroischaemic foot usually occurs on the margins of the foot and the first sign is a red mark which blisters and then develops into a shallow ulcer with a base of sparse pale granulations or yellowish closely adherent slough. Although ulcers occur on the medial surface of the first metatarso-phalangeal joint and over the lateral aspect of the fifth metatarso-phalangeal joint, the commonest sites are the apices of the toes and also beneath the nails if allowed to become overly thick.

Management

Mechanical, wound, microbiological, vascular and educational control are important.

Mechanical control

In the neuropathic foot the aim is to redistribute plantar pressures, while in the neuroischaemic foot, it is to protect the vulnerable foot margins.

Neuropathic foot

The most efficient way to redistribute plantar pressure is by the immediate application of some form of cast,[20] for example the Aircast, total contact cast and Scotchcast boot.

The Aircast[21] is a removable bivalved cast and the halves are joined together with velcro strapping. It is lined with four air cells which can be inflated with a hand pump through four valves to ensure a close fit. The total contact cast should be reserved for plantar ulcers that have not responded to other casting treatments. It is a close fitting plaster of Paris and fibreglass cast applied over minimum padding. In a trial of 40 patients randomized to total contact cast or standard management, cast treatment was associated with a significant increase in ulcer healing at three months.[22] The Scotchcast boot[23] is a simple removable boot made of stockinette, felt and fibreglass tape which is effective in redistributing plantar pressure. If casting techniques are not available, temporary ready made shoes with a plastozote insole such as a Drushoe can off load the site of ulceration.

The five year cumulative rate of ulcer recurrence is 66 per cent.[24] In the long term, cradled or moulded insoles are designed to redistribute weight bearing away from the vulnerable pressure areas and prevent recurrence. In a controlled trial of therapeutic shoes compared with patient's own shoes, the risk of ulcer recurrence at one year was 27 per cent in the intervention group and 58 per cent in the control group.[25]

Neuroischaemic feet

Ulcers in neuroischaemic feet are often associated with tight shoes which lead to frictional forces on the foot margins. A high street shoe that is sufficiently long, broad and deep and fastens with a lace or strap high on the foot may be sufficient. Alternatively, a ready made stock shoe which is wide fitting may be suitable.

Wound control

Wound control consists of three parts; debridement, dressings and stimulation of wound healing.

Debridement

Debridement is the most important part of wound control and is best carried out with a scalpel. It allows removal of callus and devitalized tissue and enables the true dimensions of the ulcer to be perceived. It reduces the bacterial load of the ulcer even in the absence of overt infection, restores chronic wounds to acute wounds and releases growth factors to aid the healing process.[8] It also enables a deep swab to be taken for culture. The larvae of the green bottle fly are sometimes used to debride ulcers, especially in the neuroischaemic foot.[26]

Dressings

Sterile, non-adherent dressings should cover all ulcers to protect them from trauma, absorb exudate, reduce infection and promote healing. There is no evidence to support a particular dressing.[3] The following dressing properties are essential for the diabetic foot: ease and speed of lifting, ability to be walked on without disintegrating and good exudate control. Dressings should be lifted every day to ensure that problems or complications are detected quickly, especially in patients who lack protective pain sensation.

Stimulation of wound healing

Techniques to stimulate wound healing include the use of platelet derived growth factor (Regranex), bio-engineered wound dressings such as Dermagraft or Apligraf, hyaluronic acid esters such as Hyaff and vacuum assisted wound closure.

Platelet derived growth factor (Regranex) stimulates fibroblasts and other connective tissue cells located in the skin and is beneficial in enhancing wound healing processes of cell growth and repair. A multicentre, double blind, placebo controlled study of 118 patients demonstrated that Regranex gel 30 mcg/g healed significantly more chronic diabetic ulcers compared with placebo gel (48 per cent versus 25 per cent, $p=0.016$) and also decreased healing times by nine weeks compared with placebo gel.[27] A pivotal study in 382 patients demonstrated that Regranex gel 100 mcg/g healed 50 per cent of chronic diabetic ulcers which was significantly greater than 35 per cent healed with placebo gel. Regranex gel 100 mcg/g also significantly decreased time to healing by six weeks.[28]

Dermagraft is an artificial human dermis manufactured through the process of tissue engineering. Human fibroblast cells obtained from neonatal foreskin are cultivated on a three-dimensional polyglactin scaffold. As fibroblasts proliferate within the scaffold, they secrete human dermal collagen, growth factors and other proteins, embedding themselves in a self-produced dermal matrix. This results in a metabolically active dermal tissue with the structure of a papillary dermis of newborn skin. A randomized controlled multi-centre study of 281 patients with neuropathic foot ulcers demonstrated that at 12 weeks, 50.8 per cent of the Dermagraft group experienced complete wound closure which was significantly greater than in the controls, of whom 31.7 per cent healed. Furthermore, at week 32, Dermagraft patients still had a statistically significant higher number of healed ulcers, 58 per cent compared with 42 per cent in controls.[29]

Apligraf consists of a collagen gel seeded with fibroblasts and covered by a surface layer of keratinocytes. Recent studies have shown that treatment of diabetic neuropathic ulcers with Apligraf was associated with a significantly reduced healing time of 42.5 days compared with 91 days in the control group.[30]

Hyaluronic acid is a major component of the extracellular matrix.[31] It is a polysaccharide that facilitates growth and movement of fibroblasts but is unstable when applied to tissues. When it is esterified it becomes more stable and, when in contact with wound exudate, produces a hydrophilic gel which covers the wound. This creates a hyaluronic acid rich tissue interface which promotes granulation and healing.

Hyaff is a commercially available ester of hyaluronic acid. A pilot study of 30 diabetic patients randomized to treatment with Hyaff or standard care showed promising results in the treatment of neuropathic foot ulcers, especially those with sinuses.[32]

An extension of this new treatment is the Vivoderm Autograft System. A biopsy is taken from healthy skin of the patient and the keratinocytes are cultured on an hyaluronic acid ester membrane, which is then used as a delivery system to the wound for the cultured epidermal cells.

Finally, in the technique of vacuum assisted closure (VAC), the VAC pump applies gentle negative pressure to the ulcer through a tube and foam sponge which are applied to the ulcer over a dressing and sealed in place with a plastic film to create a vacuum. Exudate from the wound is sucked along the tube to a disposable collecting chamber. The negative pressure improves the vascularity and stimulates granulation of the wound.

Microbiological control

When the skin of the foot is broken, the patient is at great risk of infection as there is a clear portal of entry for invading bacteria. At every patient visit, the foot should be examined for local signs of infection, cellulitis or osteomyelitis. If found, antibiotic therapy is indicated.

However, a uniformly agreed practice on the place of antibiotics in clinically non infected ulcers has not been established. In a recent investigation, 32 patients with new foot ulcers were treated with oral antibiotics and 32 patients without antibiotics.[33] In the group with no antibiotics, 15 patients developed clinical infection compared with none in the antibiotic group ($p<0.001$). Seven patients in the non-antibiotic group needed hospital admission and three patients came to amputation (one major and two minor). Seventeen patients healed in the non-antibiotic group compared with 27 in the antibiotic group ($p<0.02$). When the 15 patients in the non-antibiotic treated group who developed clinical infection were compared to the 17 who did not, there were significantly more ischaemic patients in the former. Furthermore, out of the 15 patients who became clinically infected, eleven had positive ulcer swabs at the start of the study compared with only one patient out of 17 in the non-infected group ($p<0.01$). From this study, it was concluded that diabetic patients with clean ulcers associated with peripheral vascular disease and positive ulcer swabs should be considered for early antibiotic treatment.

Thus for the neuropathic ulcer, at the first visit, if there is no cellulitis, discharge or probing to bone, then debridement, cleansing with saline, application of dressing and daily inspections will suffice. For the neuroischaemic ulcer, at the initial visit, if the ulcer is superficial, oral amoxycillin 500 mg thrice daily and flucloxacillin 500 mg four times daily may be prescribed (or erythromycin 500 mg four times daily or cephadroxyl 1 g twice daily if the patient is penicillin allergic). If the ulcer is deep, extending to the subcutaneous tissue, trimethoprim 200 mg twice daily and metronidazole 400 mg thrice daily may be added.[8]

The patient is reviewed, preferably at one week, together with the result of the ulcer swab. If the ulcer show no sign of infection and the swab is negative, treatment is continued without antibiotics. However, in the cases of severe ischaemia (pressure index below 0.5), antibiotics may be prescribed until the ulcer is healed. If either the neuropathic or neuroischaemic ulcer has a positive swab, the patient may be treated with the appropriate antibiotic according to sensitivities until the repeat swab, taken at weekly intervals, is negative.

Vascular control

If an ulcer has not responded to optimum treatment within six weeks and ankle brachial pressure index is less than 0.5 and the Doppler waveform is damped, or transcutaneous oxygen is less than 30 mmHg or toe pressure is less than 30 mmHg, then angiography is indicated. This can be performed by a Duplex examination, which combines the features of Doppler waveform analysis with ultrasound imaging to produce a picture of arterial flow dynamics and morphology.[8] Alternatively, transfemoral angiography can be performed, together with digital subtraction angiography to assess the distal arteries.

Angioplasty is a valuable treatment to improve arterial flow in the presence of ischaemic ulcers and is indicated for the treatment of isolated or multiple stenoses as well as short segment occlusions less than 10 cm in length.[34] If lesions are too widespread for angioplasty, arterial bypass may be considered. However, this is a major, sometimes lengthy, operation, not without risk, and is more commonly reserved for the foot with severe tissue destruction which cannot be managed without the restoration of pulsatile blood flow.

Educational control

Patients should be instructed on the principles of ulcer care stressing the importance of rest, footwear, regular dressings and frequent observation for signs of infection.

Stage 4 – foot ulcer and cellulitis

Presentation

Infection is caused by bacteria which invade the ulcer from the surrounding skin. Staphylococci and streptococci are the most common pathogens.[35] However, infection due to gram negative and anaerobic organisms occur in approximately 50 per cent of patients and infection is often polymicrobial.[36] The most common manifestation is cellulitis. However, this stage covers a spectrum of presentations, ranging from local infection of the ulcer to spreading cellulitis, sloughing of soft tissue and finally, vascular compromise of the skin. This is seen as a blue discolouration, when there is an inadequate supply of oxygen to the soft tissues. This spectrum occurs in both neuropathic and neuroischaemic feet, although in the presence of severe neuropathy and ischaemia, signs of inflammation are often diminished. Infection of the soft tissues may be complicated by underlying osteomyelitis.

Infected ulcer

Local signs that an ulcer has become infected include colour change of the base of the lesion from healthy pink granulations to yellowish or grey tissue, purulent discharge, unpleasant smell and the development of sinuses with undermined edges or exposed bone. There may also be localized erythema, warmth and swelling. In the neuroischaemic foot, it may be difficult to differentiate between the erythema of cellulitis and the redness of ischaemia. Although the redness of ischaemia is usually cold, it is not always so. It is most marked on dependency. The erythema of inflammation is warm.

Cellulitis

When infection spreads there is widespread intense erythema and swelling. Lymphangitis, regional lymphadenitis, malaise, 'flu-like' symptoms, fever and rigors may develop. In the presence of neuropathy, pain and throbbing are often absent, but, if present, usually indicate pus within the tissues. Palpation may reveal fluctuance suggesting abscess formation, although discrete abscesses are relatively uncommon. Often there is a generalized sloughing of the ulcer and surrounding subcutaneous tissues, which liquefy and disintegrate. Subcutaneous gas may be detected by direct palpation of the foot and the diagnosis is confirmed by the appearance of gas in the soft tissue on the radiograph. Although clostridial organisms have previously been held responsible for this presentation, non-clostridial organisms are more frequently the offending pathogens. These include Bacteroides, Escherichia coli and anaerobic streptococci. Only 50 per cent of episodes of severe cellulitis will provoke a fever or leucocytosis.[37] A substantial number of patients with a deep foot infection do not have severe symptoms and signs indicating the presence of deep infection. However, when increased body temperature or leucocytosis is present, it usually indicates substantial tissue damage.[38]

Osteomyelitis

The diagnosis of osteomyelitis is strongly suggested if a sterile probe, inserted into the ulcer, reaches bone. In the initial stages, plain X-ray may be normal. Localized loss of bone density and cortical outline may take at least 14 days to develop. Radionuclide bone scanning using technetium-99m diphosphonate is very sensitive but not specific for osteomyelitis. Gallium or indium scans may improve specificity but MRI may be most helpful in demonstrating loss of bony cortex.[39] Chronic osteomyelitis of a toe has a swollen, red, sausage-like appearance.[40]

Management

Infection in the diabetic foot needs full multidisciplinary treatment. It is vital to achieve microbiological, wound, vascular, mechanical and educational control, for if infection is not controlled it can spread with alarming rapidity, causing extensive tissue necrosis and taking the foot into stage 5.

Microbiological control

General principles

At presentation, the organisms responsible for infection cannot be predicted from the clinical appearance. The wound should be swabbed for culture and broad spectrum antibiotics prescribed without delay in all stage 4 patients. Deep swabs or tissue should be taken from the ulcer after initial debridement and further deep tissue samples taken for culture if the patient undergoes operative debridement. Ulcer swabs should be taken at every follow up visit. Bacterial species not normally pathogenic can cause true infection in a diabetic foot when part of a mixed flora. As the diabetic patient has a poor immune response even bacteria regarded as skin commensals may cause severe tissue damage. This includes gram negative organisms such as Citrobacter, Serratia, Pseudomonas and Acinetobacter. Gram negative bacteria isolated from an ulcer swab should not be automatically regarded as insignificant. If there is fever and systemic toxicity, blood should be cultured. Close contact with the microbiologist is advised and it is helpful to do laboratory bench rounds to discuss management.

Antibiotic treatment

Infection in the neuroischaemic foot is often more serious than in the foot which has a good arterial blood supply; a positive ulcer swab in a neuroischaemic foot has serious implications, which influence antibiotic policy.

Antibiotic treatment is discussed both as initial treatment and at follow up: dosage should be determined by the level of renal function and serum levels when available. No single agent or combination has emerged as most effective.[3] Chantelau randomized patients with neuropathic ulcers (some with cellulitis) to oral amoxycillin plus clavulinic acid or matched placebo. At 20 days follow up, there was no significant difference in outcome.[41] Lipsky randomized 56 patients with an infected lesion to oral clindamycin or oral cephalexin in an outpatient setting and at two weeks, there was no difference in outcome.[42] Grayson randomized 93 patients to intravenous imipenem/cilastatin or intravenous ampicillin/sulbactam and, cure had been effected after five days in 58 per cent and 60 per cent respectively.[36]

The regimen outlined in Box 1 has been developed in our practice, based on many years of treating the diabetic foot, with a significant reduction in amputations.

Wound control

Diabetic foot infections are almost always more extensive than would appear from initial examination and surface appearance. Initial debridement is indicated to determine the true dimensions of the lesion and obtain samples for culture. Callus often overlies the ulcer and must be removed, to reveal the extent of the ulcer, allow drainage of pus and removal of infected sloughy tissue.

Cellulitis should respond to intravenous antibiotics, but the patient needs daily review to ensure that erythema is resolving. In severe episodes of cellulitis, the ulcer may be complicated by extensive infected subcutaneous soft tissue. At this point, the tissue is not frankly necrotic but has started to break down and liquefy. It is best for this tissue to be removed operatively. The definite indications for urgent surgical intervention are a large area of infected sloughy tissue, localized fluctuance and expression of pus, crepitus with gas in the soft tissues on X-ray and purplish discolouration of the skin, indicating subcutaneous necrosis.

The role of hyperbaric oxygen in the management of wounds is not yet established but two small randomized controlled trials found that systemic hyperbaric oxygen reduced the absolute risk of foot amputation in people with severely infected ulcers compared with routine care.[3]

Vascular control

It is important to explore the possibility of revascularization in the infected neuroischaemic foot. Improvement of perfusion will not only help control infection but will also promote healing of wounds after operative debridement.

Mechanical control

Patients should be on bed rest with heel protection using foam wedges.

Educational control

The patient should be advised about the importance of rest in severe infection. If the patient has mild cellulitis and is treated at home he should understand the signs of advancing and progressing cellulitis so as to return early to clinic. Patient education provided after the

Box 1 Antibiotic regimen for the stage 4 diabetic foot

- Local signs of infection in the ulcer or mild cellulitis
  - Initial treatment
    - Oral amoxycillin flucloxacillin, metronidazole and trimethoprim. Erythromycin for flucloxacillin in penicillin allergic patients
    - Intramuscular ceftriaxone for cellulitis, on the borderline of mild to severe
  - Subsequent management (with reference to previous visit's swab)
    - If no signs of infection and no organisms isolated, stop antibiotics unless the patient is severely ischaemic with a pressure index below 0.5, when continuing antibiotics until healing should be considered
    - If no signs of infection are present but organisms are isolated, focus antibiotics and review in one week
    - If signs of infection are present but no organisms are isolated, continue with original antibiotics
    - If signs of infection are still present, and organisms are isolated, focus antibiotic regime according to sensitivities
    - If methicillin resistant staphylococcus aureus (MRSA) is grown, but there are no local or systemic signs of infection, use topical mupirocin 2% ointment (if sensitive)
    - If MRSA is grown, with local signs of infection, consider oral therapy with two of the following: sodium fusidate, rifampicin, trimethoprim and doxycycline, according to sensitivities, together with topical mupirocin 2% ointment
- Foot with severe cellulitis
  - Initial treatment
    - Intramuscular (IM) ceftriaxone and oral metronidazole as an outpatient. At one week, if cellulitis is controlled, continue regimen
    - If cellulitis is increasing, admit for intravenous antibiotics, using quadruple therapy: amoxycillin, flucloxacillin, metronidazole and ceftazidime or erythromycin or vancomycin for the penicillins (with doses adjusted according to serum levels). Assess need for surgical debridement
  - Subsequent management
    - Daily assessment to gauge the initial response to antibiotic therapy. Appropriate antibiotics should be selected when sensitivities are available, if the foot is not clearly responding
    - If no organisms are isolated but the foot remains severely cellulitic, repeat deep swab and continue quadruple antibiotic therapy
    - If MRSA is isolated, vancomycin (dosage to be adjusted according to serum levels) or teicoplanin

are indicated. These antibiotics may need to be accompanied by either sodium fusidate or rifampicin orally. Intravenous therapy can be changed to the appropriate oral therapy when the signs of cellulitis have resolved

- Osteomyelitis
  - Initial treatment
    - Antibiotics as for infected ulcer and cellulitis
  - Subsequent management
    - Antibiotic selection guided by the results of deep swabs. Antibiotics with good bone penetration include sodium fusidate, rifampicin, clindamycin and ciprofloxacin
    - Continue antibiotics for at least 12 weeks
    - If ulcer persists after three months (with continued probing to bone and the bone is fragmented on X-ray) resection of the underlying bone is probably indicated in the neuropathic foot

management of acute foot complications decreases ulcer recurrences and major amputations.[43]

Stage 5 – foot ulcer and necrosis

Presentation

This stage is characterized by the presence of necrosis. It is classified as either wet necrosis due to infection (Fig. 5) or dry necrosis due to ischaemia (Fig. 6). In wet necrosis, the tissues are grey or black, moist and often malodorous. Adjoining tissues are infected and pus may discharge from the ulcerated demarcation line between necrosis and viable tissue. Dry necrosis is hard, blackened, mummified tissue and there is usually a clean demarcation line between necrosis and viable tissue.

Necrosis presents in both the neuropathic and the neuroischaemic foot and the management is different.

Neuropathic foot

In the neuropathic foot, necrosis is invariably wet, and is usually caused by infection complicating an ulcer, leading to a septic vasculitis of the digital and small arteries of the foot. The walls of these arteries are infiltrated by polymorphs leading to occlusion of the lumen by septic thrombus.

Necrosis can involve skin, subcutaneous and fascial layers. In the skin, it is easily evident but in the subcutaneous and fascial layers it is not so apparent. The bluish-black skin discolouration may be the 'tip of an iceberg' of deep necrosis in subcutaneous and fascial planes, so-called necrotizing fasciitis.

Neuroischaemic foot

Both wet and dry necrosis can occur in the neuroischaemic foot. Wet necrosis is also caused by a septic vasculitis. However, reduced arterial perfusion to the foot resulting from atherosclerotic disease of the leg arteries is an important predisposing factor.

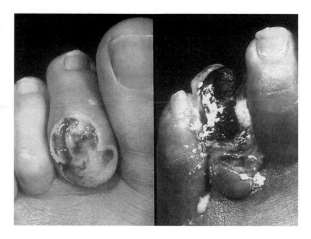

Fig. 5 (a) severe infection of toe; (b) wet necrosis of the toe.

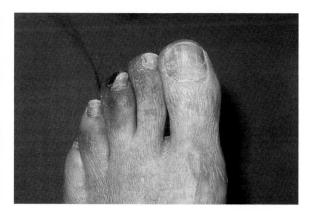

Fig. 6 Dry necrosis of the 3rd toe, secondary to severe ischaemia.

Dry necrosis is usually secondary to a severe reduction in arterial perfusion and occurs in three circumstances: severe chronic ischaemia, acute ischaemia and emboli to the toes. In the first, a gradual but severe reduction in arterial perfusion results in vascular compromise of the skin, leading to blue toes which usually become necrotic unless the foot is revascularized. Acute ischaemia is usually caused either by thrombosis in the superficial femoral or popliteal artery or by emboli from proximal atherosclerotic plaques to the iliac, femoral or popliteal arteries. It presents as a sudden onset of pain in the leg associated with pallor of the foot, quickly followed by mottling and slatey grey discolouration. Blue discolouration of the toes followed by necrosis can also occur. Paraesthesiae and ischaemic pain may be reduced or absent because of sensory neuropathy and this may delay presentation. Emboli to the digital circulation results in a bluish or purple discolouration of the toes which is quite well demarcated but which quickly proceeds to necrosis. If it escapes infection, the toe will dry out and mummify. Microemboli present with painful petechial lesions in the foot that do not blanch on pressure.

Digital necrosis in the patient with renal impairment

Digital necrosis is a relatively common problem in patients with advanced diabetic nephropathy. It may result from a septic neutrophilic vasculitis but can occur in the absence of infection. It may be precipitated by trauma.

Management

Patients should be admitted for urgent management to achieve wound, microbiological, vascular, mechanical and educational control.

Wound control

The neuropathic foot

Operative debridement is almost always indicated for wet gangrene. It is important to remove all necrotic tissue, down to bleeding tissue, and to open all sinuses. Deep necrotic tissue should be sent for culture. Although necrosis in the diabetic foot may not be associated with a definite collection of pus, the necrotic tissue still needs to be removed. The neuropathic foot, with good arterial circulation, the wound always heals as long as infection is controlled. Wounds should not be sutured. Skin grafting may be the best way to accelerate healing of large tissue deficits. When there is extensive loss of tissue, modern reconstructive surgical techniques have proved useful.[44]

The neuroischaemic foot

In the neuroischaemic foot, wet necrosis should also be removed when it is associated with severe spreading sepsis. This should be done whether pus is present or not. In cases when the limb is not immediately threatened, and the necrosis is limited to one or two toes, it may be possible to control infection with intravenous antibiotics and proceed to urgent revascularization with digital or ray amputation at the same operation. Wounds in the neuroischaemic foot may be slow to heal even after revascularization, and wound care needs to continue as an outpatient procedure in the diabetic foot clinic. With patience, outcomes may be surprisingly good.

If revascularization is not possible for digital necrosis, then a decision must be made to either amputate the toe in the presence of ischaemia or allow the toe, if infection is controlled, to convert to dry necrosis and autoamputate. Surgical amputation should be undertaken if the toe is painful or if the circulation is not severely impaired, that is, a pressure index above 0.5 or a transcutaneous oxygen tension greater than 30 mmHg.[8]

Microbiological control

Wet necrosis

Wound swabs and tissue specimens and deep tissue taken at operative debridement must be cultured. Intravenous antibiotic therapy (amoxycillin, flucloxacillin, metronidazole and ceftazidime) should be given. Erythromycin or vancomycin (dosage adjusted according to serum levels) may be used instead of amoxycillin and flucloxacillin. Intravenous antibiotics can be replaced with oral therapy after operative debridement and when infection is controlled. When the wound is granulating well and swabs are negative then the antibiotics may be stopped.

Dry necrosis

When dry necrosis develops secondary to ischaemia, antibiotics should be prescribed if discharge is present or the wound swab is positive, and continued until there is no evidence of clinical or microbiological infection.

When toes have gone from wet to dry necrosis and are allowed to autoamputate, antibiotics should be stopped only if the necrosis is dry and mummified, the foot is entirely pain-free, and there is no discharge exuding from the demarcation line. Daily inspection is essential. Regular swabs should be sent for culture and antibiotics should be restarted if the demarcation line becomes moist or swabs grow organisms.

Vascular control

After operative debridement of wet necrosis, revascularization is often essential to heal the tissue deficit. In dry necrosis, which occurs in the background of severe macrovascular disease, revascularization is necessary to maintain the viability of the limb. When dry necrosis is secondary to emboli, a possible source should be sought.

In some patients, increased perfusion following angioplasty may be useful. However, unless there is a very significant localized stenosis in iliac or femoral arteries, angioplasty rarely restores the pulsatile blood flow to the foot which is necessary to keep the limb viable in severe ischaemia or restore considerable tissue deficits secondary to necrosis. This is best achieved by arterial bypass.

Peripheral arterial disease is common in the tibial arteries, and distal bypass with autologous vein has become an established method of revascularization. A conduit is fashioned from either the femoral or popliteal artery down to a tibial artery in the lower leg, or the dorsalis pedis artery on the dorsum of the foot. Patency rates and limb salvage rates after revascularization do not differ between diabetic patients and non-diabetic patients, and an aggressive approach to such revascularization procedures should be promoted.[45]

Mechanical control

During the peri- and postoperative period, bed rest with elevation of the limb will relieve oedema and afford heel protection. After operative debridement in the neuroischaemic foot, non-weight bearing is advised until the wound is healed especially when revascularization has not been possible. In the neuropathic foot, non-weight bearing is advisable initially and then off-loading of the healing postoperative wound may be achieved by casting. Autoamputation can take several months, during which the patient needs a wide fitting shoe to accommodate the dressings.

Educational control

For patients in hospital, advice is similar to that given for severe cellulitis. For patients undergoing autoamputation at home, it is important to rest the foot and keep it dry and covered with a dressing and bandage. Patients should be advised to return to the clinic immediately if the foot becomes swollen, painful, develops an unpleasant smell or discharges pus.

Conclusion

This chapter has outlined a simple classification of the diabetic foot into the neuropathic and neuroischaemic foot and defined six specific stages in its natural history. It has described a simple plan of management for each stage which requires a well organized multi-disciplinary approach that provides continuity of care between primary and secondary sectors.[46] Secondary care should be focussed on a diabetic foot clinic to which rapid referrals should be possible. Such clinics have reported a reduction in amputations and should be available to all diabetic patients.[47]

References

1. **Edmonds ME**. Progress in care of the diabetic foot. *Lancet*, 1999; **354**: 270–2.

2. **Mason JM, O'Keefe C, McIntosh A, Hutchinson A, Booth A, Young R**. A systematic review of foot ulcer in patients with type 2 diabetes mellitus I: prevention. *Diabetic Medicine*, 1999; **16**: 801–12.

3. **Mason JM, O'Keefe C, Hutchinson A, McIntosh A, Young R, Booth A**. A systematic review of foot ulcer in patients with type 2 diabetes mellitus II: treatment. *Diabetic Medicine*, 1999; **16**: 889–909.

4. **Hunt D, Gerstein H**. Foot ulcers in diabetes. *Clinical Evidence*, 1999; **2**: 231–7.

5. **Pinzur MS, Slovenkai MP, Trepman E**. Guidelines for diabetic foot care. *Foot and Ankle International*, 1999; **20**: 695–702.

6. *International Consensus on the Diabetic Foot*. The International Working Group on the Diabetic Foot, 1999.

7. **American Diabetes Association**. Consensus development conference on diabetic foot wound care. *Diabetes Care*, 1999; **22**: 1354–60.

8. **Edmonds ME, Foster AVM**. *Managing the diabetic foot*. Oxford: Blackwell Science, 2000.

9. **Edmonds ME, Foster AVM**. Classification and management of neuropathic and neuroischaemic ulcers. In: Boulton AJM, Connor H, Cavanagh PR, eds. *The Foot in Diabetes*, 2nd edn. Chichester: John Wiley, 1994.

10. **Flynn MD**. The diabetic foot. In: Tooke JE, ed. *Diabetic Angiopathy*. London: Arnold, 1999.

11. **Johnson CLW**. Infection and diabetes mellitus. In: Pickup J, Williams G, eds. *Textbook of Diabetes*, vol 2. Oxford: Blackwell Science, 1997: 70.1–70.14.

12. **Rith-Najarian SJ, Stolusky T, Godhes DM**. Identifying diabetic patients at risk for lower extremity amputation in a primary healthcare setting. *Diabetes Care*, 1992; **15**: 1386–9.

13. **Hurley JJ, Woods JJ, Hershey FB**. Non invasive testing: practical knowledge for evaluating diabetic patients. In: Levin MF, O'Neal LW, Bowker JH, eds. *The Diabetic Foot*. St Louis: Mosby, 1993: 321–40.

14. **Tovey FI**. The manufacture of diabetic footwear. *Diabetic Medicine*, 1984; **1**: 69–71.

15. **Litzelman DK** *et al.* Reduction of lower extremity clinical abnormalities in patients with non-insulin dependent diabetes mellitus. *Annals of Internal Medicine*, 1993; **199**: 36–41.

16. **McCabe CJ, Stevenson RC, Dolan AM**. Evaluation of a diabetic foot screening and protection programme. *Diabetic Medicine*, 1998; **15**: 80–4.

17. **Sanders LJ, Frykberg RG**. Diabetic neuropathic osteoarthropathy: the Charcot foot. In: Frykberg RG, ed. *The High Risk Foot in Diabetes*. New York: Churchill Livingstone, 1991: 227–38.

18. **Selby PL, Young MJ, Boulton AJM**. Bisphosphonates: a new treatment for diabetic Charcot neuroarthropathy. *Diabetic Medicine*, 1994; **11**: 28–31.

19. **Papa J, Myerson MS, Girard P**. Salvage with arthrodesis in intractable diabetic neuropathic arthropathy of the foot and ankle. *Journal of Bone and Joint Surgery. American Volume*, 1993; **75a**: 1056–66.

20. **Armstrong DG, Lavery LA**. Evidence based options for off loading diabetic wounds. *Clinics in Podiatric Medicine and Surgery*, 1998; **15**: 95–104.

21. **Kalish SR, Pelcovitz N, Zawada S, Donatelli RA, Wooden MJ, Castellano BD**. The Aircast walking brace versus conventional casting methods. *Journal of the American Podiatric Medical Association*, **77**: 589–95.

22. **Mueller MJ** *et al.* Total contact casting in treatment of diabetic plantar ulcers. Controlled clinical trial. *Diabetes Care*, 1989; **12**: 384–8.

23. **Burden AC, Jones GR, Jones R, Blandford RL.** Use of the 'Scotchcast boot' in treating diabetic foot ulcers. *British Medical Journal*, 1983; **286**: 1555–7.

24. **Apelqvist J, Larsson J, Agardh C-D.** Long term prognosis for diabetic patients with foot ulcers. *Journal of Internal Medicine*, 1993; **233**: 485–91.

25. **Uccioli L** *et al.* Manufactured shoes in the prevention of diabetic foot ulcers. *Diabetes Care*, 1995; **18**: 1376–8.

26. **Rayman A, Stansfield G, Woollard T, Mackie A, Rayman G.** Use of larvae in the treatment of the diabetic necrotic. *Diabetic Foot*, 1998; **1**: 7–13.

27. **Steed DL.** The Diabetic Ulcer Study Group. Clinical evaluation of recombinant human platelet-derived growth factor for the treatment of lower extremity diabetic ulcers. *Journal of Vascular Surgery*, 1995; **21**: 71–81.

28. **Wieman TJ, Smiell JM, Su Y.** Efficacy and safety of a topical gel formulation of recombinant human platelet derived growth factor – BB (Becaplermin) in patients with non healing diabetic ulcers: a phase III, randomized, placebo-controlled, double-blind study. *Diabetes Care*, 1998; **21**: 822–7.

29. **Naughton G, Mansbridge J, Gentzkow G.** A metabolically active human dermal replacement for the treatment of diabetic foot ulcers. *Artificial Organs*, 1997; **21**: 1203–10.

30. **Pham HT** *et al.* Evaluation of graftskin (Apligraf R), a human skin equivalent for the treatment of diabetic foot ulcers. *Diabetes*, 1999; **48** (suppl. 1): A18.

31. **Chen WYJ, Abatangelo G.** Functions of hyaluronan in wound repair. *Wound Repair and Regeneration*, 1999; **7**: 79–89.

32. **Foster AM, Bates M, Doxford M, Edmonds ME.** The treatment of indolent neuropathic ulceration of the diabetic foot with Hyaff. *Diabetic Medicine*, 1999; S94.

33. **Foster A, Mccolgan M, Edmonds M.** Should oral antibiotics be given to clean foot ulcers with no cellulitis? *Diabetic Medicine*, 1998; **15**(suppl. 2): S10.

34. **Edmonds ME, Walters H.** Angioplasty and the diabetic foot. *Vasc Med Rev*, 1995; **6**: 205–14.

35. **Lipsky BA.** A current approach to diabetic foot infections. *Current Infectious Disease Reports*, 1999; **1**: 253–60.

36. **Grayson ML.** Diabetic foot infections: antimicrobial therapy. In: Eliopoulos GM, ed. *Infectious Disease Clinics of North America*. Philadelphia: WB Saunders, 1995: 143–62.

37. **Armstrong DG, Lavery LA, Sariaya M, Ashry H.** Leukocytosis is a poor indicator of acute osteomyelitis of the foot in diabetes mellitus. *Journal of Foot and Ankle Surgery*, 1996; **4**: 280–3.

38. **Eneroth M, Apelqvist J, Stenstrom A.** Clinical characteristics and outcome in 223 diabetic patients with deep foot infections. *Foot Ankle Int*, 1997; **18**: 716–22.

39. **Longmaid III HE, Kruskal JB.** Imaging infections in diabetic patients. In: Eliopoulos GM, ed. *Infectious Disease Clinics of North America*, Philadelphia: WB Saunders, 1995; 163–82.

40. **Rajbhandari S, Sutton M, Davies C, Tesfaye S, Ward JD.** Sausage toe: a reliable sign of underlying osteomyelitis. *Diabetic Medicine*, 2000; **17**: 74–7.

41. **Chantelau E, Tanudjaja T, Altenhofer F, Ersanili Z , Lacigova S, Metzger C.** Antibiotic treatment for uncomplicated neuropathic forefoot ulcers in diabetes: a controlled trial. *Diabetic Medicine*, 1996; **13**: 156–9.

42. **Lipsky BA, Pecoraro RE, Larson SA, Hanley ME, Ahroni JH.** Outpatient management of uncomplicated lower-extremity infections in diabetic patients. *Archives of Internal Medicine*, 1990; **150**: 790–7.

43. **Malone JM, Snyder M, Anderson G, Bernhard VM, Holloway GA, Bunt TJ.** Prevention of amputation by diabetic education. *American Journal of Surgery*, 1989; **158**: 520–4.

44. **Armstrong MD, Villalobos RE, Leppink DM.** Free tissue transfer or lower extremity reconstruction in the immunosuppressed diabetic transplant recipient. *Journal of Reconstructive Microsurgery*, 1997; **13**: 1–5.

45. **Pomposelli FB** *et al.* Dorsalis pedis arterial bypass: durable limb salvage for foot ischaemia in patients with diabetes mellitus. *Journal of Vascular Surgery*, 1995; **21**: 375–84.

46. **Edmonds M** *et al.* Report of the diabetic foot and amputation group. *Diabetic Medicine*, 1996; **13**: S27–42.

47. **Larsson J, Apelqvist J, Agardh CD, Stenstrom A.** Decreasing incidence of major amputation in diabetic patients: a consequence of a multidisciplinary foot care team approach? *Diabetic Medicine*, 1995; **12**: 770–6.

10 The metabolic syndrome

Harold E. Lebovitz

The metabolic syndrome has been recognized as a clinical entity for over 50 years. In 1956, Vague described central obesity as a predisposing factor in the development of diabetes mellitus, atherosclerosis and gout. Reaven, in his 1988 Banting lecture, focussed on the importance of insulin resistance and a related cluster of metabolic abnormalities that were associated with an increase in coronary artery disease.[1] This cluster included resistance to insulin-stimulated glucose uptake, glucose intolerance, hyperinsulinaemia, increased very-low-density lipoprotein (VLDL) triglyceride, decreased high-density lipoprotein (HDL) cholesterol and hypertension. He called this cluster syndrome X and raised the possibility that resistance to insulin-stimulated glucose uptake and hyperinsulinaemia were involved in the aetiology of the metabolic abnormalities and the clinical diseases associated with them. Obesity and particularly visceral obesity have been recognized as a major contributor to the syndrome since precise techniques to quantitate regional body composition became available. The syndrome has been referred to over the last decade as the insulin resistance syndrome. A WHO expert committee has recently recommended this syndrome should be termed the metabolic syndrome. Two large databases (The European group for the study of insulin resistance and the Danish twin register) have confirmed that insulin resistance is significantly correlated with the various components of the syndrome and that the prevalence of the syndrome in Caucasian populations is 16 per cent. This syndrome, which is associated with type 2 diabetes mellitus, hypertension and coronary artery disease, is one of the major health problems facing society today.

Definition and consequences of insulin resistance

Insulin resistance in the context of the metabolic syndrome means a decrease in the effect of various doses of insulin on glucose metabolism when compared to that which occurs in normal individuals. This can be a shift in the dose-response curve toward higher concentrations of insulin or a decrease in the maximal obtainable effect of insulin or a combination of both. Associated with the insulin resistance to glucose metabolism is, resistance of adipose tissue lipolysis to insulin suppression and resistance of endothelial cell nitric oxide (NO) production to insulin stimulation and vascular vasodilatation.[2,3] Insulin action on growth and mitogenesis, as well as insulin's stimulation of ovarian testosterone production, appear to be normal in those individuals who have insulin resistance of glucose metabolism.[4,5]

Figure 1 is a simplified scheme of intracellular insulin action which illustrates how some actions of insulin can be resistant and others not. When insulin binds to the extracellular domain of its receptor, tyrosine residues in the intracellular domain of the insulin receptor are auto-phosphorylated. Following this activation of the insulin receptor, there are two major intracellular phosphorylation–dephosphorylation cascades which are initiated.[6] One involves phosphorylation of tyrosine residues on insulin receptor substrates (IRS), followed by binding of phosphoinositide-3-kinase (PI-3-kinase) to the IRS molecule with subsequent phosphorylation and activation of PI-3-kinase. The activated PI-3-kinase triggers the phosphorylation–dephosphorylation of a number of other molecules which eventually regulate various aspects of glucose and lipid metabolism. For example, they stimulate the translocation of the molecules of the glucose transporter GLUT-4 from an intracellular storage site into the plasma membrane. This increases glucose transport into the cell. The other pathway involves phosphorylation of Shc (an adapter protein) which then activates the RAS–RAF–MAP kinase pathway to stimulate the growth, gene activation and mitogenic effects of insulin. The consequence of insulin resistance on muscle glucose uptake and suppression of hepatic glucose production causes a compensatory increase in insulin secretion (causing hyperinsulinaemia) which is to overcome the effects of the resistance and to maintain normal glucose metabolism. This compensatory hyperinsulinaemia causes exaggerated effects at those sites of insulin action which are not resistant.

There are several clinical examples of dissociation between the two pathways of insulin action. In the syndrome of pseudoacromegaly,

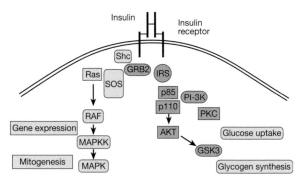

Fig. 1 Intracellular insulin action.

insulin stimulation of PI-3-kinase activity is markedly reduced and severe resistance to insulin effects on *in vivo* glucose metabolism can be demonstrated.[7] In contrast, insulin stimulation of mitogen-activated protein (MAP) kinase phosphorylation and thymidine incorporation into DNA is normal. Fibroblasts from patients with polycystic ovarian syndrome show normal insulin stimulation of DNA synthesis, but markedly impaired stimulation of glucose incorporation into glycogen.[8] Type 2 diabetic patients show a marked decrease in insulin-stimulated PI-3-kinase activity in muscle (presumably mediating the decreased effect of insulin on glucose metabolism), however serine-threonine kinase (AKT) activity is normally stimulated by insulin.

Measurement of insulin resistance

Understanding the relationships between insulin resistance and the various metabolic abnormalities and disease processes included in the metabolic syndrome requires methods to identify and quantitate insulin action on glucose metabolism. Box 1 lists many of the techniques which have been used. The gold standard for measuring *in vivo* insulin sensitivity is the euglycaemic hyperinsulinaemic clamp. A constant infusion of exogenous insulin and a labelled glucose tracer are infused over several hours. The plasma glucose is measured every few minutes and is maintained constant by a variable glucose infusion. The study is done at normal fasting plasma glucose levels. The amount of glucose infused to offset a given dose of insulin is a measure of whole body insulin sensitivity. Dilution of tracer concentration allows an estimation of glucose entry into the circulation, the amount of exogenous glucose given is known and both hepatic glucose production and insulin-mediated glucose disposal can be calculated. The euglycaemic hyperinsulinaemic clamp technique is however costly and labour intensive and not well suited for population studies.

The insulin suppression test administers a constant infusion of glucose and insulin and measures the steady state plasma levels. Endogenous insulin and glucagon secretion are suppressed by adding somatostatin to the infusion. The steady state plasma glucose level achieved is the measure of insulin sensitivity but the hormonal milieu of the subject has been disturbed.

The Bergman minimal model uses data collected after administering a bolus of glucose intravenously and frequently sampling blood for glucose and insulin (12 or 24 samples). A computer model calculates insulin sensitivity (S_I) and glucose effectiveness (S_G).

Box 1 Methods used to quantitate insulin action on glucose metabolism

- Complex techniques requiring many samples
  - Euglycaemic hyperinsulinaemic clamp
  - Insulin suppression test
  - Bergman's minimal model
- Simple techniques requiring multiple samples
  - Insulin tolerance test
  - Oral glucose tolerance test
- Techniques utilizing fasting plasma samples
  - Homeostasis Model Assessment (HOMA)

In diabetic subjects, the glucose bolus must be followed by tolbutamide or insulin 20 minutes later, otherwise the plasma insulin levels are too low for the model to be valid. The one-compartment model originally described by Bergman overestimates glucose effectiveness and underestimates insulin sensitivity. Several two-compartment models have been described which appear to correct some of these errors. The correlation coefficient between insulin sensitivity measured by the minimal model and that measured by the euglycaemic hyperinsulinaemic clamp is 0.62. A major advantage of the minimal model technique is its ease of applicability to large numbers of patients. Measurement of the glucose and insulin response to an oral glucose load or oral glucose tolerance test (OGTT), can also give useful indications of insulin responsiveness, but these are complicated by differences in insulin secretory capacity.

The Homeostasis Model Assessment (HOMA) is derived from the relationship between the fasting plasma glucose and fasting plasma insulin. These relationships were modelled mathematically based upon the known characteristics of the β-cell response to glucose in normal individuals. Insulin sensitivity derived from the HOMA model has been shown in population studies to correlate quite well with that derived from euglycaemic hyperinsulinaemic clamps or the minimal model of Bergman[9] but is not useful in assessing insulin sensitivity in an individual.

Mechanism of insulin resistance

Insulin resistance resulting from abnormalities in the genes regulating the various proteins in the insulin action cascade is rare. The overwhelming majority of individuals with insulin resistance are obese and sedentary. The mechanisms by which obesity causes insulin resistance are being elucidated. Insulin resistance is highly correlated with the size of the visceral adipose tissue pool, while subcutaneous adiposity has relatively little influence. Increases in visceral adipose tissue are associated with increases in hepatic triglyceride. Visceral adipose tissue has a higher metabolic activity than subcutaneous and its products drain directly to the liver. The triglyceride content of muscle cells also correlates with insulin resistance.

Adipose tissue releases several active metabolic factors including non-esterified fatty acids (NEFA), tumour necrosis factor α and leptin. Elevated concentrations of NEFA have been known since the 1960s to cause insulin resistance.[10] Obese patients have higher plasma NEFA levels than normal weight individuals because of the increase in size of adipose tissue pools and the resistance of their adipose tissue to the anti-lipolytic effects of insulin.

The mechanism by which NEFA cause insulin resistance was initially thought to involve increased fatty acid oxidation, generating citrate which in turn inhibited phosphofructokinase and interfered with glycolysis. More recently, it has been demonstrated with elegant nuclear magnetic resonance studies that NEFA inhibit insulin-mediated glucose transport.[11] Elevated NEFA levels decrease the action of insulin to stimulate IRS-1 associated PI-3-kinase activity. PI-3-kinase activity plays a major role in facilitating the translocation of GLUT-4 glucose transporters to the plasma membrane. Blocking the action of PI-3-kinase therefore would decrease insulin-mediated translocation of GLUT-4 and reduce insulin-mediated glucose transport.

Tumour necrosis factor-α is released from adipose tissue and inhibits PI-3-kinase and IRS-1 by causing phosphorylation of some of their serine and threonine residues. Such changes inhibit tyrosine phosphorylation and thus decrease insulin signalling activity in the PI-3-kinase pathway. These effects of tumour necrosis factor-α can be readily demonstrated in animals or *in vitro*. In humans, the data are less clear, since infusion of antibodies to the tumour necrosis factor-α do not reduce insulin resistance. However, it is produced locally from adipocytes within muscle and its effects are likely to be paracrine.

Fetal malnutrition as a possible cause of the metabolic syndrome

Low birthweight and low weight at one year of age correlate with the development of type 2 diabetes, four or five decades later in many different populations. A similar relationship with low birthweight has been shown also for hypertension, visceral obesity, dyslipidaemia, a procoagulant state and coronary artery disease. It is suggested that fetal malnutrition leads to the metabolic disease syndrome later in life but the mechanisms are unknown. Phillips and co-workers have shown that fasting plasma cortisol concentrations in men are inversely correlated with birthweight and positively correlated with systolic blood pressure; fasting and two hour plasma glucose concentrations during an oral glucose challenge; plasma triglyceride levels and insulin resistance.[12] They have speculated that fetal malnutrition leads to an imprinting of the hypothalamic–pituitary–adrenal axis which may cause altered cortisol secretory patterns throughout life. Additionally, fetal malnutrition is thought to lead to deficient β-cell development, which pre-determines β-cell failure in later life.

What is the metabolic disease syndrome?

The concept of the metabolic disease syndrome was generated initially from data derived from large prospective or cross-sectional epidemiological studies in the 1980s and 1990s which investigated either coronary artery disease or type 2 diabetes. Both types of studies used plasma insulin levels in non-diabetic populations as a surrogate for insulin sensitivity. The cardiovascular epidemiological studies suggested that endogenous hyperinsulinaemia might be an independent risk factor for coronary artery disease and that it was associated with higher plasma VLDL triglycerides and lower plasma HDL cholesterol. The prospective type 2 diabetes studies indicated that hyperinsulinaemia was frequently associated with impaired glucose tolerance and was a strong predictor of the development of type 2 diabetes. These two sets of studies identified a cluster of metabolic abnormalities which were associated and were evidently the same cluster. For example, Haffner's data from the San Antonio Heart Study showed that the development of type 2 diabetes was preceded by higher plasma insulin, higher plasma triglycerides, higher fasting and two hour plasma glucoses on OGTT, higher systolic and diastolic blood pressure and lower plasma HDL cholesterol when compared to a control population who did not develop type 2 diabetes.[13]

Another approach in assessing the components of the metabolic disease syndrome has been to identify discrete populations of insulin-sensitive and insulin-resistant type 2 diabetic patients and to determine the metabolic abnormalities which are unique to those who have insulin resistance.[14,15] Table 1 lists the results of such analyses. The metabolic disease syndrome consists of changes in the distribution and increases in the quantity of adipose tissue, a specific type of dyslipidaemia and a procoagulant state. The relationship of increased blood pressure to the metabolic disease syndrome is quite complex and somewhat variable.

At the present time it is unclear whether there is a single underlying cause of the metabolic disease syndrome and, if so, what it might be. Many studies now suggest that obesity and in particular visceral obesity might play a major role in causing the metabolic syndrome in some individuals. However, at best this could only account for some of the cases. Recent epidemiological studies show that there are several clusters within the metabolic disease syndrome and that they are variably associated with hyperinsulinaemia and insulin resistance. New components of the metabolic disease syndrome are being proposed continually.

The important clinical issues relative to the metabolic disease syndrome may be posed as follows:

(1) to what degree does the metabolic syndrome predict the development of type 2 diabetes?

(2) to what degree does the metabolic disease syndrome predict coronary artery disease, cerebrovascular disease and peripheral vascular disease?

(3) which, if any, of the components of the metabolic disease syndrome are caused by insulin resistance and/or hyperinsulinaemia?

(4) does insulin resistance, itself, independent of the other components of the metabolic disease syndrome, cause vascular disease?

Table 1 Metabolic differences found between insulin resistant and insulin sensitive type 2 diabetics

	Haffner *et al.*	Banerji *et al.*
Obesity		
BMI	↑	↑
Waist circumference	↑	↑
Body fat		↑
Visceral fat		↑
Subcutaneous fat		0
Lipids		
LDL cholesterol	↑	↑
HDL cholesterol	↓	↓
Triglycerides	↑	↑
LDL size	↓	
Blood pressure		
Systolic	0	0
Diastolic	0	0
Coagulation state		
Fibrinogen	↑	
PAI-1	↑	
Carotid IMT	0	

IMT: Intimal media thickness; PAI-1: plasminogen activator inhibitor-1.

↑: Greater in insulin resistant subjects.

↓: Less in insulin resistant subjects.

0: No difference between insulin resistant and insulin sensitive subjects.

Insulin resistance has been shown to play a major role in the development of two diseases (type 2 diabetes and polycystic ovarian syndrome) and by significantly different mechanisms. Type 2 diabetes develops when insulin resistance creates a secretory stress on β-cells which are genetically (or otherwise) constituted to have limited functional reserve. Polycystic ovarian syndrome occurs when insulin resistance causes compensatory hyperinsulinaemia in a woman whose ovaries are normally responsive to insulin and have a cytochrome P450c17 variant that results in excess androgen production when stimulated by high insulin levels.

Vascular disease in the metabolic disease syndrome may be the result of a summation of the components of the metabolic disease syndrome inflicting their detrimental effects. Insulin normally causes vasodilatation of vessels through the PI-3-kinase pathway which stimulates NO production and insulin effects on smooth muscle cell migration and growth and matrix protein synthesis through the MAP kinase pathway are minimal. Insulin resistance with compensatory hyperinsulinaemia moves the insulin effect on vascular tissues toward increased MAP kinase activity and promotes atherogenic actions on the vessels. The dyslipidaemia, hypertension and procoagulant state accelerate the vascular damage.

Treatment of the metabolic disease syndrome should focus not only on treating the glucose, lipid, blood pressure and coagulation abnormalities but needs now to consider treating the insulin resistance itself.

Components of the metabolic disease syndrome

The major components of the metabolic disease syndrome which accompany insulin resistance are central obesity, the characteristic dyslipidaemia, the procoagulant state, hypertension and the more recently described endothelial cell dysfunction.

Central obesity

Cross-sectional studies in the early 1980s showed that cardiovascular risk factors such as hypertension, hypertriglyceridaemia, hyperinsulinaemia and glucose intolerance were more pronounced in subjects with an android type of obesity. Population based prospective studies in Gothenburg, Sweden, indicated that central obesity as estimated by the waist–hip ratio was a much greater predictor of the subsequent development of type 2 diabetes and cardiovascular endpoints such as myocardial infarction, angina pectoris, stroke and death than was generalized obesity as estimated by body mass index (BMI).[16]

The availability of computerized axial tomography (CT scans) and magnetic resonance imaging (MRI) has permitted precise measurements of body composition and adipose tissue distribution. Non-diabetic women show a very high correlation between central adiposity and insulin resistance ($r=-0.89$). Higher quantities of central adiposity are associated with increased fasting plasma NEFA levels, lipid oxidation and hepatic glucose production. Changes in insulin resistance in individuals gaining or losing weight are significantly correlated with changes in visceral but not subcutaneous adipose tissue depots.[17] Total body fat, subcutaneous body fat and visceral fat are however significantly correlated with each other and it

is not always possible in very obese individuals to determine which adipose tissue depot is the independent correlate to a metabolic event. Therefore, while most studies indicate that visceral obesity is the major determinant of insulin resistance, not all studies agree, and some place equal importance on abdominal subcutaneous adipose tissue as on visceral adipose tissue.

The waist–hip ratio has been used to estimate the ratio of visceral adipose tissue to subcutaneous adipose tissue. Correlating the anthropomorphic data with either CT scans or MRI indicate that waist circumference alone is a better surrogate for central obesity than waist–hip ratio.

Fat deposition within muscle may be another important aspect of adipose tissue distribution that is altered in obesity and might be linked to insulin resistance. Increases in visceral adiposity are associated with increases in both liver and intra-muscular fat.

The relationship between insulin resistance and visceral adipose tissue depots, is the same in diabetic individuals as in non-diabetic individuals, has no gender difference and is curvilinear, with the greatest decrease occurring with small increases in adipose tissue. Visceral adipose tissue depots measured as per cent of total body fat vary among individuals by as much as 7–10 fold and this is probably genetically determined. Relatively small changes in the visceral adipose tissue depot in individuals with a BMI below 30 kg/m^2 can cause profound changes in insulin sensitivity.[18]

The limbic–hypothalamic–pituitary–adrenal axis in patients with visceral obesity is hypersensitive. Some data are available to suggest that visceral obesity could be a consequence of abnormal cortisol regulation with exaggerated stress responses. The increased cortisol secretion could contribute to both central obesity and insulin resistance.

The mechanism by which visceral obesity contributes to the dyslipidaemia of the metabolic disease syndrome relates to its increased rate of release of NEFA as compared to other fat depots and its release of the NEFA directly into the portal vein.

Sufficient data are available in the literature to support the hypothesis that an increase in visceral adiposity could be the underlying cause of the metabolic disease syndrome in many individuals. Reduction of intra-abdominal fat by calorie restriction, exercise or thiazolidinediones ameliorates the insulin resistance and the other components of the metabolic disease syndrome.

Dyslipidaemia

The classic dyslipidaemia associated with insulin resistance is an elevation in VLDL triglycerides, a decrease in HDL$_2$ cholesterol and an increase in small dense LDL particles.

While the increase in VLDL triglyceride particles in central obesity with insulin resistance might be thought to be due to increased insulin mediated hepatic fatty acid esterification or a reduction in adipose tissue lipoprotein lipase (LPL), neither hypothesis is supported by available data. The liver is resistant to insulin action and plasma triglyceride removal is not defective. Adipose tissue LPL activity per cell is elevated in obesity. A more plausible explanation is that the delivery of increased quantities of long-chain NEFA directly into the liver through the portal vein results in increased apoprotein B-100 (ApoB) secretion by the liver. A significant proportion of newly synthesized ApoB in the liver cell is ordinarily degraded before secretion. Long-chain fatty acid uptake by the hepatocyte diverts ApoB away from degradation by the endoplasmic reticulum toward secretion. This could explain the increased small VLDL particles with a decreased ratio of VLDL triglyceride to ApoB which is observed in insulin resistance states.

Low HDL cholesterol is associated with central obesity and insulin resistance. The major cause of the low HDL cholesterol appears to be an increased rate of degradation. HDL_2 cholesterol seems to be specifically reduced in insulin resistant states.

Central obesity with insulin resistance and increased NEFA levels is associated with increased hepatic lipase activity. This increased activity leads to removal of lipids from HDL and LDL particles and makes them smaller and denser.

One can tie the central obesity and insulin resistance to the dyslipidaemia of insulin resistance through an increase in portal vein NEFA causing an increase in hepatic ApoB secretion and increased hepatic lipase activity.[19] These changes result in hypertriglyceridaemia, small dense LDL particles and decreased HDL_2 cholesterol. Hyperglycaemia in the type 2 diabetic patient exaggerates this dyslipidaemia by increasing triglyceride synthesis and decreasing LPL-mediated triglyceride removal. Cholesterol ester transfer protein acting on these triglyceride rich particles may lead to more small dense LDL particles and further reduce HDL cholesterol.

Procoagulant state

People with the metabolic disease syndrome are at increased risk for the development of coronary artery disease and strokes. Studies of the coagulation–fibrinolytic system have identified three factors which are abnormal in individuals with insulin resistance: increased levels of plasminogen activator inhibitor-1 (PAI-1); increased von Willebrand factor and increased plasma fibrinogen levels.[20]

PAI-1 is a rapid acting agent which inhibits the conversion of plasminogen to plasmin thereby decreasing fibrinolysis. Elevated levels of PAI-1 shift the balance of the thrombotic-fibrinolytic system in favour of vascular occlusion. PAI-1 is produced by endothelial cells, liver and adipose tissue. Population studies have shown a strong correlation between plasma PAI-1 activity and insulin resistance and hyperinsulinaemia. PAI-1 synthesis is stimulated by insulin, proinsulin-like peptides, triglyceride rich lipoprotein particles and oxidized LDL cholesterol. Several studies have demonstrated that PAI-1 production is stimulated by insulin resistance independent of insulin.[21] Drugs such as metformin or thiazolidinediones which decrease insulin resistance decrease PAI-1 levels. The consistent relationship between PAI-1 levels and the other components of the metabolic disease syndrome are ample evidence to include it as an independent component of the syndrome. The mechanism for the increase in PAI-1 has been postulated to be related to overproduction by endothelial cells as well as the liver. Numerous studies have identified PAI-1 as a significant risk factor for coronary artery disease.

von Willebrand factor is synthesized and secreted primarily by endothelial cells. In population studies, von Willebrand factor concentrations correlate with both plasma insulin levels and insulin resistance. The increase in von Willebrand factor in insulin resistant states may reflect the degree of endothelial dysfunction and could be accompanied by other changes such as an increase in production of adhesion molecules.

Increases in plasma fibrinogen levels are also associated with insulin resistance. Fibrinogen is synthesized in the liver. Several reports have emphasized the positive correlation between fibrinogen levels and plasma insulin levels.[21] The data from the Insulin Resistance Atherosclerosis Study clearly show that higher plasma fibrinogen levels are independently correlated with fasting plasma insulin and with insulin resistance.

Hypertension

Hypertension has been a component of the metabolic disease syndrome since the cluster was first described. Despite this, little is known about the relationship of hypertension to the other components of the syndrome and its relationship to insulin resistance and hyperinsulinaemia.[22] While the association of essential hypertension with insulin resistance had been suspected from epidemiological studies, it was the observation by Ferrannini et al. in 1987, that patients with essential hypertension were insulin resistant as determined by the euglycaemic hyperinsulinaemic clamp that focussed attention on this component of the metabolic disease syndrome.[2] The available data indicates that blood pressure is significantly correlated with insulin resistance in normal weight Caucasians. No significant correlation between blood pressure and insulin resistance is observed in most studies involving obese individuals or in many racial populations other than Caucasians. An example of the type of data available comes from the San Antonio Heart Study. In individuals who were normotensive at baseline, fasting plasma insulin was a weak univariate predictor of hypertension eight years later. An increase in baseline fasting plasma insulin that was associated with more than a two fold increase in developing diabetes was associated with only a 21 per cent increase in the odds of developing hypertension. In multivariate analysis adjusting for age, sex, ethnic group, BMI and fat distribution, insulin was no longer a significant risk factor for hypertension.[22]

The effects of insulin which might be expected to increase blood pressure include acute increase in renal sodium resorption, activation of the sympathetic nervous system and proliferation of vascular smooth muscle cells. In contrast, infusions of insulin decrease vascular resistance and cause vasodilation. Other confounding issues have been raised concerning whether the measured insulin resistance is a consequence of a decrease in muscle perfusion because of a decrease in the ability of insulin to augment blood flow. Some investigators have proposed that hypertension could cause insulin resistance rather than the reverse. This would be the result of closure of small vessels by capillary hypertrophy leading to reduced blood flow impairing delivery of insulin to the local muscle bed.

The data concerning hypertension as a component of the metabolic disease syndrome can be summarized as follows: hypertension is a major component of the metabolic disease cluster. Its underlying mechanism and its relationship to the other components of the syndrome are likely to be different than those of the other components.

Endothelial dysfunction

Endothelial dysfunction appears to be an integral part of the insulin resistant complex which makes up the metabolic disease syndrome.[3,4] The ability of insulin to stimulate NO-mediated vasodilatation amplifies the metabolic effects of insulin by increasing blood flow to the target tissues. Insulin resistance reduces the production of NO by endothelial cells. The mechanism involves inhibition of

PI-3-kinase activation. Elevated plasma NEFA impair endothelium dependent NO production and vasodilatation. It is likely that the elevated plasma NEFA occurring with central obesity and insulin resistance contribute to the impaired endothelial function seen in insulin resistant states. As noted earlier the potent vasoprotective effects of NO mitigate various atherogenic processes. Insulin resistance by impairing NO production and increasing mitogenic activity at the endothelial and vascular smooth muscle cell switch the balance toward an atherogenic state.

Other potential components

Microalbuminuria is a condition in which the albumin excretion rate is higher than normal but less than that which is characteristic of clinical proteinuria. Microalbuminuria has been shown to be both a risk factor for the development of diabetic nephropathy and for macrovascular disease in both diabetic and non-diabetic populations. Several studies have suggested that microalbuminuria is associated with insulin resistance and other components of the metabolic disease syndrome. In the Insulin Resistance Atherosclerosis Study 15 per cent of non-diabetic subjects had microalbuminuria.[23] In logistic regression analysis a weak relationship was observed between increasing insulin sensitivity and a decreasing prevalence of microalbuminuria. This relationship was partially dependent on blood pressure, plasma glucose levels and obesity. Mesangial cells have some properties similar to those of vascular smooth muscle cells. While there are no data indicating a possible mechanism by which insulin resistance or hyperinsulinaemia leads to the development of microalbuminuria, one might speculate that this could be related to an increase in activity in the insulin mitogenic pathway.

A clinical entity which is an insulin resistant mediated metabolic cluster which overlaps considerably with the metabolic disease syndrome is the polycystic ovary syndrome.[5] These young women have insulin resistance, hyperinsulinaemia and many of the other components of the metabolic disease syndrome. Additionally, because of their presumed genetic abnormality in the ovary which makes it more susceptible to insulin stimulated androgen production, they have amenorrhoea or irregular menses, infertility and hirsuitism. This clinical entity is associated with increased prevalence of type 2 diabetes and macrovascular disease. It should probably be considered a subtype of the metabolic disease syndrome.

Summary

The metabolic disease syndrome may have arisen as a result of changes in lifestyle. The genetic basis of the syndrome probably relate to our ancestors' ability to survive in a much more hostile environment. The increase in caloric intake and fat, coupled with a decrease in physical activity has led to a condition known as insulin resistance in a large percentage of our population. This insulin resistance alone or coupled with other abnormalities such as central obesity in some way fosters the development of a cluster of metabolic abnormalities which culminate in the major chronic diseases of our time: diabetes, hypertension and coronary artery disease.

Many potent drugs are available to treat the hyperglycaemia, hypertension, dyslipidaemia and the procoagulant state. Is that enough or do we need to treat the insulin resistance itself? We do not know the answer to that question, but there are some data to suggest that the answer will be 'yes' and, we do need to do more. We have agents available that can treat the insulin resistance and more are in development. The importance of the metabolic disease syndrome is that it focusses this cluster of risk factors at the forefront of clinical thought and should stimulate us to do better in caring for a large number of people who are at a very high risk to develop clinical sequelae of metabolic abnormalities.

References

1. **Reaven GM**. Banting lecture 1988: role of insulin resistance in human disease. *Diabetes*, 1988; **37**: 1595–607.

2. **DeFronzo RA, Ferrinnini E**. Insulin resistance: a multifaceted syndrome responsible for NIDDM, obesity, hypertension, dyslipidaemia, and atherosclerotic cardiovascular disease. *Diabetes Care*, 1991; **14**: 173–94.

3. **Laight DW, Carrier MJ, Anggard EE**. Endothelial cell dysfunction and the pathogenesis of diabetic macroangiopathy. *Diabetes/Metabolism Research Reviews*, 1999; **15**: 274–82.

4. **King GL, Wakasaki H**. Theoretical mechanisms by which hyperglycaemia and insulin resistance could cause cardiovascular disease in diabetes. *Diabetes Care*, 1999; **22**(suppl. 3): C31–7.

5. **Dunaif A**. Insulin resistance and the polycystic ovary syndrome: mechanism and implications for pathogenesis. *Endocrine Reviews*, 1997; **18**: 774–800.

6. **Virkamaki A, Ueki K, Kahn CR**. Protein–protein interaction in insulin signaling and the molecular mechanisms of insulin resistance. *Journal of Clinical Investigation*, 1999; **103**: 931–43.

7. **Dib K** et al. Impaired activation of phosphoinositide-3-kinase by insulin in fibroblasts from patients with severe insulin resistance and pseudoacromegaly. *Journal of Clinical Investigation*, 1998; **101**: 1111–20.

8. **Book CB, Dunaif A**. Selective insulin resistance in the polycystic ovary syndrome. *Journal of Clinical Endocrinology and Metabolism*, 1999; **84**: 3110–6.

9. **Bonora E** et al. Homeostasis model assessment closely mirrors the glucose clamp technique in the assessment of insulin sensitivity. *Diabetes Care*, 2000; **23**: 57–63.

10. **Boden G**. Role of fatty acids in the pathogenesis of insulin resistance and NIDDM. *Diabetes*, 1996; **45**: 3–10.

11. **Dresner A** et al. Effect of free fatty acids on glucose transport and IRS-1-associated phosphotidylinositol 3-kinase activity. *Journal of Clinical Investigation*, 1999; **103**: 253–9.

12. **Phillips DIW** et al. Elevated plasma cortisol concentrations: a link between low birth weight and the insulin resistance syndrome. *Journal of Clinical Endocrinology and Metabolism*, 1998; **83**: 757–60.

13. **Haffner SM, Stern MP, Hazuda HP, Mitchell BD, Patterson JK**. Cardiovascular risk factors in confirmed prediabetic individuals. Does the clock for coronary heart disease start ticking before the onset of clinical diabetes. *Journal of the American Medical Association*, 1990; **263**: 2893–8.

14. **Chaiken RL, Banerji MA, Pasmantier RM, Huey H, Hirsch S, Lebovitz HE**. Patterns of glucose and lipid abnormalities in black NIDDM subjects. *Diabetes Care*, 1991; **14**: 1036–40.

15. **Haffner SM** et al. Insulin sensitivity in subjects with type 2 diabetes. *Diabetes Care*, 1999; **22**: 562–8.

16. **Larsen B, Svardsudd K, Welin L, Wilhelmsen L, Bjorntorp P, Tibblin G**. Abdominal adipose tissue distribution, obesity and risk of cardiovascular disease and death: 13 year follow-up of participants in the study of men born in 1913. *British Medical Journal*, 1984; **288**: 1401–4.

17. **Goodpaster BH, Kelley DE, Wing RR, Meier A, Thaete FL**. Effects of weight loss on regional fat distribution and insulin sensitivity in obesity. *Diabetes*, 1999; **48**: 839–49.

18. **Banerji MA, Lebowitz J, Chaiken RL, Gordon D, Kral JG, Lebovitz HE.** Relationship of visceral adipose tissue and glucose is independent of sex in black NIDDM subjects. *American Journal of Physiology*, 1997; **273**: E425–32.

19. **Brunzell JD, Hokanson JE.** Dyslipidaemia of central obesity and insulin resistance. *Diabetes Care*, 1999; **22**(suppl. 3): C10–3.

20. **Yudkin JS.** Abnormalities of coagulation and fibrinolysis in insulin resistance. Evidence for a common antecedent? *Diabetes Care*, 1999; **22**(suppl. 3): C25–30.

21. **Festa A** *et al.* Relative contribution of insulin and its precursors to fibrinogen and PAI-1 in a large population with different states of glucose tolerance. The Insulin Resistance Atherosclerosis Study. *Arteriosclerosis, Thrombosis and Vascular Biology*, 1999; **19**: 562–8.

22. **Stern MP.** The insulin resistance syndrome. In: Alberti KGMM, Zimmet P, deFronzo RA, Keen H, eds. *International Textbook of Diabetes Mellitus*, 2nd edn. Chichester: John Wiley, 1997: 255–83.

23. **Mykkanen L, Zaccaro DJ, Wagenknecht LE, Robbins DC, Gabriel M, Haffnerr SM.** Microalbuminuria is associated with insulin resistance in nondiabetic subjects. *Diabetes*, 1998; **47**: 793–800.

Index

Main index entries are shown in **bold**.
Page numbers in *italics* refer to tables.